Peace and Conflict Studies
A Theoretical Introduction

Peace and Conflict Studies
A Theoretical Introduction

Masatsugu Matsuo

Professor,
Institute for Peace Science,
Hiroshima University

KEISUISHA

Copyright © 2005 Masatsugu Matsuo
First printed in May 2005
Published by Keisuisha Co., Ltd.
1-4 Komachi, Naka-ku, Hiroshima 730-0041
Japan
ISBN4-87440-881-8 C3031

To My Wife, Kiyoko

Preface

This book originated in my class of peace studies at the Graduate School for International Development and Cooperation, Hiroshima University. It is intended to be a graduate level introduction to, and a critical review of, peace studies. But it deals only with limited topics and limited aspects of the discipline.

First, the book will not cover the entire range of research topics of peace studies. Its focus is predominantly upon war and armed conflict. I regret some inevitable omissions of such topics as poverty, development, environment, human rights, gender issues and so on. Secondly, it does not go into the details of the human damages and sufferings caused by war and armed conflict, for example, damages and sufferings of Atomic bombs dropped upon Hiroshima and Nagasaki. The book only provides a bird's eye view of war and conflict from above, but not from below. Thirdly, this book mainly discusses theoretical aspects of the issues, leaving factual details mainly to other works and references.

No one can deny the importance of the issues which are left untouched in this book. The narrow focus is partly due to the limit of space and partly due to my inability. But it is also partly due to my understanding of the research priority of peace studies. Peace studies began as a discipline which sought to explore the causes of war and the conditions of peace. I believe that this should still be the core of peace studies. Therefore, the book deals almost exclusively with war and armed conflict.

The book consists of eight chapters. The first two chapters examine the concept of peace and follow the development of peace studies. Then the third chapter provides a general introduction to studies on war. The following three chapters deal with major themes of war and conflict studies. First, the fourth chapter addresses the issues of very great wars. The fifth chapter examines the relationship between arms race and war. The sixth chapter discusses the issue of local conflict, especially the issue of internal conflict. The next chapter, chapter 7, is an attempt at the reexamination of war and armed conflict in a broader and more abstract perspective of conflict and cooperation. The last chapter gives a theoretical prospect of peace studies.

I am grateful to many people who made the research, writing, and publication of the book possible. They are too numerous to list here individually. I heavily drew upon many works of peace studies and international relations. I was encouraged and stimulated by graduate students, especially, Maxym Alexandrov and Vladimir Rouvinski, who attended my class and my seminar. I would also like to express my special thanks to the late Professor Hiroharu Seki, who first introduced me to peace studies. Last but not least, I am particularly grateful to the Satake Foundation for making the publication of this book possible.

Hiroshima

April, 2005

Masatsugu Matsuo

Institute for Peace Science,
Hiroshima University

Table of Contents

list of tables ix
list of figures x

1 Introduction: What Is Peace Studies? — 1
   1.1 What Is Peace Studies? — 1
   1.2 What Is Peace? — 7

2 Development of Peace Studies — 13
   2.1 Birth of Peace Studies — 13
      2.1.1 Early Years — 13
      2.1.2 Forerunners and the Birth of Peace Studies — 14
   2.2 Development of Peace Studies — 16
      2.2.1 Periodization — 16
      2.2.2 First Stage: Till the End of 1960s — 18
      2.2.3 First Crisis to the Second Stage — 22
      2.2.4 Synthesis by Galtung: The Theory of Violence — 24
      2.2.5 Structural Violence: Pros and Cons — 28
      2.2.6 The Third Stage — 34
      2.2.7 Peace Studies as a World Learning Process — 38

3 Studies on War and Conflict: General — 40
   3.1 War and Peace Studies: Pioneering Works — 40
   3.2 Collection of the Empirical Data on War — 45
   3.3 Understandings of War — 48
   3.4 A Case of A Systemic Factor: Polarity — 53

4 Studies on Great Wars — 58
   4.1 General Introduction — 58
   4.2 Lateral Pressure — 59
   4.3 Cycles of Great Wars — 62
      4.3.1 Economic Cycles and Great Wars — 63
      4.3.2 Cycles of Great Wars — 66
      4.3.3 Retrospect on Studies on Great Wars — 74

5 Arms Race — 77
   5.1 Introduction: Significance of Arms Race — 77
   5.2 Security Dilemma — 79
   5.3 Richardson Model — 82
   5.4 Unilateral Model — 87
   5.5 Arms Race and War Revisited — 90
   5.6 Disarmament Efforts — 94
      5.6.1 Disarmament and Arms Control — 94
      5.6.2 Nuclear (Weapon) Free Zones — 99
      5.6.3 Nuclear Non-Proliferation Regime — 100
      5.6.4 Nuclear Disarmament as a Process Utopia — 102

6 Internal Conflict — **105**
- 6.1 General Introduction: What Is Internal Conflict? — 105
- 6.2 Realities of the "Local Wars" in the Postwar World — 108
- 6.3 Local Conflicts in the Post-Cold War Era — 110
- 6.4 New Trends in the Post-Cold War Era — 115
- 6.5 Nature of Internal Conflict — 117
- 6.6 Causes of Internal Conflict — 119
  - 6.6.1 General Introduction — 119
  - 6.6.2 General Theories of Conflict — 122
  - 6.6.3 Major Factors of Internal Conflict — 124
    - (1) Structural Factors — 126
    - (2) Politico-Military Factors — 128
    - (3) Economic Factors — 132
    - (4) Ethnic or Cultural Factors — 136

7 Conflict and Cooperation in International Society — **138**
- 7.1 Collective Action Dilemmas — 138
- 7.2 Game Theory — 142
- 7.3 Prisoner's Dilemma — 144
  - 7.3.1 Prisoner's Dilemma — 144
  - 7.3.2 Games of Conflict and Cooperation — 149
- 7.4 Solving Prisoner's Dilemma — 155
- 7.5 Cooperation under Anarchy — 163
  - 7.5.1 Neoliberal Institutionalism vs. Neorealism — 163
  - 7.5.2 Possibility of Cooperation — 166

8 Theoretical Postscript: Whither Peace Studies? — **171**
- 8.1 Peace Studies and War — 171
- 8.2 Peace and Security — 173

References — 178

List of Tables

1	Changes in the Number of Academic Articles on Non-Proliferation	5
2	Concepts of Peace among Different Cultures	8
3	Shrinking Spheres of Peace for the Japanese	11
4	Periodization of Early Peace Studies	16
5	Early Institutionalization of Peace Studies	17
6	Structural Violence in Terms of Life Expectancy (1970)	31
7	Number of Deaths due to Direct Violence and Structural Violence	31
8	Increase in the "Intensity" of Wars	40
9	Magnitude, Severity, and Intensity of War	41
10	Percentage of Civilian (Non-Combatant) Deaths	41
11	Magnitude of War	42
12	Genocides and Politicides since World War II	44
13	Typical Lists of Wars	48
14	Democratic Peace	52
15	Power Polarity and Cluster Polarity	55
16	"Global Wars"	72
17	Arms Race and the Outbreak of War (1816-1965)	77
18	Escalation from Arms Race to War (1816-1965)	78
19	Models of the Arms Race	79
20	Richardson Model of Arms Race (Richardson Equations)	82
21	Arms Race and War: Varying Results	92
22	Major Bilateral Arms Control and Disarmament Negotiations between US and USSR (or Russia)	96
23	Strategic Nuclear Disarmament Agreements between the United States and the Soviet Union/Russia	97
24	Major Arms Control and Disarmament Treaties concerning Weapons of Mass Destruction	98
25	Wars and Conflicts after the World War Two (1945-1989) (Wars, Civil Wars, Invasions, Interventions)	105
26	Number of Refugees and Internally Displaced Persons (estimate as of January 1, 2001)	106
27	Local Wars (1945-1976)	109
28	Regional Distribution of Local Wars (1945-1976)	110
29	Post-Cold War Armed Conflicts, 1989-2000	111
30	Ethnic Conflicts: Beginnings and Endings	112
31	Regional Distribution of Armed Conflicts after the End of the Cold War	112
32	Conflict Termination in the Post-Cold War Era, 1989-1996	114
33	Underlying Causes of Internal Conflict	125
34	Military and Social Expenditures (1991)	130
35	Number of Military-Controlled Regimes	131
36	Characteristics of Military Regimes	132
37	Development and Military Capability	135
38	A Sample Payoff Matrix of a Game	143
39	Prisoner's Dilemma: Original Model	145

40	Prisoner's Dilemma: US-USSR Arms Race	146
41	Prisoner's Dilemma: Environmental Cooperation	147
42	General Form of Mixed Motive Games	149
43	Stag Hunt	151
44	Chicken Game: Nuclear War	152
45	Prisoner's Dilemma: Generalized Form	157
46	Expected Payoff Matrix for Infinitely Repeated Prisoner's Dilemma	161
47	Neoliberalism vs. Neorealism	164
48	Security: Referents and Sources of Threat	174

List of Figures

1	Process Utopia and End-point Utopia	6
2	Spheres of Peace	9
3	Peace as the Absence of War	20
4	Revised Concept of Peace	23
5	Violence and Peace	25
6	Operationalization of Structural Violence	29
7	Two Perspectives on Violence: War and Poverty: Boulding vs. Galtung	33
8	Changes of the Relationship among the Notions "Peace," "Development," and "Human Rights"	37
9	Path to the First World War	51
10	Polarity and the Incidence and Scale of Wars	56
11	Lateral Pressure and the Process Leading to War	60
12	Kondratieff's Long Waves and Wars	64
13	Economic Cycles and Battle Fatalities	65
14	Hegemonic Cycle	70
15	Long Cycles and Naval Power	73
16	Security Dilemma: Spiral Model	81
17	Arms race leading to World War II based on Richardson Model	84
18	The Arms Race between the Two Superpowers during the Cold War	86
19	Conflict, Crisis and War	93
20	Processes of Conflict and the International Community	117
21	Two Types of Internal Conflict	118
22	Environmental Scarcity and Armed Conflicts	120
23	Regime Types and Internal Conflict	128
24	The Tragedy of the Commons	140
25	Peace and Security Studies	177

Peace and Conflict Studies
A Theoretical Introduction

1. Introduction: What Is Peace Studies ?

1.1 What Is Peace Studies ?

It is rather a conventional way to begin a textbook with the definition and history of the discipline. We follow this established custom here, and begin with the definition of peace studies and its brief history and development.

Peace Studies is a young discipline. Even the name "peace studies" is not an established one. Other names were used formerly, and are still used often alongside with "peace studies." "Peace research" was the common name in the earlier days. And "peace science" has been used by a group of researchers who founded "Peace Science Society, International," and who have shared a strong behavioral orientation. Recently, however, many scholars have begun to adopt the name "peace studies." In this book we will follow the current majority practice.

In most of the cases, a textbook on some subject, say, linguistics or biology, will usually begin with the definition of the discipline. A linguistic textbook will begin, for example, with a definition of linguistics as "a science of language, an academic enterprise for the better understanding of what language is."

We would like to do the same in the case of peace studies. We wish we could say that peace studies is an academic discipline for the better understanding of what peace is. But this is only partially true. There is a serious difference between empirical sciences like linguistics on the one hand and peace studies on the other. No one can deny the existence of language or languages. In a sense, language is just there, whether we want it to exist or not. On the contrary, can we seriously argue that peace exists? We can only give a very weak "yes" if at all. Perhaps it existed or exists only in some small part of the world in the human history if it ever exists. Our answer to the question is usually "No" writ large. Peace studies is not a discipline which studies what already exists, but one that studies what should or ought to exist. This is a peculiar characteristic of peace studies.

With this reservation, we can tentatively define peace studies as "*an academic discipline analyzing factors hindering and preventing peace and exploring conditions promoting it.*" In this definition nothing is said about *what peace is*. For the time being, we should be content to leave the definition of peace itself in the black box, assuming that there is some desirable but not yet realized social condition(s) which can be referred to as "peace."

This is a reflection of the nature of peace which we discussed above. It is a state of affairs to be created rather than that which already exists or has existed. This character of peace studies has two important implications.

First, we, peace researchers, should always concern ourselves about the question of what peace is. It is because not only barriers and obstacles to peace but also means and measures of establishing peace depend largely upon the definition of what peace is. In this sense, the development of peace studies has been centered upon this question.

Secondly, we should also consider what it means to study what should be or what ought to be rather than what is (Wiberg 1988: 30).

Suspending the definition of peace itself for the time being, peace studies can be characterized by the following properties. Needless to say, these are not properties peculiar to peace studies alone, but shared by other scientific disciplines as well.

First of all, as long as peace studies is an academic discipline, it should meet the scientific requirements of objectivity like any other research or any other "science." Peace studies should be objective in the sense that what it states can and should be proved or disproved by some objective and empirical means and data. Even if peace studies was born of ardent desire for the world without war or any other human suffering, or however ardently individual peace researchers long for peace, such desire itself cannot become a science or an academic enterprise. Such desire or longing may be a necessary condition for peace studies as an academic research, but it can never be a sufficient condition. To be sure, peace studies have been sometimes criticized for thinking (perhaps wishfully) that by deploring the tragedy and immorality of war or by simply advocating peace we can bring about peace (for example, Quester 1989: 102). The criticism may be true of some peace movements, but not of peace studies.

As we saw above, peace studies is not only about what does exist but also about what ought to be, or something which should be created. Even though the image of what ought to be or what is desirable is neither clear enough at present nor unanimously agreed upon, the current situations around the world leave many things to be desired in view of such an ideal. Remember the definition of peace studies we gave above. It aims to clarify or examine what prevents peace. It should be able to point to deficiencies, what the present world of ours is lacking, from the perspective of what is better or desirable. In this sense, peace studies should be critical of the present state of affairs. This is one of the responsibilities which peace studies has undertaken upon itself by its self-definition. Thus, peace studies should not only be empirically objective but also critical in this sense (Takayanagi 1983: 4-5).

Peace studies is further characterized by another property. While the critique of the present state of affairs derives rather from the first half of the goal of peace studies, that is, examination of factors preventing peace, this characteristic is related more to the latter half of the goal, namely, exploration of the conditions conducive to peace. Whatever the definition of the term "peace" may be, peace studies believes that peace is better than war (and, in a wider definition of peace, equity and justice are better than inequality and injustice). Peace studies seeks to contribute to the creation of domestic and international society which does not need any kind of war and armed conflicts (and which also eliminates social injustices and inequalities and realizes social equity and justice). In a word, peace studies envisages a social state in which war and armed conflict are abolished (and social justice is achieved as well). Peace studies is committed to contribute to the realization of such a world (Takayanagi 1983: 5). In this sense, peace studies is committed to a certain value judgment. It is clearly value-oriented.

By the way, such a commitment to a value judgment has traditionally been severely criticized following Max Weber's famous dictum of "value free(ness)." The dictum requires that researchers should be neutral to social and political values. Researchers should be free from worldly interests in their research. Peace studies seems to clearly violate this because peace studies is committed to a certain value, that of realizing peace.

The value orientation of peace studies can be easily seen in studies on war. War is a very important subject of peace studies. But peace studies is not the only discipline that is interested in the study of war. There are several academic disciplines engaged in understanding and analysis of war. International relations studies in general and strategic studies in particular also share the academic research interest in war. While the primary research goal of peace studies is to minimize the costs and damages of armed conflicts, and to prevent and eliminate them if possible (Boulding 1978: 135), some disciplines attach much greater importance to victory than to the costs or damages, and aim ultimately to win the war at any human and material cost (Seki 1981: 268-269).

In view of this characteristic, some have attached the term "normative" to peace studies (Seki 1981: 291). The normative nature of peace studies is, as we saw above, derived from the nature of our research subject, peace.

The issue of normativity has another implication as well. The importance of empirical and objective analyses cannot be overemphasized, and they are an essential requirement of a scientific discipline. But, if our research activity is limited to objective investigation, though it is very laudable and is very difficult to achieve in actual situations, we often fall into an intellectual trap of limiting ourselves to what has already happened. Exclusive concentration on objectivity often tends to limit our understanding to "what is" and to the past phenomena. As Yoshikazu Sakamoto says,

> "Our empirical understanding is bounded by the facts which happened already. Strictly speaking, the task of truly empirical sciences is to analyze the phenomena *ex post facto*, that is, after they happened. If we are engaged exclusively in this task, therefore, we cannot evade a kind of perceptual or intellectual conservatism. ...We cannot get out of the trap in which reality precedes us and we only follow it." (Sakamoto 1976: 49-50, translation and emphasis mine)

In this way, the emphasis on the objectivity tends to bound and limit our knowledge and understanding to the past phenomena. Consequently, our study may become, at the worst, a form of accepting the present state of affairs after things have happened, for example, after a nuclear war happened. (If past phenomena can be assumed to recur, or if we can extrapolate the past regularities to the future, there will be no such problem).

In the past, peace studies may have been clearly a dependent variable in an important sense. It was a variable dependent upon the political situation of the time (Takayanagi 1989: 305). Table 1 shows one example in which reality preceded peace studies and it only followed the reality. The table shows the rise and fall of the relative number of academic articles which dealt with the issue of nuclear non-proliferation. With the occurrence of several important events in the 1960s, we saw the rise of interest in the proliferation issues, as is exemplified by the rise of the relative number of articles addressing them. But the attention and interest declined sharply in the 1970s.

Table 1 Changes in the Number of Academic Articles on Non-Proliferation
source : adapted from Matsuo et al (1978), 502
Figures are percentages of the articles on non-proliferation

Year	No. of Articles	Major Events
1963	7.1	Partial Test Ban Treaty Nuclear Test by China
1964	13.8	French Withdrawal from NATO
1965	11.9	
1966	12.9	
1967	13.5	Nuclear Weapon-Free Zone Treaty in Central and South America
1968	11.1	Non-Proliferation Treaty
1969	7.4	
1970	5.9	
1971	3.8	
1972	2.9	

In this way, peace studies often followed the actual situation only after it had happened, without making attempts at anticipating the future or giving future visions. In order to avoid this kind of cognitive pitfall, therefore, it is necessary to anticipate and envisage a more desirable and better future. In this sense, peace studies is value-oriented and future-oriented. What is more, peace studies is normative in that it proposes a norm or ideal in the form of a desirable future world. It concerns with what ought to be, in a word. And, in this sense, peace studies is Utopian, partially at least.

We are, however, not denying that there are advantages as well in "chasing headlines." For example, a researcher can see the policy relevance of his or her research, find a clue to model or theory improvement, or identify a new question (Diehl 2002: 10-11).

To be Utopian, however, does not mean at all that peace studies attempts to propose or advocate a Utopian state of affairs which has no possibility of realization. In the modern world, many visions, plans and projects of a desirable future world, were proposed. A survey shows that there were as many as 450 peace plans and projects in Europe since the early fourteenth century (Wiberg 1988: 48, note 8). Among them, we can mention such well-known works by great thinkers and scholars as: Sir Thomas More's *Utopia* (1516), Desiderius Erasmus's *Encomium Moriae* (1509), Hugo Grotius's *De jure belli ac pacis* (1625), Abbe de Saint-Pierre's *Projet de paix perpetuelle* (1713), Immanuel Kant's *Zum ewigen Frieden* (1795), etc (see also Kende 1989, van den Dungen and Wittner 2003).

While these works are very imaginative and creative in describing the desirable world as the terminal point of human history, they usually say little or nothing about the ways and processes along which we can reach the final point. Thus almost all of them had virtually little or no effects upon the real world. What is required of peace studies is not this kind of Utopia. The real challenge is to bridge the apparently unbridgeable gap between the present and the distant desirable future. More concretely, the important task of peace studies is to think of ways and means starting from the present and finally reaching the future goal. In this context, the concept of "process Utopia" is crucial to peace studies (Takayanagi 1989: 320).

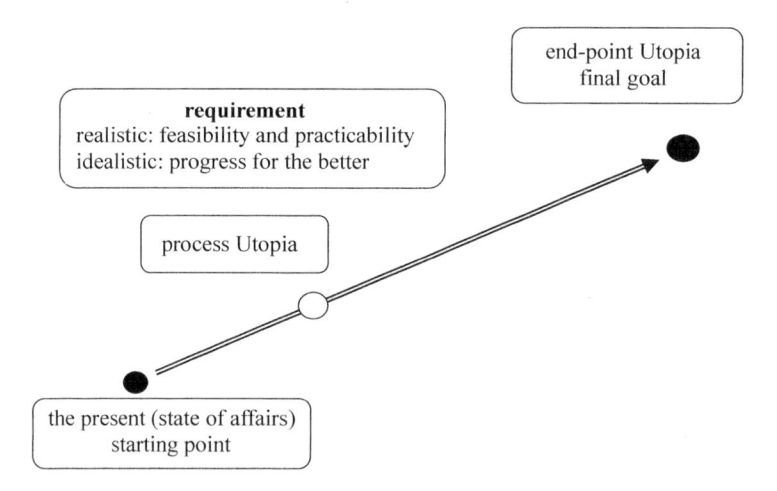

Figure 1 Process Utopia and End-point Utopia

end-point Utopia
final goal

requirement
realistic: feasibility and practicability
idealistic: progress for the better

process Utopia

the present (state of affairs)
starting point

The concept of "process Utopia" is, however, not an invention of peace studies. The distinction between two kinds of Utopia, between "end-point Utopia" and "process Utopia," was first proposed by Joseph Nye (Nye 1987, Booth 1991: 536). The former, the end-point Utopia, refers to the final point of human history or human development. By definition, it will be achieved only in the distant future if at all. On the contrary, the latter, process Utopia, refers to a state of affairs at some point in future which can be achieved, or a certain stage leading finally to the end-point Utopia. Figure 1 above illustrates the relationship between these two kinds of Utopias.

Needless to say, the process Utopia has its own drawbacks. It is because the concept contains an inherent tension or dilemma between what is possible and what is desirable or between what is realistic and what is idealistic. We will take up the issue in some detail later in 5.6.4 when we discuss recent nuclear disarmament process.

1.2 What Is Peace?

We have, as it were, suspended the definition of peace, though it is the most important concept for peace studies. The question of "what peace is" is crucial for peace studies, because the discipline aims to ultimately realize the goal of "peace." When we say that peace studies is value oriented or normative, it does not make any sense if the value, "peace" in our case, is empty, without any definition or meaning. Moreover, not only the research priorities and methodologies vary greatly depending upon the definition of peace. But the means and processes leading to the final goal are also largely determined by the definition.

Around 1970, for example, some peace researchers argued that peace should be seen primarily as the liberation and emancipation of the oppressed people of the world, and that violent or armed revolutions should be legitimate means of achieving such a goal. But their argument, especially their advocacy of violent means for achieving the goal of peace, did not convince the majority of peace researchers, who believed in the minimization of the use of force. The group finally parted company with peace studies. In this way, the definition of the goal of peace largely determines the means to the end. This is why the definition of peace is so crucial to peace studies, and peace studies has addressed the issue in earnest. Consequently, the development of the discipline of peace studies can be seen as the process of enrichment and deepening of the concept of peace. And we can go so far as to say that peace studies has been developed around the semantics of peace.

Before proceeding to the examination the definition of peace in peace studies, let us briefly examine popular concepts of peace in a broader context as a starting point.

Meanings, images or views of peace differ vastly among civilizations, cultures, nations, ethnic communities and so on, and, of course, over time. Indeed, the concept of peace is characterized by its diversity, though, needless to say, we can observe common qualities or properties as well. Moreover, the diversity of the meanings of peace is actually two-fold. First, there is a great variety in the substances or components of peace, or what is called peace values. The substances of peace or peace values are not uniform or homogeneous over time and space. But we can also observe differences in other respects as well. Among civilizations, cultures, nations, there are clear differences in the spheres or spaces of peace as well as in the substances.

Table 2 shows one example of the differences in the substance of peace. The table compares the words corresponding to English "peace" in classical civilizations such as Ancient Judaism, Greece, Rome, China (including Japan), and India. For the sake of comparison, it highlights the components of the meanings which were emphasized in each of them (Ishida 1969).

Table 2 Concepts of Peace among Different Cultures
source: Ishida (1969), 135

	will of God justice	prosperity	order	tranquility of mind
Ancient Judaism	shâlôm			
Greece		eirene		
Rome			Pax	
China(Japan)			ho p'ing/p'ing ho(heiwa)	
India				šânti

For example, in the case of "shâlôm" of the Ancient Judaism, "will of God or justice" and "prosperity" are the most important meanings of peace. It may also mean other things as well, but they are less important.

It is evident from the table that the emphasized components of peace greatly differ from one civilization to another. Some civilizations, like the ancient Jewish civilization, emphasize the importance of "the will of God" or "justice" as the critical element of peace, while others emphasize the tranquility or quietness of the mind. Still others emphasize the economic prosperity or "order and stability." In addition, even from this kind of simple comparison, we can easily see the merits and demerits of each of the peace concepts. For example, as we go upward from the bottom to the top, the concept of peace will tend increasingly to accept a holy war or just war, that is, war for the cause of God, justice, or peace. But as we go down from the top to the bottom, the peace concept will be more and more indifferent to war and injustice.

Table 2 showed the variety of the substances or contents of peace, or what can be called peace values, among civilizations. It is clear from the table that the substances of peace or peace values are not uniform or homogeneous over time and space. But, among civilizations, cultures, nations, there are clear differences in the spheres of peace as well. The Norwegian peace researcher, Johan Galtung, classified the peace concepts of the world into three types as is shown in Figure 2. The criterion of the typology is what can be called the sphere of peace, that is, where peace can exist. The three types of the sphere of peace are: universalist, ingroup-oriented, inward-oriented (Galtung 1981).

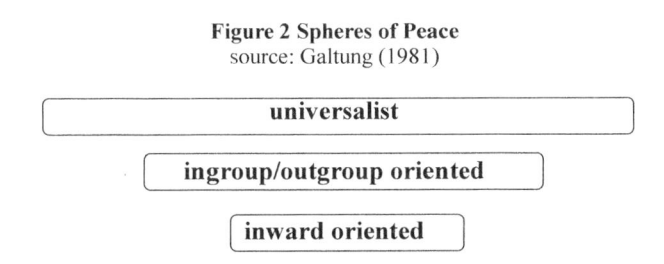

Figure 2 Spheres of Peace
source: Galtung (1981)

| universalist |
| ingroup/outgroup oriented |
| inward oriented |

The universalist concept of peace is typically represented by the Roman "Pax." This concept of peace regards the world as an indivisible whole, not divided into parts. Hence the label "universalist." The world is one universe and peace can exist only in the whole of this universe, but not in some parts of it. The universalist concept of peace can lead to the world peace, but it may also lead to the domination of the world by one empire, in which some center of power rules and controls the whole world as in the case of the Roman Empire. If the concept gives a particular priority to the notion of order, this concept of peace will be nothing more than the stability of domination or hegemony as is exemplified by the expression "Pax Romana," "Pax Britannica" or more recent "Pax Americana."

The second category, the ingroup-oriented concept of peace is characterized by two properties. First, this concept makes a sharp distinction between the in-group, "we" or "us" on the one hand, and the out-group, "others" or "them," on the other. Secondly, this peace concept pays attention to the peace only within the in-group. Out-groups are usually ignored or considered to be normally or perpetually in the state of war. In this case, peace exists only within the group or only where the group inhabits. This concept of peace has been almost universal in a variety of human collectivities, raging from huge religious groups to small communities.

Perhaps, one of the clearest examples is the classical Islamic cosmology. According to the classical (and oversimplified) Islamic world view, the world is divided into two parts: house of Islam ("Dar al-Islam") and house of war ("Dar al-harb"). The house of Islam is where Muslims live under the complete rule of the Islamic laws (sharia). On the contrary, the house of war means non-Islamic areas inhabited by heretics and heathens, and ruled by heretic rulers, and therefore not benefited by the Islamic laws.

The dichotomy of the in-group oriented peace concept reminds us of many current divisions of the world such as "developed" and "developing" countries, "rich" and "poor" countries, "core" and "periphery," and "zone of peace" and "zone of war" (for the last distinction, see Kozhemiakin 1998, Singer and Wildavsky 1996, etc.) among others.

This kind of division does not only involve the global divide, but it may be manifested in a very small sphere of peace in some cases. For example, the sphere of peace of the Japanese people has a tendency to shrink into a smaller and smaller sphere in space and in time. In the case of the Japanese, the in-group or "us" as a sphere of peace may shrink into a very small unit both spatially and temporarily, until, for example. the family or home is the only place where peace has some significance. The following few citations are typical, though rather extreme, cases where the sphere of peace is diminished to the minimum in space and time. They are taken from actual testimonies and diaries at the end of the Second World War. The small spatial and temporal size of the sphere of peace is in a stark contrast with the vast geographical scale of the dichotomy of Islamic cosmology we mentioned above (Matsuo 1983: 24-25, Matsuo 1985).

Table 3 Shrinking Spheres of Peace for the Japanese
translation and emphasis mine

[Hiroshima, Morning, August 6, 1945] I got up at six as usual. The sun was shining as brightly as if there had not been no warnings of air raids last night. It was again a **peaceful** morning. (*A-Bomb Experiences*[*1], 202)

[at a hometown in Hiroshima] I arrived at Itsukaichi town near twelve o'clock. Window glasses were broken by the Bomb. But it was **peaceful** in my hometown. (*Student Mobilization*[*2] 143)

We heard of the defeat. ... A glimpse of the horrible scene like heaps on heaps of rotten fish, at which we were quite helpless, convinced everyone of our complete defeat. ... My wound was not cured very much. So I made my mind to go back to my mother's house, which was left unburned. I was lying on the "futon" laid on a rubber-wheel cart, and when I saw **peace** restored after many years, tears dropped down in spite of myself due to fond remembrances. (*A-Bomb Experiences,* 52)

[*1] Hiroshima City Publication Committee for the A-Bomb Experiences (1965), *The A-Bomb Experiences*, Tokyo: Asahi Shimbun

[*2] Showa 18th Graduates of History Department of Tokyo Imperial Univeristy (1968), *Records of Student Mobilization*, Tokyo: Chuo Koron Sha

The in-group-oriented concept of peace often leads to indifference to the peaceless state of affairs outside, or even to the hostility against out-groups. In an extreme case, such a concept could contribute to the war alleged to protect the peace of the in-group from the threats posed by the out-group(s).

The inward-oriented concept of peace gives priority to the tranquility or quietness of the mind of an individual, that is, the inner peace of an individual or so-called "peace of mind." Too much emphasis on the peace of mind may often lead to indifference or acquiescence to outside violence and injustice.

When we consider the conditions of peace, we should think of some way in which these three spheres could complement each other. If many people suffer from mental stress and frustration, it cannot be called true peace. If many families, villages and towns, communities and countries are afflicted by armed conflicts and wars, then it cannot be called peace either. If states are frequently at war with each other, then, of course, it cannot be called peace.

The brief examination of the traditional concepts of peace raises two questions about the definition of peace, which is our primary research priority. First, what is, or ought to be, the substance(s) of peace in peace studies? Next, what should be the sphere(s) of peace? Since the definition of peace is crucial to peace studies, as we pointed out above, answers to these questions given by peace studies in its development will be examined in detail in the next chapter, which deals with the development of peace studies.

2. Development of Peace Studies

2.1 Birth of Peace Studies

2.1.1 Early Years

Most of the scientific fields can trace their history far back to the ancient world. It is the same with peace studies if it is rather broadly conceived. If we take up studies on war and strategy, we can name *History of the Peloponnesian War* by an ancient Greek, Thucydides (or Thoukydides, (460(455)-400, BC) and the study of strategy by an ancient Chinese, Sunzi (or Sun-tzu, around the 6th century, BC).

We have briefly touched upon the Utopian nature of peace studies, and mentioned a few peace plans and projects in the previous chapter. Their authors can also be included in the camp of earlier ancestors of peace studies.

Even if we limit our attention to recent times and to academic studies, we can find a considerable number of pioneering works in the nineteenth and the early twentieth centuries. Most of these works were engaged in empirical and statistical studies on the human and material costs of war, military expenditures and so forth. For example, a group called Massachusetts Peace Society is said to have estimated, as early as the beginning of the nineteenth century, the amount of the military expenditures and how they could have been converted to civilian purposes if they were not wasted (Wiberg 1988: 32). Similarly, there were many who advocated the necessity of a science of peace in these periods. But it was not until much later, when the world had experienced the tragedies of the two World Wars, that these earlier attempts and appeals culminated in the birth of a new academic field called peace studies.

According to John David Singer, these earlier scholars and their research belonged to "the first stage" of the development of studies on interstate war, which is the stage characterized by intelligent speculation (Singer 2000: 4). Indeed, Thucydides has been regarded as the spiritual founding father of the realist school of international relations discipline (Cashman 1993: 232). And the study of international relations as a discipline began as a study of war and peace. Founding fathers of the discipline such as Quincy Wright, Hans Morgenthau, E. H. Carr and Raymond Aron were all devoted to the study of war and peace as the titles of their classic books suggest (Grieco 2002: 65).

And they can, in a sense, be regarded as forerunners of peace studies (Singer 2000: 4).

2.1.2 Forerunners and the Birth of Peace Studies

The next stage is what Singer calls "the second stage" in which scientific method became prevalent. In the historical developments directly leading to the birth of peace studies, the most important milestone was the publication of *Towards a Science of Peace* by Theodore Lentz in 1955. The book made various proposals for research objects and research methodologies of a new science of peace (Boulding 1978: 127, 128). And it is said to have directly led to the birth of peace studies as it gave an impetus to many scholars to turn their attention to issues of peace. When we look back at the birth of the discipline, we cannot ignore the direct influence of several scholars. Besides Lentz, among the forefathers of peace studies, three names are particularly important. They are Pitrim Sorokin (1889-1968), Quincy Wright (1890-1970), and Lewis Richardson (1881-1953) (Singer 2000: 4-5).

Singer argues that we should include the fourth name, in addition to the above three. "The fourth horseman" was the Polish economist, Jean de Bloch, whose six-volume *Future of War*, published in as early as 1899, was a truly quantitative history of warfare over several centuries (Singer 2000: 5). But we will deal only with the former three here.

Pitirim Sorokin is well-known for his *Social and Cultural Dynamics*, in which he conducted a historical survey of thousands of years of wars and revolutions. He was the first to propose the notion of the "intensity of war (or conflict)." The notion of intensity has now become an important indicator in empirical and quantitative studies on war and armed conflict. It indicates the scale and size of war in terms of the amount of budget, number of soldiers, number of victims and so forth. "Intensity" of war will be examined in some detail in the next chapter.

Probably, it is the latter two of the three, Wright and Richardson, who had a much greater influence upon the early peace studies. They introduced a scientific (actually quantitative or "behavioral") method into the study on war, and demonstrated that causes and realities of war can be studied with scientific rigor and objectivity. In this sense, they truly deserve the name of founders of peace studies.

Quincy Wright made a comprehensive survey of past studies on peace and war, and conducted a systematic analysis of the data so collected, in an attempt to identify the causes of war and the conditions of peace. The result was published as a voluminous book, *A Study of War.* In this book, for example, he showed with concrete figures that the casualties of war, especially those of civilians or non-combatant citizens, rose enormously since the First World War. Perhaps this is one of the best known of his studies on war. Following Wright, we will later show how the percentage of non-combatant casualties rose in recent years in 3.1.

Lewis Richardson, an English meteorologist, had an immeasurable influence on the later peace studies, especially in the United States, through the two posthumous books of his. They were *Statistics of Deadly Quarrels* and *Arms and Insecurity.* In the former, *Statistics of Deadly Quarrels,* he collected data on 295 wars since 1820, classified and analyzed them, and showed that the casualties of war had increased literally exponentially during the hundred years in consideration. In the latter, *Arms and Insecurity*, he proposed a mathematical model of arms race, which has now become known as *Richardson model* or *Richardson equations*. He successfully applied this model to the arms race among major powers leading to the Second World War. The Richardson model will be examined in detail later in 5.3.

The pioneering studies on war by Wright and Richardson had a tremendous influence upon the subsequent development of peace studies, especially in the United States. This was partly due to the academic situation there. In the United States the so-called behavioral science was at its height around the time. The approach of behavioral science is characterized by its methodological emphasis upon the research procedure beginning with systematic data collection, followed by the formulation of explicit model or hypothesis based on them, and ending with the proof or disproof of the hypothesis or model by statistical or quantitative methods.

The legacies of Wright and Richardson inherited by peace studies can be summarized in the following three points. First, these scholars placed studies on war, especially realities and damages of war, at the core of the research. Secondly, they attempted at objective, quantitative analyses on the basis of the collection of vast historical and empirical data on wars. Thirdly, they, especially Richardson, employed mathematical models. These "legacies" were inherited and theoretically further elaborated by the early peace studies centered in the United States.

2.2 Development of Peace Studies

2.2.1 Periodization

Lentz' proposals and research achievements of Wright and Richardson acted as a direct impetus to the birth of peace studies as an academic discipline around 1960.

The development or history of peace studies since then can be roughly divided into the following three stages. The periodization in Table 4 is not a definitive one. But many scholars have made similar divisions. The periodization is basically the same as those proposed or suggested, for example, by Håkan Wiberg (Wiberg 1988) and by Yoshikazu Sakamoto (Sakamoto 1990). Take note here that our periodization below ends with the third stage. Though some may argue that the end of the Cold War marked a kind of watershed in the development of peace studies, at present it is still not clear whether it ushered in a new stage of peace studies or not.

Table 4 Periodization of Early Peace Studies

stage	Duration	peace concept	main research theme	areas of focus
First	before 1970s	absence of war	war	developed world
Second	1970s	absence of violence	development	developing world
Third	1980s and after		human rights	world

The division into three stages is based primarily on the definition of peace prevailing in peace studies at the time. It also corresponds to the research priority as derived from the definition. In terms of the research priority, the three stages could be represented by war, development, and human rights, respectively. Each of the stages also corresponds roughly with major geographical, or rather geopolitical, area which is the main target of the research. Or if we use our term, "sphere of peace," each of the stages has its own sphere of peace: developed countries, developing countries, and the world, respectively.

The transition from one stage to the next was not smooth. According to Wiberg, peace studies faced a "crisis" at each turn of stages (Wiberg 1993: 10). It is these crises that brought about the transitions. We will see shortly what they were.

Now, let us briefly follow the development of peace studies according to the division given in the table. The development of an academic discipline is accompanied by, and is virtually determined by, the so-called institutionalization. In concrete terms, institutionalization means the establishment and development of research institutes, research associations, educational institutions, (channels of) publication of academic journals and books etc. However, we will not go into the detail of institutionalization except in the discussion of the earliest period. Instead, we will append below a brief chronology of the early institutionalization of peace studies in Table 5.

Table 5 Early Institutionalization of Peace Studies
source : adapted from Okamoto (1982), 134-135 etc

year	Inauguration of academic societies, institutions, and journals
57	*Journal of Conflict Resolution* [USA]
59	Center for Research on Conflict Resolution, University of Michigan (CRCR) Peace Research Institute, Oslo (PRIO)
61	Groningen Polemological Institute [Netherlands]
63	Peace Science Society, International (PRSI → PSSI) [USA]
64	*Peace Research Abstracts Journal* [Canada] *Journal of Peace Research* [Norway]
65	International Peace Research Association (IPRA)
66	Japan Peace Research Group Stockholm International Peace Research Institute (SIPRI)
67	*Peace Research in Japan* [Japan]
70	Consortium on Peace Research, Education and Development (COPRED) [USA] Deutsche Gesellschaft fur Friedens- und Konfliktforschung (DGFK) [West Germany] *Bulletin of Peace Proposals* [Norway] → *Security Dialogue*

( ) indicates acronyms, [ ] indicates the country

Let us have a look at a few indications of the institutionalization of peace studies. Toward the end of the 1980s, there were more than three hundred peace research and training institutions around the world according to UNESCO's statistics

(UNESCO 1988). The figure can be viewed as one of the indicators demonstrating the considerable advance of institutionalization of peace studies. In this connection, Kenneth Boulding, a distinguished economist and one of the founding fathers of peace studies, proposed interesting criteria for measuring the maturity of an academic discipline. According to him, one can measure the maturity of an academic field in terms of the two criteria, namely, research achievements and education capabilities, of the discipline. More concretely, one can ask whether there are a sufficient number of reference books (including textbooks) on the subject and whether one can hold an examination on the subject. In the 1980s, more than one hundred American universities offered peace studies classes (Wien nd). And a recent survey in Japan shows that more than one hundred and fifty universities and colleges offer classes related to peace issues, even if they are not classes of peace studies proper (Okamoto 1997: 226). As these examples show, institutionalization is an important aspect of the development of an academic discipline.

2.2.2 First Stage: Till the End of 1960s

It is said that peace studies was born around 1960. The first stage of the development of peace studies is roughly from the late 1950s to the 1960s. The stage saw inaugurations of research institutes, academic journals and academic associations, especially in the United States and Western Europe. In the United States, for example, the first academic journal, *Journal of Conflict Resolution,* was inaugurated in 1957, and the Center for Research on Conflict Resolution was established in 1959 in the University of Michigan. In Northern Europe, Johan Galtung established Peace Research Institute, Oslo (PRIO), in the same year. A few years later, the institute began to publish *Journal of Peace Research*, one of the most authoritative journals in this field.

In 1961, Bert Röling, one of the judges of the Tokyo Tribunal, established The Polemological Institute in Groningen, the Netherlands. In 1965, the institute hosted the inaugural conference of International Peace Research Association (IPRA), the international academic association for peace studies. In 1966, Stockholm International Peace Research Institute (SIPRI) was founded. The institute is well known for its systematic collection of data on armaments and disarmament, and the publication of the yearbook, *SIPRI Yearbook*. In the same year, the Japan Peace Research Group was formed in Japan. For the development of peace studies in Japan, see Matsuo (1995).

Roughly at the same time, Peace Science Society, International (PSSI) was established in 1963. This is another peace studies academic association based mainly in the United States. It is more inclined to mathematical or quantitative research methodologies.

We should also mention the name of the Polemological Institute in France. The institute was established as early as 1945 by the efforts of Gaston Bouthoul and others, quite independently of the main trends of peace studies we saw above. It achieved unique academic results, which were best represented by the publication of *Sociology of War*.

The early peace studies was strongly motivated by the reflection on the tragedies of the Second World War and by a sense of crisis of human survival caused by the danger of a total nuclear war between the two superpowers. Reflecting these motivations, the research focused almost exclusively on war, especially on the causes of war and its prevention. This preoccupation with war manifested itself in the definition of peace implicitly embraced by peace researchers at the time.

In the early years of peace studies, it was assumed that peace is the opposite of war. Peace was defined as *the absence of war*. This concept of peace came later to be called negative peace for reasons we will explain below. If we follow the definition of peace as the absence of war, the most urgent task of peace studies is to prevent war, especially a nuclear war in the context of the age, that is, US-USSR confrontation at the height of the Cold War.

In this formulation, if there is a war, there is no peace. And if there is no war, there is peace. Peace and war are, as it were, in the "zero-sum" relationship. This formulation of the relationship between peace and war soon came to be perceived as too narrow and inflexible, because it did not allow of the possibility of a "grey zone." Accordingly, attempts were made to extend the relationship a little, making it a little closer to reality. These attempts usually took into consideration the fact that there might be a state lying somewhere between peace and war. Figure 3 shows one of these attempts at the extension of the definition of peace.

Figure 3 Peace as the Absence of War
Source: Darnton (1973), 113.

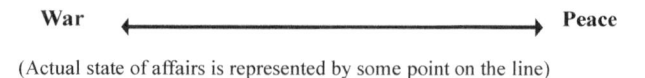

War ⟵――――――――――――――⟶ Peace

(Actual state of affairs is represented by some point on the line)

In this figure, the actual state is represented by a point on the line, or the spectrum, between the two poles of peace and war. Even in this scheme, however, the degree of peace is determined solely by the degree or extent of war (Darnton 1973: 113). The relationship between peace and war described by this figure can be compared to a balance with peace on one scale and war on the other (Boulding 1978: 43). Boulding made another attempt at elaborating the relationship between peace and war in this direction. He first postulated two variables. The one, "strength," is a set of factors promoting peace, and the other, "strain," is a set of factors contributing to war. He assumed that the actual state is determined by the relative values of the two variables, "strain" and "strength." He divided the state of war and peace further into four stages according to the relative intensity of "strain" and "strength," that is, by the relative intensity of peace promoting factors and war promoting factors (Boulding 1978: 43 etc).

Compared with the richness of everyday concept of peace we saw in the previous chapter, the concept of peace defined and used in peace studies may seem extremely poor in its content. It is partly because an academic discipline cannot attend to every aspect of the phenomena it is interested in, but it has instead to focus as narrowly as possible upon those aspects of the research object that it considers to be most significant. This process is usually called abstraction. Though it may sound paradoxical, an academic discipline often aims to understand and explain complex phenomena by disregarding or bracketing many aspects or elements of them. Of course, this kind of analytical method has its own deficiencies. We may end up with only a partial, fragmented and often distorted understanding of the phenomena, never achieving a holistic idea of the matter in question, never understanding the matter in its entirety. But, as a first approximation at least, the selection of apparently important aspects of the research object is inevitable. And this is what peace studies did at its birth.

The assumption of peace as the absence of war rather automatically determined the primary research themes in this period. The main research themes were wars and their causes including psychological and ideological aspects. In addition, more general issues of conflict and conflict resolution were also important themes of research.

The dominant methodology in this period was the so-called behavioral approach. It was characterized by the collection of empirical data (hence the name "positivism," or "positivistic"), the formulation of formal or mathematical models, and the testing of the hypotheses or models on the basis of empirical data. The collection and analysis of vast amount of empirical and historical data on war and other armed conflicts also characterized the research in this period. These efforts were direct legacies of the pioneering works by Wright and Richardson.

In retrospect, peace studies in this period had two tacit assumptions about its primary research theme, war. The early peace studies was not only war-centered, but also state-centered. First of all, "war" was implicitly assumed to be among major powers. Only major wars were thought to be worth the name of "war," though it is quite understandable when we consider the historical background of the time. This assumption left two important research areas almost completely out of consideration: the developing world and the local conflicts which swept it. For instance, internal conflicts were ignored by the Correlates of War Project, launched at the University of Michigan, which sought to accumulate the data on war in a scientific and more rigorous method (Geller and Singer 1998: 12). Even this ambitious enterprise limited its data collection exclusively to wars between states, categorically excluding intrastate wars from its attention. Thus, systematic studies on local wars were virtually neglected until the seminal works of Istvan Kende (1971, 1978) appeared in the 1970s, rather from the then periphery of peace studies.

Secondly, war was assumed to be symmetric, that is, fought between roughly equal powers. According to this assumption, the Vietnam War was an anomaly. As we will see shortly, the validity of the implicit assumption of the early peace studies became problematic in part due to the events like the Vietnam War and the Spring of Prague, where clearly non-major powers and non-state actors were involved in conflict and violence.

2.2.3 First Crisis to the Second Stage

In 1970s, peace studies advanced to its second phase of development. The transformation of peace studies, however, was not an automatic or endogenous one arising from within the discipline. The outside events and changes in world affairs, and especially interpretations and perceptions of them, played a great role in the transition. From 1945 to the 1960s, there were no major wars contrary to the fear of researchers though there were many local wars, which we will take up later. But, on the other hand, the so-called "North-South problem" (the term was first used in 1959 by the British banker, Sir Oliver Frankes) emerged, or more precisely, came to be perceived, as an urgent issue facing the whole world. It became what we now call part of global problematique. The problem is most visible in the great gaps between the developed and developing countries. And peace researchers could not be indifferent to the tragic and miserable situations in developing countries represented by famines, poverty, underdevelopment, and gross human rights violations. It is against this background that many peace researchers began to ask whether the absence of war really meant peace.

There was another important factor which promoted the transition. In a sense, the factor imposed itself upon students of international relations, and particularly students of peace studies. The factor was represented by asymmetric conflicts like the Vietnam War and the invasion of Czechoslovakia by the Warsaw Treaty Organization armies which crushed the Spring of Prague in 1968. These armed conflicts were quite different from symmetric conflicts in which roughly equal parties fought each other. Before these events, peace studies implicitly assumed that wars were symmetric and were fought between two roughly equal parties, especially two major powers or alliances of them. These asymmetric conflicts raised new issues in the international system, new to peace studies at least, which was unwittingly entrapped by what can be called a "Westphalian" fallacy.

In a word, peace studies was obliged to face squarely with unequal and unjust realities in the international relations which threatened to undermine its previous definition of, and assumption about, war and peace. It was against this background that voices of strong objection were raised to the traditional peace studies centered around empirical studies on "war." More and more scholars came to cast doubt on the validity of the definition of peace as the absence of war. Many asked if peace can and should be really defined in this way. This was the "first crisis" of the young peace studies (Wiberg 1993: 10).

In this situation, various attempts were made to expand the traditional definition of peace. Figure 4 shows one of the attempts at the extension of the definition (Darnton 1973: 113).

Figure 4 Revised Concept of Peace
Source: Darnton (1973), 113

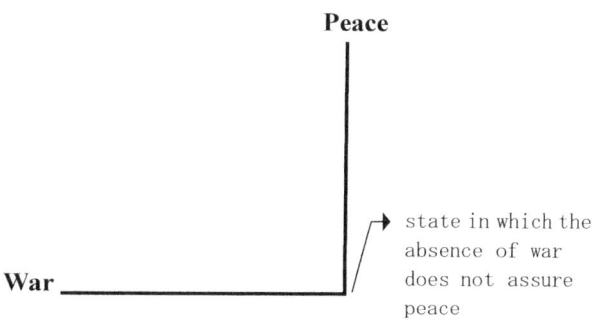

```
              Peace
                |
                |
                |
                |      → state in which the
                |     /   absence of war
  War _____|____/    does not assure
                          peace
```

(Actual state of affairs is represented by some point on the orthogonal lines)

In this figure, a particular state of affairs is represented by a point on either of the orthogonal lines. The degree of peace or war can be measured by the distance from the origin. But the figure shows the crucial departure from the traditional thinking about peace and war. The figure makes it clear that even if there is no war, the degree of peace varies, and it can be very small or even zero in an extreme case. The point where two lines cross indicates that, contrary to the conventional wisdom, and contrary to the original definition of peace, even if there is no war, there is no peace.

But it was Sugata Dasgupta, an Indian researcher, who went far beyond the absence of war and proposed a radically new concept of peace. He proposed the notion of *"peacelessness"* as a critical alternative to the prevalent concept of peace defined as the absence of war (Dasgupta 1968). The notion of "peacelessness" refers to the current situations, especially in developing countries, where, in spite of the absence of war, human beings are suffering just as much from poverty, malnutrition, disease, illiteracy, discrimination, oppression and so on, as from war. Even though there is no war, people cannot live their lives with dignity and happiness. In a word, they cannot live in peace. Needless to say, the proposal of the notion was greatly motivated by the reflection on the miserable situations of the South.

Thus, in the late 1960s and early 70s, peace studies faced two serious problems: the North-South Problem and asymmetric conflicts. And underlying both was the common fundamental issue of the unequal structure of the international society. This issue led to heated debates and divide within peace studies. A serious confrontation ensued between the protagonists of the "old agenda" focusing on war and those of the "new agenda" focusing on "structural violence" (Wiberg 1993: 10).

At one extreme, some argued that peace studies had been incapable of the analysis of, and much less solution of, the North-South problem and the Vietnam War, and that it should, therefore, give priority to the criticism and analysis of structural factors in the international society which brought about war and poverty, taking sides with the weak and oppressed. As we saw in the previous chapter, some went even further and argued that peace studies should aim to dismantle the existing unequal structure of the international society, even by violent means. At the other extreme, others argued that the prime task of peace studies should be objective empirical studies on war as before.

2.2.4 Synthesis by Galtung: The Theory of Violence

Peace researchers' efforts to cope with the new global situation culminated in the concept of "violence" proposed by Johan Galtung in a now classical article (Galtung

1969). It was his concept of violence that theoretically synthesized these seemingly incompatible issues of war and poverty and achieved a new integration. To be precise, what he proposed was a new concept of peace and violence, and not the concept of "structural violence" proper as is often popularized. Galtung's theory of violence was intended to solve the dilemmas undermining peace studies at the time, by providing a broader theoretical framework which integrates the issues of war and poverty into a higher (or deeper) synthesis. The key to the synthesis was the new concept of violence. Figure 5 shows schematically the formulation of the relationship between peace and violence proposed by Galtung. As is shown in the figure, Galtung defined peace as the absence of violence, and not as the absence of war (Galtung 1969: 167). Of course, the usefulness and validity of the definition depends exclusively upon the definition of violence. What, then, is violence?

Figure 5 Violence and Peace
source: adapted from Galtung (1969), 183

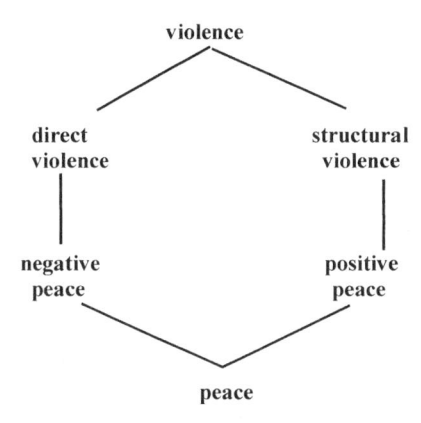

```
              violence
             /        \
       direct          structural
       violence        violence
          |               |
       negative        positive
       peace           peace
             \        /
              peace
```

Galtung defined violence as everything which prevents the full realization of innate somatic and mental human potentials. To put it in a little different way, violence is anything which produces a gap between the physical and mental potentials of human beings and their actual conditions (Galtung 1969: 168). For example, when the life expectancy was thirty years in the Paleolithic age, it may not have been due to violence.

But in our world such a low life expectancy is a clear indication of the existence of violence (Galtung 1969: 169). In this way, the poverty, underdevelopment, oppression and other social ills afflicting billions of people in developing countries can be seen as manifestations of violence.

Galtung argued that violence is the key factor common both to war and social injustice. In everyday language, it does not matter whether one is killed in war or by famine. The result is a premature death, which is the deprivation of one of the human potentials. In this way, peace came to be defined as the absence of violence, instead of as the absence of war. Galtung succeeded in providing a theoretical framework which embraced both war and poverty, both the North and the South. Now peace studies was capable of dealing in a theoretically consistent manner with the issues both of war and poverty, the urgent issues of the North and the South.

As in the case of the stone age life expectancy, Galtung's concept of violence clearly presupposes the distributive justice. His theory presupposes an ideal state in which the goods and services available are distributed equally. In this sense, the issue of violence, especially that of structural violence, is also an issue of social justice.

Galtung further divided violence into two categories: direct violence and structural violence (Galtung 1969: 170), as is shown in Figure 5. The direct violence is produced by visible human actors. The structural violence is produced without any particular human agency, but impairs and reduces the human potentials in the forms like poverty and discrimination. This type of violence was named "structural" because, in most of the cases, poverty, starvation, discrimination, human rights violations and so forth are all manifestations of violence due to, or embedded in, the structures of domestic and international societies. And, as we hinted above, structural violence can be seen also as manifested in "social injustice" (Galtung 1969: 171).

Incidentally, when we accept the notion of structural violence, another interesting issue arises. What is the relationship between direct and structural violence? How direct and structural violence are related to each other? Only one aspect of the issue has been pursued extensively so far, that is, the question whether structural violence leads to direct violence. Do inequality and poverty breed armed conflict?

Recently, some have asked, "Does grievance breed war?" At present, there is no definitive answer to the question. We will take up the issue in some detail in 6.6.3 (3).

In parallel with the division of violence into direct and structural violence, peace defined as the absence of violence is also divided into two categories of negative and positive peace (Galtung 1969: 183). Negative peace is defined as the absence of direct violence like war and armed conflict. The notion of the negative peace largely retains the previous definition of peace as the absence of war. Positive peace is defined as the absence of structural violence. In other words, positive peace refers to the state in which social justice is attained and human potentials are fully realized.

Once peace was defined in this way as the absence of violence, new vistas for studies were opened. Since the elimination of structural violence became an important goal of peace studies, issues of poverty and development, inequality and injustice, especially in developing countries, now became major research themes. The new research focused upon politics, economy and the military in developing countries. Thus, the concept of structural violence not only deepened the meaning of peace, but also opened new research possibilities. Here, however, we will only point out major theoretical contributions (or some may prefer the term confusion for reasons that will become clear below) of the theory of structural violence. Its contribution can be summarized in the following way.

First, the concept of structural violence led to the deepening of the concept of peace and to the expansion of peace studies by opening the new research fields. It opened our eyes to the present deprivation of the common people in developing countries, forced victims of structural violence, and gave rise to the recognition that the satisfaction or fulfillment of the basic human rights and needs of the people is a very important component of peace. It was for this reason that particular attention was paid to the state of development or underdevelopment (or what some call "maldevelopment") in developing countries. In other words, the notion of structural violence highlighted the issues of development and social justice as necessary conditions of peace.

Secondly, research stimulated by the concept of structural violence made clear that the structural violence is inseparably linked to the structure of today's international society as well as to the domestic political, economic and social structures of developing countries.

Thirdly, such recognition of the linkage between domestic and international societies contributed to the formation of a global perspective in peace studies. A global perspective here means a particular mode of understanding issues in which one assumes the world constitutes a single system or one single whole and one understands an issue, for example, the issue of underdevelopment, in the context of this single system.

2.2.5 Structural Violence: Pros and Cons

To be sure, the theory of violence, or popularly the theory of structural violence, was a great contribution to peace studies. But, it was also true that many criticisms were raised against the theory. The criticisms can be divided into three types. The first is that of overexpansion, the second is that of fuzziness, and the third is that of theoretical confusion.

First, some accused the theory of expanding the research themes of peace studies endlessly. If we adopt the definition of violence proposed by Galtung, peace studies must address every social problem which in some way or other prevents the full realization of inherent physical and mental human potentials. In fact, peace studies has come to deal not only with war and underdevelopment, but also with environmental degradation, sexism, and so on.

Secondly, another criticism of Galtung's theory of violence is centered upon its fuzziness. Against this criticism, some scholars attempted to counter it by proposing an objective measure of structural violence and applying it to actual data. Let us look at one example of these attempts.

Galtung's theory of violence views early deaths or premature deaths as caused by violence, whether they are caused by war or by other factors like famine. As we know well, people in developing countries can only enjoy shorter lives on the average than those in developed countries. They are, in a sense, killed by something, long before their natural deaths. Galtung called this "something" structural violence. In this sense, a premature death is an extreme case of violence, to be precise, an extreme case in which human beings are deprived of their inherent physical potential. Then, the length of life or life expectancy can be regarded as one indicator of violence, especially that of structural violence. If we compare the actual life expectancy with the hypothetical life expectancy in an ideal situation where all the goods and services are equally distributed, then we can obtain an approximate measure of the amount of the structural violence in the country or society in question. Figure 6 illustrates this kind of comparison. Here we assume that in an ideal society one can live as long as one's physical possibility and the present technological and material levels allow.

Figure 6 Operationalization of Structural Violence
source: Hoivik (1977), 64

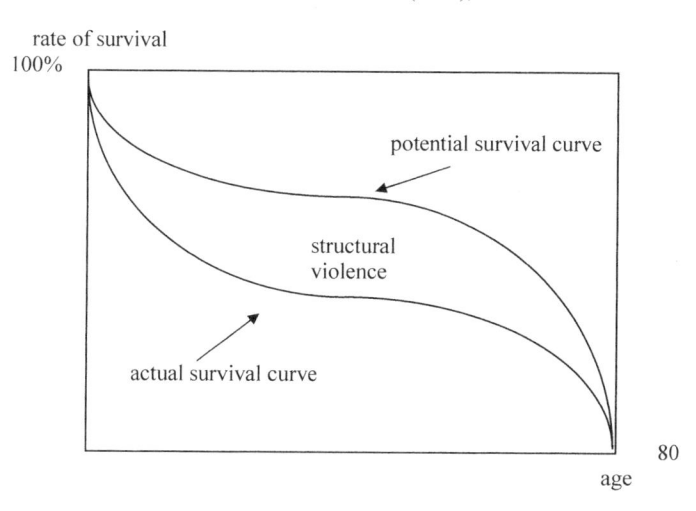

In figure 6, there are two "survival" curves. The curves show the probability or rate of survival at each age. Suppose now that the lower curve represents the actual survival rate, and that the upper curve represents the survival rate in a hypothetical, ideal situation. The former is called actual survival curve, and the latter potential survival curve. The potential survival curve is a hypothetical one (though, in fact, it was based partially on the actual data of developed countries), which is realized only when all the resources, goods and services are distributed equally and every one can enjoy the length of life equally under the constraints of technological and material levels. Moreover, the curve can be regarded approximately as one which is realized when structural violence is eliminated as far as the length of life or life span is concerned.

If we think in this way, then the size of the area bounded by the two curves indicates, though approximately (because there are premature deaths due to direct violence), the amount of structural violence in the society or country in question. The smaller the size of the area is, the smaller the amount of structural violence will be, and vice versa. In this way, we can operationalize the notion of structural violence and demonstrate the validity of the concept.

Yet, in addition to the difficulty of defining the ideal state, it is at present very difficult to obtain the actual survival possibility at each of the age, especially in developing countries which are at the focus of research on structural violence. Consequently, a simpler method of approximation was devised (Köhler and Alcock 1976: 343-356). Incidentally, note that the United Nations Development Programme (UNDP) uses a similar but more ambitious indicator called Human Development Index (HDI) (UNDP 2001: 240 etc). As its inclusion to the index shows, life expectancy is regarded as one of the major indicators which can measure the quality of life.

The following two tables, tables 6 and 7, are products of similar efforts toward the operationalization of structural violence. Table 6 gives the approximate estimation of the amount of structural violence by region calculated on the basis of the 1970 data. According to this estimate, the index of structural violence is 26 percent for the whole world. This means 18 million deaths. In other words, 18 million people were forced in one single year to die earlier than their natural death. The figure can be compared with the total number of deaths in the Second World War, 50 million. Even if we do not agree with the concept of structural violence, we cannot be indifferent to the fact.

It is also evident from Table 6 that structural violence is overwhelmingly concentrated in developing countries. The comparison between developed and developing countries in the next table again makes clear the great gap in the structural violence. Moreover, Table 7 shows that not only structural violence but also direct violence is concentrated in developing countries. People in developing countries have been afflicted both by direct and structural violence. They are not only poverty-stricken, but also war-stricken.

Table 6 Structural Violence in Terms of Life Expectancy (1970)
source: extracted from Hoivik (1977), 71

region	life expectancy	index of structural violence (%)	amount of structural violence*
World Total	53	26	18,100
Central Africa	40	44	2,610
Southern Africa	48	33	160
Northern Africa	50	31	530
South Asia	49	32	9,850
Mainland East Asia	50	31	4,640
Other East Asia	60	17	170
Japan	71	1	20
Latin America	60	17	790
Oceania	65	10	30
North America	70	3	90
Soviet Union	70	3	100
Europe	71	1	90

* in thousands

Table 7 Number of Deaths due to Direct Violence and Structural Violence (estimates for 1965)
source: adapted from Köhler and Alcock (1976), 349

	direct violence (wars)	structural violence
developed	2,200	754,000
developing	112,800	17,396,000

What we have seen is only the tip of the iceberg named structural violence. Such serious problems as discrimination, political oppression, human rights abuses are only reflected in the tables above as far as they influence the actual life span of the people. The tables above show the amount of structural violence only as it is measured in terms of life expectancy.

It should be noted that these attempts at the operationalization and demonstration of structural violence have been severely criticized for their theoretical assumptions, for their lack of precision and rigor, and for the flaws in their estimation methods. For example, if we take life expectancy as a measure of structural violence, we would be obliged to conclude that structural violence in developing countries has been greatly reduced, since the life expectancy in developing countries has been considerably improved in these thirty or forty years. In spite of various difficulties, these attempts have attained their purposes, say, heuristic purposes, because they were successful in exposing important facts and issues in a very simple form.

Thirdly, of the criticisms raised against Galtung's concept of violence, one of the most profound and incisive was that made by Kenneth Boulding (1977). Boulding argues that Galtung overemphasizes phenomena and results, and overlooks causes and processes which bring about the effects. As is illustrated in Figure 7, Galtung, in essence, places emphasis upon the phenomena or effects. In contradistinction, Boulding places greater emphasis on the structures and processes leading to the consequences or effects. Galtung pays attention rather exclusively to the violence as a result, as the property common to the results. Galtung should be duly praised for the discovery of the commonality, whether we call it violence or not. On the contrary, Boulding emphasizes causes, that is, processes and structures leading to the results, rather than the results themselves.

According to Boulding, the processes and structures producing the direct violence or war on the one hand, and the processes and structures producing the structural violence on the other, may overlap considerably and may be mutually related, as is shown in Figure 7, but these are basically different processes and structures and should be clearly distinguished theoretically. Boulding argues that the same results do not necessarily mean that they are produced by the same factors. Even if the results are the same, they may be caused by the different factors. On the basis of the distinction between causes of war and causes of poverty, Boulding argued that peace studies should concentrate its efforts upon the former.

Both war and poverty share the common property of depriving human beings of their inherent potentials. Nevertheless, Boulding sees war and poverty as resulting from essentially different causes, through essentially different processes and structures. Wars are caused by processes and structures quite different form those producing poverty, and there are specific *structures,* international or domestic, which breed wars. Therefore, the use of term "structural" is quite problematic, because Galtung applies the term only to structures producing poverty while there are structures producing wars. His use of the term gives the impression that poverty alone is produced by structural factors.

Moreover, the term structural violence has the effect of concealing the differences between the processes and structures producing war and poverty. Thus, Boulding concludes that the term "structural violence" is only worth the name of *metaphor* at best (Boulding 1977: 83).

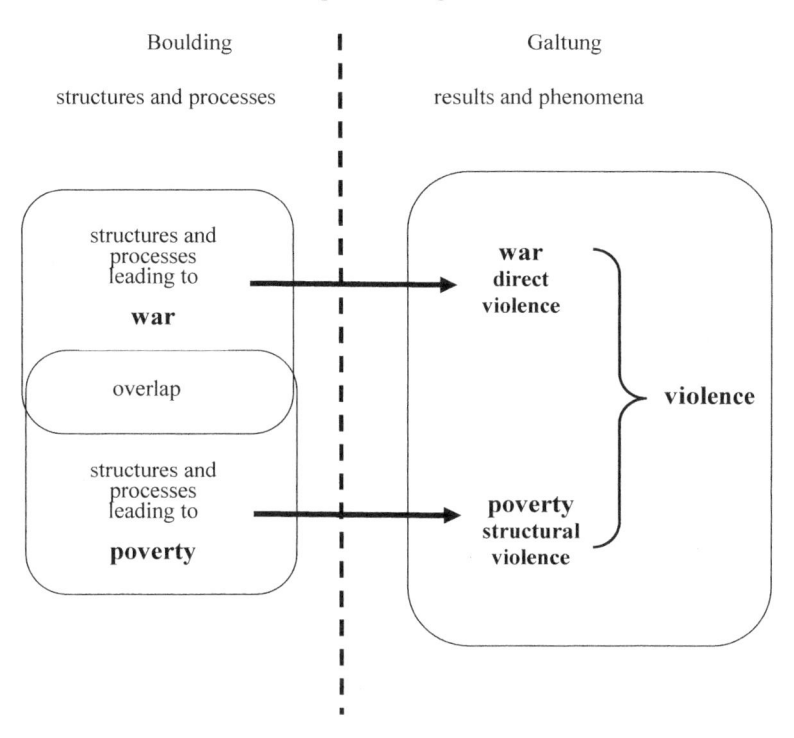

**Figure 7 Two Perspectives on Violence: War and Poverty
Boulding vs. Galtung**

```
            Boulding              |         Galtung
      structures and processes    |    results and phenomena

      ┌─────────────────────┐     |     ┌─────────────────────┐
      │  structures and     │     |     │      war            │
      │  processes          │─────┼────▶│      direct         │
      │  leading to         │     |     │      violence       │ ⎫
      │     war             │     |     │                     │ ⎪
      │  ┌──────────┐       │     |     │                     │ ⎬ violence
      │  │ overlap  │       │     |     │                     │ ⎪
      │  └──────────┘       │     |     │                     │ ⎭
      │  structures and     │     |     │     poverty         │
      │  processes          │─────┼────▶│     structural      │
      │  leading to         │     |     │     violence        │
      │     poverty         │     |     │                     │
      └─────────────────────┘     |     └─────────────────────┘
```

To be sure, in some respect, Boulding's criticism was utilitarian in the same way as other criticisms in that he was opposed to the endless expansion of peace studies which the concept of violence seemed to produce. He argues that it is better to limit our attention to direct violence, because such a narrow and rigorous focus will reward us with much richer academic results, and he concludes that, therefore, peace studies should concentrate upon the issues of war.

In spite of the criticisms by Boulding and others, the theory of structural violence won the support and sympathy of the overwhelming majority of peace researchers. The theory of structural violence was a real contribution to peace studies as it not only deepened the meaning of peace, but also provided a new integrated theoretical framework and opened new research vistas. Most significant of all, the concept of peace was defined on the basis of the full realization of human potentials, in other words, human rights in the broadest and most fundamental sense of the word. The idea that human rights in this sense is the most important element of peace, and hence the most important research goal for peace studies, seems to have come to be shared by the majority of peace students.

On the other hand, the ready acceptance of the theory of structural violence was accompanied by the danger of fragmentation of the discipline. For one thing, the concept of violence proposed by Galtung was too broad and too all-embracing. As long as human rights in the above sense continued to be the research priority of peace studies, every urgent problem of our world should be included in its research agenda. War, conflict, poverty, disease, inequality, discrimination, social injustice, political oppression, and environmental degradation should all be important research subjects for peace studies. Thus, peace studies was precipitated toward fragmentation, losing sight of its common core.

Needless to say, it was not in vain. Peace studies may have gone a little astray but was not wandering aimlessly in a barren wilderness. As Chadwick Alger demonstrates, though in much later days, important peace approaches or "tools" were found, such as "economic development," "economic equity," "ecological balance," "governance of the global commons," "feminist perspectives," "peace education," and "people's movements" (Alger 1999: 30-39).

2.2.6 The Third Stage

The transition to the third stage was again motivated largely by factors external to peace studies. Toward the end of the 1970s, the Soviet Union's invasion of Afghanistan marked the beginning of what is called a "New Cold War" after the decade of détente. The plan to deploy intermediate nuclear forces (INF) or what then was called theater missiles (or theater nuclear weapons) in Western Europe drove peace studies back to the realities of war, especially nuclear war.

Indeed, a researcher confessed in the early 1980s that they might have been blinded to true problems, that is, cold facts of nuclear war, by the attraction of structural violence. A voice was heard to say "we have been missing our real target in all these years when we focused on structural violence rather than on the war making capacities of our societies" (Krippendorf 1981: 109).

At the same time, as Boulding warned, peace studies seemed to lose its way. While the focus on structural violence deepened and expanded our understanding of peace, and achieved excellent academic results, it also brought about the overexpansion or dilution of research themes. A researcher deplored the current state of the art in peace studies, saying that peace research has grown in so many different directions that "a synthesis, in the sense of forging different traditions together" is lacking (Wiberg 1981: 147). Peace studies had now become "a black hole" absorbing every social problem and like "[after the fall of] the tower of Babel" (Wiberg 1993: 10-11). Thus, in some quarters at least, the necessity of a new integration of the discipline or "some common core theory" (Wiberg 1993: 11) was felt in the face of the fragmentation of peace studies carried too far. This was the second crisis of peace studies.

As a result, peace studies had to face the issue of war once again. Yet this time the challenge was no longer a simple choice between direct violence and structural violence, or between the old agenda and new. The real challenge was how to understand and explain the relationship or linkage of the two. It is a question of how to theoretically integrate or synthesize former academic achievements both on direct and structural violence. Thus, an important task of peace studies in the 1980s is to (re)construct a theoretical framework which enables us to understand diversified themes in an integrated or holistic way.

Another characteristic of this period was the increasing importance of the notion of human rights in the broadest and the most fundamental sense of the word. If "human rights" is understood to mean the full realization of inherent human potentials, then the abolition of war, the achievement of economic prosperity, the establishment of democratic political system, and the accomplishment of social justice are all necessary conditions for such a full realization. In other words, all these goals are ultimately means to the end of the future full realization of the human potentials, the realization of human rights in the broadest sense of the word. War, poverty, starvation, discrimination, oppression and even environmental degradation, are all obstacles to be eliminated and eradicated for the achievement of the final goal.

A similar view emphasizing the growing significance of the concept of human rights is advanced by Sakamoto. Sakamoto argues that leading discussions in the international society, for example, in the United Nations, reflected important changes in the perception of the relationship among the three key values: peace (here meaning the absence of war), development, and human rights (Sakamoto 1990: 241). According to Sakamoto, the leading discussions in the international society involving these concepts can be divided into three phases of evolution, as is schematically shown in Figure 8. It is important to note here that the shifts of the focus or priority were accompanied by critical changes in the perception of the mutual relationship among the three key values

In the first phase, the focus of the discussions was peace. Here the term "peace" is used in its conventional sense, "the absence of war." The goals of development and human rights were considered to be necessary and indispensable conditions for achieving the goal of peace. In other words, development and human rights were means to the goal of eliminating wars. This view has been very prevalent. Though the term "peace" is replaced by "security," the latest version of this view can be found in the report of the Secretary-General of the United Nations: *In Larger Freedom: Towards Development, Security and Human Rights for All, Report of the Secretary-General of the United Nations* (A/59/2005).

In the second phase, the focus changed to development, reflecting the recognition of the urgency of the North-South problem in that period. The three values were perceived to be independent goals on its own, with no priority among them. They were all goals to be achieved at the same time.

**Figure 8 Changes of the Relationship
among the Notions "Peace," "Development," and "Human Rights"**
source: adapted from Sakamoto (1990), 241-250

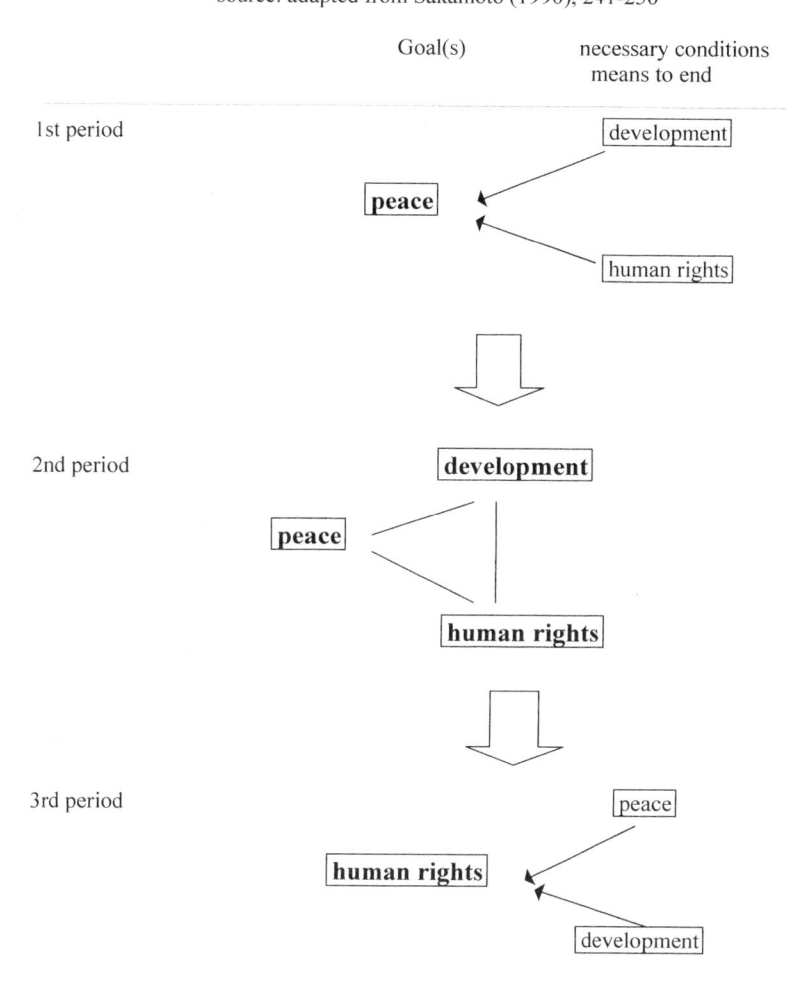

Goal(s)   necessary conditions
         means to end

1st period

```
              peace  ←  development
                    ←  human rights
```

2nd period

```
              development
        peace
              human rights
```

3rd period

```
              human rights  ←  peace
                            ←  development
```

In the third phase, a new perception of their mutual relationship emerged. Finally, in this phase, human rights came to be regarded as a value supreme to the other values. The two goals of peace and development were now viewed as means to the end of human rights. The prevalent view in this phase is, therefore, that both the elimination of war and the attainment of economic prosperity are only means for achieving the final goal of the full realization of human rights. In this context, the concept of human rights should be understood, as we saw above, in the broadest sense of the word, that is, as the realization of inherent human possibilities (Sakamoto 1990: 242 – 250).

So far, we have traced the development of the concept of peace in peace studies roughly toward the end of 1980s. After the end of the Cold War, several new concepts concerning peace in its broader sense have been proposed. They are at present in a state of theoretical or conceptual ferment. We will examine them in the last chapter.

2.2.7 Peace Studies as a World Learning Process

The development of peace studies can also be seen as part of the much broader process, big global learning process, in which human race has been learning the meaning of peace (Alger 1989: 119).

The process is seen as part of the global learning process, parallel with the development of peace studies, in which emphasis shifted from the solution of disputes by war, through the banning of war, to the elimination of structural violence. For example, the United Nations has come to recognize the importance of the issues of economic development, environment, and human rights as peace studies has learnt. Probably, however, the most suitable example of this process will be the case of war.

Only after the nightmare experiences of the two world wars, and the danger of extermination of the entire human race by a nuclear war, did human race begin a serious academic endeavor, in the form of peace studies, for analysis of the causes of war and the exploration of the prevention of war, especially nuclear war.

This process of learning corresponds to the change in the recognition of the legitimacy of war. Traditionally, war was considered to be a legitimate means of the sovereign state for solving international disputes. As we will see in the next chapter, war is often considered to be a necessary mechanism for the well-functioning of the balance of power (see 3.3). The idea is said to be traced back to Niccolo Machiavelli (1469-1527), and it is categorically expressed in the famous dictum of von Clausewitz as "a war is a continuation of politics by other means." But, through the learning process, war has lost its legitimacy gradually.

The decline and final demise of the legitimacy of war is ascribed to the too much progress of military technologies. The excessive development of military technologies has eroded the legitimacy of war, because war has become too costly both with respect to its weapons and to its human victims and material damages. It goes without saying that nuclear weapons did much to accelerate the trend.

In this way, interstate or international wars, especially nuclear wars, have now come to be regarded as illegitimate. Intrastate wars or internal wars within a sovereign state still seem, however, to retain some of the legitimacy. And we have many such conflicts throughout the world.

Of course, we must make other important reservations concerning the decline of the legitimacy of war. First, the right to defend one's country with the use of force is still regarded as legitimate. Even the use of nuclear weapons was not deemed completely illegal in self-defence, as the advisory opinion of the International Court of Justice on the legality of nuclear weapons in 1996 showed. Secondly, war and the use of force should be distinguished in this context. With the prevalence of internal wars which brought about tremendous victims, the use of force to stop gross human rights violations in internal wars seems to have regained some legitimacy. This is the issue of humanitarian military intervention. The United Nations or the UN-authorized multinational armies have used military force in Somalia, and Iraq. And NATO conducted air raids against Yugoslavia even without such an authorization from the United Nations.

Traditionally, the sovereign state has been viewed as the only legitimate possessor and user of the military force. But parallel with the decline and demise of the legitimacy of war, the trust and confidence in the sovereign state has been seriously eroded. For one thing, in our interdependent world, no single state can behave independently without due regard to other states and the whole world, and no single state can solve the urgent problems like environmental degradation or global financial crisis without the cooperation with other states. For another, actors other than state such as international organizations, multinational corporations, NGOs, even terrorist groups have become influential in the international society.

3. Studies on War and Conflict: General

3.1 War and Peace Studies: Pioneering Works

As we saw above, the early peace studies viewed peace as the absence of war, and concentrated its efforts predominantly upon the issue of war, especially wars between major powers. It was against the background of the human and material damages of the two World Wars, the atomic bombings of Hiroshima and Nagasaki, and the threat of the possible extermination of the whole human race by a nuclear war.

And it was also due to these factors that forerunners of peace studies like Sorokin, Wright and Richardson were interested in studies on war, especially the human costs of war. In a sense, they had established the precedence of the method and produced results which the succeeding generation of peace researchers could follow. Let us examine some of the major research achievements prior to the birth of peace studies. We will take up three topics: intensity of war, civilian casualties of war, and operationalization of war realities, especially of casualties.

First of all, Sorokin developed a composite index called "intensity" from the duration (in months and years) of war, number of soldiers, number of casualties or deaths, number of belligerents or combatant states etc., as is given in Table 8. The table shows clearly that the intensity of war rocketed exponentially in the twentieth century. The concept of intensity of war was to be inherited and sophisticated by the later peace studies.

Table 8 Increase in the "Intensity" of Wars
source: Originally from Sorokin, cited in Wright (1964), 56

Century	12	13	14	15	16	17	18	19	20
Intensity	18	24	60	100	180	500	370	120	3080

Melvin Small and John David Singer further sophisticated the studies on the scale and intensity of war. Drawing on the pioneering study we just examined, they proposed the following three indicators: magnitude (indicating duration of war and number of participants), severity (of the damages measured by battle deaths), and intensity (composite indicator showing the scale of war) (Small and Singer 1982: chap. 3). Table 9 shows these indicators for some of the wars.

Table 9 Magnitude, Severity, and Intensity of War
source: Small and Singer (1982), Fig 4.2, 82-95

magnitude : indicates the temporal and spatial scale of war
Magnitude is measured in terms of "nation month," which is the sum of the number of months during which each state is engaged in war

severity : shows the damages of war, casualties
Severity is expressed in the absolute or relative number of the casualties. Civilians are excluded from the definition. The index is similar to Richardson's "magnitude."

intensity = severity / magnitude

<Some historical examples>

	magnitude	severity (10,000s)	intensity
Franco-Prussian	27.0	19	6944
Sino-Japanese	16.0	2	937
Russo-Japanese	38.6	13	336
World War I	607.9	900	14074
World War II	887.9	1500	17086
Korean War	514.1	200	3680
Vietnam War	729.7	121	1666

where intensity = severity / magnitude

Quincy Wright also made a similar effort to measure the human cost of war. In his comprehensive survey of past studies on war, he demonstrated with concrete figures that the war casualties, especially the percentage of civilian deaths, rose rapidly in the twentieth century. This trend is confirmed by another statistics. The percentage of civilian deaths was 52% in the 1960s, and rose to as high as 85% in the 1980s (Sivard 1987: 28). Table 10 gives the figures.

Table 10 Percentage of Civilian (Non-Combatant) Deaths
source: Sivard 1987: 28

1960s	1980s	1990s
52	73	85

Richardson made a somewhat different attempt. He devised the indicator called "magnitude (of war)" which captured the great increase of war casualties. Actually, magnitude is a very simple indicator calculated as the common logarithm of the deaths, that is, the logarithm of the number of deaths to the base of 10 (Richardson 1960: 6). We can see the magnitudes for several wars in Table 11.

Table 11 Magnitude of War
source: Richardson (1960), 6

magnitude (μ) = log10 (N)
N = casualties, number of people who died because of the war

<some historical examples>

	Magnitude (μ)
World War I	7.4
Boer War (1899-1902)	4.4
US Civil War(1861-65)	5.8

The figure for the First World War, for instance, means that the number of the casualties was the seventh power of 10 or more. Such expressions of war casualties as this reflect the fact that war casualties have recently increased so much that they are no longer neatly expressed and comprehended by natural numbers which we use in everyday life, but only by logarithm or exponential functions.

From the above data, we can safely conclude that the rise of war casualties is an undeniable fact, whether the victims are civilians or not. This trend was a matter of great concern for the forerunners of peace studies.

Though the facts shown by these figures seem indisputable, we should, however, be very careful in interpreting their significance. There are two issues to be pointed out here: inclusion or exclusion of civilians, and absolute versus relative measurements.

First, when we examine figures of war casualties, we should be careful whether they include civilian victims or not. Various terms have been used to make this distinction: "civilian," "non-combatant," etc for the one, and "combatant," or "battle deaths" for the other. As we saw above, today civilian victims account for the greater percentage of the total casualties. Thus, the figures may vary greatly depending upon whether civilian deaths are included or not.

Secondly, we usually deal with the absolute number of the victims of war, whether it includes civilian deaths or not. When we consider the relative number of the victims in their percentage to the total population of the country or society in question, we find another, quite different aspect of the reality. In Northern Ireland, for example, 2,300 people were killed and 17,000 people were injured during the decade from 1971 to 1982 due to the so-called the Northern Ireland Conflict. If Northern Ireland had the same population as the United States, the number of the dead would have amounted to 345,000, which would have been roughly the same as the casualties in the American Civil War (Schaeffer 1989: 4). The prolonged conflict is a very serious war to the people of Northern Ireland comparable to the Civil War in the United States.

All of the studies we discussed above were concerned with presenting the scale of human costs of war in simple and clear terms. Take note that the results were expressed in numbers and figures, sometimes defined by simple mathematical formulas. These efforts meant the operationalization. Operationalization can be viewed simply as expressing the phenomena in terms of numbers and figures or mathematical terms. And operationalization requires preceding collection of data. Thus, the early peace studies, especially studies on war, were characterized by efforts to collect and operationalize empirical/historical data.

Statistics reduce the death of individuals to a simple number, without any regard to their sufferings and sorrows and those of their families, friends and so on. We should always keep this in mind when we examine casualties of war.

In the early years of peace studies and international relations studies, when the human costs of war were examined, attention was paid exclusively to the number of the casualties or direct victims of war. Recently, however, a new interest has emerged in the indirect victims or deaths of violence connected with war and armed conflict, especially in the mass murders. New terms have been coined such as "genocide," "politicide," "democide" and so forth which refer to these mass murders. They are symptoms of this emerging research concern. And the research attention is now being expanded to include many other politically-induced mass murders.

It is clear from this kind of research that the twentieth century was literally a century of mega death, or deaths by millions. Beside the Holocaust, We saw many tragedies such as the Armenian massacre during the First World War, the Ukrainian famine politically induced by the Stalin regime, the massacre by the Pol Pot regime in Cambodia, recent massacre in Rwanda among others. Ted Robert Gurr and Rudolph Rummel were pioneering in this research. Table 12 shows major cases of mass murders since the Second World War (see, also Eckhardt 1991, Harff and Gurr 1988, Rummel 1994).

Table 12 Genocides and Politicides since World War II
source: adapted from Harff (1992), 32-36
legend: P: politicide, victims defined politically
G: genocide, victims defined communally
PG: politicide against politically active communal groups
GP: mixed communal and political victims

state	type	date	Victims	number of victims (1,000s)
USSR	P	1943-47	repatriated Soviet nationals	500-1,100
USSR	G	1943-57	Chechens, Ingushi, Karachai, Balkars	230
USSR	G	1944-68	Meskhetians, Crimean Tatars	57-175
China	P	1950-51	Kuomintang cadre	800-3000
Sudan	P	1952-72	southern nationalists	100-500
Indonesia	GP	1965-66	Chinese, communists	500-1,000
Burundi	PG	1965-73	Hutu leaders, peasants	103-205
China	P	1966-75	Cultural Revolution victims	400-850
Philippines	PG	1968-85	Moro (Muslim) nationalists	10-100
Uganda	GP	1971-79	Karamojong, Acholi, Lango, Catholic clergy, political opponents of Idi Amin	100-500
Pakistan	PG	1971	Bengali nationalists	1,250-3,000
Kampuchea	GP	1975-79	Muslim Chan, old regime supporters, urban people, disloyal cadre	800-3,000
Indonesia	PG	1975-	East Timorese nationalists	60-200
Afghanistan	P	1978-79	supporters of old regime, rural supporters of rebels	1,000
Uganda	GP	1979-86	Karamojong, Nilotic tribes, Bangandans, Amin regime supporters	50-100

Notes (1) Only cases with more than 100,000 victims are listed.
(2) Cases where the estimation of the number of victims is not possible are excluded.

3.2 Collection of the Empirical Data on War

Pioneering works of the forerunners of peace studies are marked by a keen interest in the realities of war, especially in the vast human and material costs of war. Their works also involved collection of vast data on war. Their research orientation set the precedence for the early peace studies and was followed by research efforts characterized by the systematic, comprehensive collection of war data and computer-assisted quantitative and statistical analysis (Singer 2000: 5-6).

As was stated above, peace studies aims ultimately to identify causes of war. In fact, however, the complex phenomena of war are produced by a variety of factors. No single factor can explain the totality of the complexity. In order to understand and explain the complexity of war, systematic and comprehensive collection and accumulation of historical and empirical data is prerequisite. As Geller and Singer argues, we "need to know a fair amount about the *correlates* of war [that is, what is related with war] before we can speak with much authority about its causes" (Geller and Singer 1998: 2).

It is for this reason that the early peace studies endeavored to collect comprehensive data on war. A typical example of this kind of efforts was the Correlates of War Project (COW). The project was initiated by John David Singer and his colleagues in the University of Michigan, and it aimed to accumulate the data on the outbreaks of war in a scientific and more rigorous manner, in order to "provide an explanation of war in international politics grounded on data-based, empirical research" (Geller and Singer 1998: 12). The project has accumulated comprehensive data on 118 wars between sovereign states since the Vienna Conference (Small and Singer 1985: 7-9), which set the stage for the "concert of Europe" after the Napoleonic Wars. Table 9 above illustrates a small portion of the results of the project. The project has also demonstrated, as we will see later, that arms races were highly likely to result in the outbreak of war as far as the past history was concerned. Major results of the project are published in Small and Singer (1982). And Vasquez (2000) is a critical self-reflection of the project (Vasquez 2000: xiii).

Besides these research achievements, the project has enjoyed a high reputation for its comprehensiveness and reliability. Many statistical and empirical studies on war, such as studies on democratic peace, rely heavily on the data accumulated by the project.

Though we have said nothing so far, we must first have some operational criteria for the war before we can begin to collect the data. Generally speaking, most datasets concerning war have employed the deaths or casualties as the most reliable criterion, and used the number of 1,000 as the lower threshold. A much lower criterion is sometimes used for internal conflict (see Figure 31 in 6.3).

As a matter of fact, the following two criteria are combined in selecting wars and armed conflicts.

(1) whether battle casualties or total casualties in which civilian deaths are included are employed
(2) whether cumulative total or some average (usually yearly average) is used.

In most cases, absolute numbers are used, but relative numbers are important in some cases. Remember the case of Northern Ireland, where, if we employ the relative number, we can better capture the significance of the conflict to the society.

In the examination of the data on war, we should distinguish two aspects of war: outbreak or initiation of war on the one hand, and the intensity or escalation (severity, scale etc) on the other. The distinction is particularly important when we discuss causes of war. Different factors affect the two differently. Some may be the cause of the outbreak of a war, and others may be the cause of its escalation. Still others may be the cause of both. For example, as we will see below, the level of economic development of a state affects the two phases differently. International factors rather than domestic factors strongly affect the magnitude or severity of conflict but do not much affect the probability of the outbreak (Henderson and Singer 2000: 278).

In spite of its high reputation, the Correlates of War Project has been sometimes severely criticized as well. It is mainly due to its definition of war. The project assumes that the international system is basically Westphalian in that it consists only of sovereign independent states. Two results follow from the assumption. First, war is defined as fought only between and among sovereign states. The project, therefore, deals almost exclusively with interstate wars, wars between sovereign independent states. The only other type of war dealt with by the project is "extra-systemic wars," wars fought between a system member (sovereign state) and a non-member. A war of independence of the colony is a typical example of this.

As many scholars admit, however, the Westphalian system consisting of sovereign states has never covered the whole earth and it has functioned only in some parts of the world, even though today's world seems to be covered nearly completely by sovereign independent states nominally at least (Krasner 1996: 2001). There are many states which actually belong not to the Westphalian system but rather to what Susan Strange called "Westfailure" system (Strange 1999).

Secondly, "non-systemic" wars, namely, wars fought within the sovereign states or fought by non-state parties were completely left out of consideration (Small and Singer 1985: 8). One recent summary of the academic achievements of the project still maintains this narrow definition of war, declaring that its research target is "war in international politics" (Geller and Singer 1998: 12, passim). In view of these problems, the project has now extended its scope to include the so-called internal conflicts.

The Correlates of War Project is not the only attempt at a comprehensive data collection on war. Perhaps one of the most noteworthy is the work of Gaston Bouthoul and René Carrére of the Polemological Institute in France. They collected data on 366 wars and revolutions from 1714 to 1972. The single most shocking finding is the fact that there was not a single year during the time which did not see a war or revolution.

In addition, there are many other databases on war, conflicts or international crises (Cioffi-Revilla 1990: 11-38), though they are not so ambitious as COW. Though their scope is not limited to war alone, we can add to our list Charles McClelland's WEIS (Word Event Interaction Survey, 1966-1978) data, and Edward Azar's COPDAB (Conflict and Peace Data Bank, from 1948) data among others (Azar 1980, Howell 1983: 150, 157). Some of them contain "event data," which are distinguished from numerical data in their use of written texts. Most of these data are frequently used in the statistical or quantitative analyses of war and armed conflict.

In addition to these datasets, the increased interest in the local conflicts or internal conflicts have been recently reflected in the creation of such datasets on local or domestic violent conflicts as "Minorities at Risk" (Gurr 1993: 326-363), "Violent Intrastate Nationalist Conflict" (Ayres 2000: 116-117) and so on. The Uppsala dataset is the latest one covering the whole period from the end of the Second World War to the present, and is characterized by a much lower threshold of 25 annual battle deaths (Gleditsch et al 2002).

A list of wars and conflicts is the simplest way to represent the accumulation of data. Table 13 shows major lists of wars and conflicts.

Table 13 Typical Lists of Wars

name of the list	source
International Wars, 1816-1980	Small and Singer (1985) Table 1, 9-12
Wars that are included	Small and Singer (1982), 297-329
The War Data	Levy (1983), Table 4.1 88-91
Wars and War-related Deaths, 1500-1990	Sivard (1991), 22-25
Wars and War-related Deaths, 1945-1992	Sivard (1993), 21
Wars and Issues, 1648-1713, 1715-1814, 1815-1914, 1918-41, 1945-89	Holsti (1991), 48-49, 85-87, 140-42, 214-16, 274-78
Principal Wars, 1400-1559, 1917-84	Luard (1986), 421-447

For sources, see references.

3.3 Approaches to War

It goes without saying that a variety of approaches and perspectives are required in order to understand the complex phenomena like war. Before discussing causes of war, therefore, it seems better to have a broad overview on how war is understood in various approaches to international relations. We will take up realism and the world-system theory as examples.

In the realist understanding of international or interstate relations, war has been recognized as one of the legitimate foreign policy options. As we saw above, it was epitomized by von Clausewitz' axiom. According to the realist theory, war, or the use of military force as an unmistakable manifestation of power, is a legitimate option in foreign policy. The realists take the rationality of war as a prerequisite. From such a viewpoint, therefore, except for great wars which could destroy the international system itself, wars are not considered to be an anomaly or aberration. In other words, the realist theory assumes that confrontations, clashes, and wars among states are inevitable because they possess, and can employ, physical coercive power in the form of armaments or military force (Kamo, 1990: 8-9, 11-12).

The latest version of realism in international relations theory is the so-called structural realism or neorealism represented by Kenneth Waltz. Neorealism never argues in favor of the legitimacy of war, but it insists upon the inherent possibility of war in the current international system. Waltz himself recently repeated the basic tenet that war is always possible (if not legitimate or inevitable) in the modern international system because of the condition of anarchy (Waltz 2000).

Realism, including both neoliberalism and neorealism (for these terms, see 7.5.1), assumes that the current international system is characterized by anarchy, namely, "lack of a common government". To neorealists, and not to neoliberalists, anarchy means the absence of higher authority which protects a state from the use of power or the threat of the use of power by other states trying to destroy or dominate the state in question. Under the condition of anarchy, there is always a possibility of attack from other states (Grieco 1988: 487, 495, 497-498), and no central authority exists which provides protection to states. Consequently, neorealists argue that war is not an anomaly, and is possible if not legitimate.

Similarly, both in theory and in practice of the balance of power, war is not just possible but inevitable. Many theorists think, as Kenneth Waltz argues, that the merit of the balance of power lies not in the prevention of war or the maintenance of peace as the absence of war. But it rather lies in the guaranteeing of the security (or the survival) of the states involved by thwarting the ambition of a state seeking the hegemony in world politics. War is the usual and most frequently resorted means of preventing an ambitious state from achieving hegemony and domination over other states. In the theory and practice of the balance of power, therefore, wars "occupy the highest place as an ultimate means of maintaining the balance of power as a system" (Takayanagi 1991: 138).

Accordingly, and ironically enough, an age when the balance of power functioned well was an age of war, while an age when the balance of power clearly broke down was an age of peace, at least an age without major wars. An age of the balance, whether it is real or imaginary, is an age of war. An age of peace is an age in which one state is clearly superior in power to others (Takayanagi 1991: 144 -145). The idea is tantamount to that of the "hegemonic stability theory," which we will discuss in 4.3.2.

The realist theory is not the only theory which emphasizes the possibility of war in the international system. Immanuel Wallerstein's world-system theory similarly treats the world as a single system. And in this theory again, war is viewed as an integral, inseparable part of the political and economic development of the capitalist world economy. In this sense, war is neither a politically motivated deviation nor an economic externality. War is not a radical deviation from the normal working or functioning of the capitalist world-system. Profit and protection, namely, the search of profitable trade and the protection of the trade through military force (Schaeffer 1989: 2), go together, as the saying goes; "trade follows the flag." Accordingly, war is not an anomaly or aberration, as long as ethical or moral issues are set aside. In this way, the realist theory of international relations and the world-system theory (and others of course) clearly admit the inevitability or rationality of war, though they do not advocate the legitimacy or necessity of just war or holy war.

So far, we examined how war is understood in two theories of international relations. They both emphasize systemic or structural factors in that they view war as almost inevitable because of the nature of the system they postulate. It goes without saying, however, that wars are not caused by systemic or structural factors alone. Even if we limit our attention to interstate wars and their causes, a recent survey of the research in the past decades enumerates more than 10 factors which heighten the probability and intensity of war (Geller and Singer 1998: 193-194). Moreover, as the time span of research is expanded, say, to the whole modern period beginning from fifteenth or sixteenth century, it will be accompanied with the discovery of such new variables or factors as economic development, population growth, technological innovations etc.

In this respect, Waltz' book, *Man, the State and War: A Theoretical Analysis*, will provide us with a good starting point. To analyze causes of war, Waltz distinguishes three images: the first, second, and third images. He begins his examination of causes of war with an individual, that is, with the human nature (first image), then proceeds to the examination of the nature of state (second image), especially of the political system (often called regime type), and finally concludes his examination with the assertion of the supremacy of systemic or structural causes (third image). Joseph Nye's explanation of the First World War illustrated in Figure 9 is an excellent example of this pattern.

Figure 9 Path to the First World War
source: adapted from Nye (2002), 72

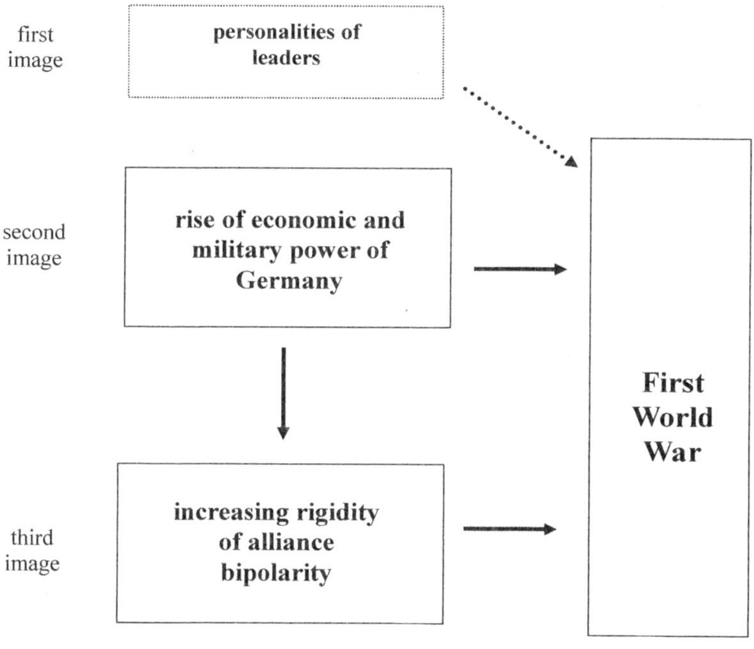

first image — **personalities of leaders**

second image — **rise of economic and military power of Germany**

third image — **increasing rigidity of alliance bipolarity**

→ First World War

Nye's analysis and similar analyses take all the three images of Waltz into consideration, and provide us with convincing pictures of the paths leading to the outbreak of war, the First World War in this case.

Yoshikazu Sakamoto and Richard Falk also present a comprehensive model of world military order, though they exclude the first image. Their model consists of five components: (1) military-industrial complex, (2) arms race between the two blocks, (3) arms transfer from developed to developing countries, (4) arms race between developing countries, and (5) militarization in developing countries (Sakamoto and Falk 1980: 3-5). Though their model was originally intended for the explanation of the Cold War period, it still retains its explanatory power. Though separately, we will discuss three of them ((1), (2), and (5)) as major causes of international or internal armed conflict.

When we discuss interstate wars, however, we will focus upon the "big picture," and deal mainly with systemic or structural causes of war. It is not because we embrace the neorealists' view that the modern international system is structured in such a way that the condition of anarchy makes wars always possible (if not inevitable). But it is rather because not a small number of scholars, whether neorealist or otherwise, have argued that some historical situations in the international system do not permit a state to avoid being involved in war.

Nevertheless, when we discuss causes of war, we cannot ignore the second image, that is, state level factors. When the international society is regarded as a system consisting of the structure and the units which make up the system, there is a long polemics concerning the relative importance of the structure and the unit, as an explanatory variable of international relations in general and war in particular. This is the "levels of analysis" problem.

In fact, in sharp contrast with systemic or structural approaches, other scholars have emphasized internal or domestic factors as the causes of war. One recent instance is the "democratic peace" thesis. Table 14 summarizes the argument in a schematic way.

Table 14 Democratic Peace

	democracies	non-democracies
democracies	no war	war
non-democracies	war	war

The proponents of the democratic peace thesis argue, on the basis of apparently convincing statistical analyses, that democratic countries never fight each other, or that democracies never fight democracies.

Though it is not the claim of the democratic peace thesis itself (because it does not assert that democracies never fight wars), if the regime type or the character of the political system of a state determines whether the state wages a war or not, then it is not the structure of the international system, but the internal character of the state, that is the major cause of war. This corresponds with the second image of war. This means that, even when we focus exclusively upon interstate war, factors internal to the state cannot be ignored. In the case of internal or intrastate conflicts, the relevance of these factors becomes much greater. We will deal with causes of internal conflict separately in chapter 6.

There is another important level of analysis in identifying causes of war. From a perspective of the dichotomy between the system and the unit, the phenomena of arms races seem to lie in between. It is because they are interactions between units under a specific system. Arms races have been regarded as one of the most important causes of war, and peace studies has proposed several models of arms race. Therefore, we will deal with the issue in chapter 5.

3.4 A Case of A Systemic Factor: Polarity

Polarity refers to the distribution of power among the members of the international system. And it is perhaps the most widely discussed aspect of the system (Cashman 1993: 232). The concepts of "poles" (or polarity) and "hegemon" (or hegemonic state) are frequently employed in studies on the role of structure of the international system in the occurrence of war. The discussion of wars in the balance of power system is one example. Since the concept of polarity has been applied to all scales of war between states, we will take up polarity as a case of a systemic or structural factor and examine in some detail whether or how it affects the initiation and intensity of interstate war in general. It is not because polarity offers a clear answer to the question. At present no definitive conclusion is reached. It is rather because we want to show that we find serious difficulties in applying even an apparently very simple factor like polarity.

The term "pole" usually refers to major states which have great political, economic, and military power and therefore have a great influence in the international society. The term "hegemon" or "hegemonic state" refers to a single dominant pole or great power such as the British Empire in the 19th century and the United States in the 20th century. In addition, hegemony means superiority or leadership over other major powers and other states. The hegemon alone, by definition, can exercise this leadership in the international system.

The polarity means the distribution of power, or simply the number of poles in the system. In terms of the number of poles, the international system is conventionally classified into three categories: unipolar, where only a single hegemon exists, bipolar, where two powers are overwhelming, as in the case of the Cold War between the United States and the Soviet Union, and, finally, multipolar, where more than two powers exist, as in the case of the Concert of Europe in the 19th century after the Congress of Vienna. The so-called balance of power is a typical example of the last category. Many studies have tried to find which category is most conducive or least conducive to the occurrence of war.

In addition, poles can be blocs or alliances of member states as well as consisting of a single member. But usually the resultant classifications are the same trichotomy into unipolar, bipolar, and multipolar systems. When poles consist of alliances of states, the term "cluster polarity" is employed. It actually refers to the number of mutually exclusive alliances or blocs. In contrast to the cluster polarity, simple polarity is often called "power polarity." Some historical examples of polarity are given in Table 15.

In the studies of the relationship between polarity and war, however, actually two interrelated questions are involved. The first is which system is most stable. And the second is which system is most free from war. Note here that in almost all of the discussions of the system stability, the stability means the absence of war. Though it is often used in this sense, the term "stability" also means the system's ability to endure over time (Cashman 1993: 235). It is because, even if wars occur, the system can survive. We should distinguish between system stability and the absence of war and we will limit our attention to the latter question, because we are interested here in the issue of war.

Table 15 Power Polarity and Cluster Polarity
source: adapted from Wayman (1985), 120

| | | polarization of blocs or alliances (cluster polarity) ||
		multipolarity	bipolarity
distribution of military power (power polarity)	multipolarity	Post-Napoleonic Europe (1812-1900) Interwar Europe (1919-1939)	Pre-World War I (1900-1914) World War II (1941-1945)
	bipolarity	Post-Sino-Soviet split (1962-1989)	Early Cold War (1947-1962)

In addition, we should also take note that it is quite another matter whether the stability or peace of the system maintained by major powers is a desirable thing or not, to the common people and to the people of other countries usually subordinated to the major powers. For example, Kiichi Fujiwara argues that there are cases of despotic or autocratic peace like the Concert of Europe or the recent ASEAN in contrast with democratic peace (Fujiwara 2000).

Now let us examine some research results concerning the relationship between polarity and war. First, Richard N. Rosecrance argues that, as is illustrated in Figure 10, in the multipolar system wars occur more frequently but they are less intense, while in the bipolar world wars occur less frequently but they are more intense (Tanaka 1989: 245).

On the other hand, Jack S. Levy reached the opposite conclusion. He classified the international system after the fifteenth century into the three categories above, and then compared wars involving major powers in terms of the duration, severity, and casualties. And he reached the conclusion that, as long as the number of occurrences of wars is concerned in the past history, the multipolar system was actually the most stable, but wars in the multipolar system were much more intense on the average than those in the bipolar system (Levy 1985b: 58). This conclusion is quite the opposite of the conclusion by Rosecrance.

But, as we will see in the next chapter, Robert Gilpin and most of cycle theorists advanced another thesis on the stability of the system. According to this thesis, and contrary to the above two conclusions, the unipolar system, where a hegemon dominates, is the most stable. In other words, the thesis claims that when there is one single hegemonic power, wars occur less frequently than when there are several great powers. The thesis has come to be called "hegemonic stability" theory. We will touch upon it later.

Figure 10 Polarity and the Incidence and Scale of Wars
source: Rosecrance (1966), 323, also partly from Tanaka 1989: 245

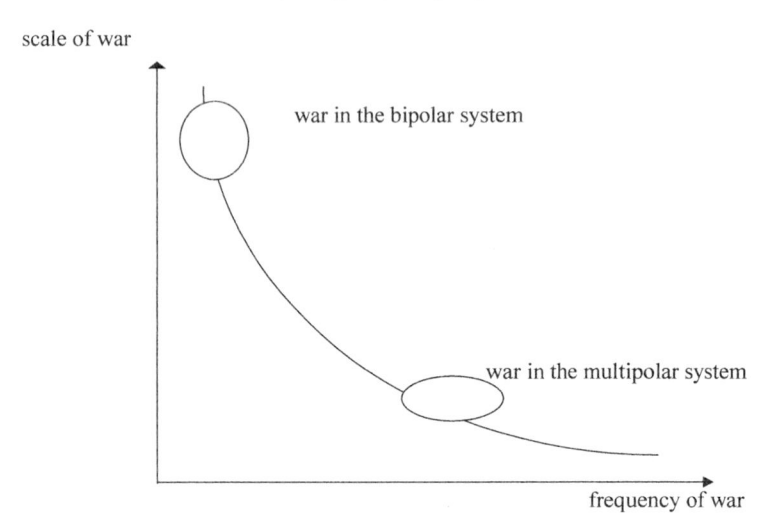

Anyway, results of previous research are rather contradictory. In view of these contradictory findings and propositions, it may be better to make several distinctions. First, as we pointed out above, the onset or outbreak of war should be distinguished from the scale or magnitude (severity or intensity, for that matter) of war. Frequency of wars is one thing, and severity quite another. A particular type of polarity may be strongly associated with either of them, but not with both.

Secondly, such association may vary over time. For example, a high concentration of power (like bipolarity) was associated with a high magnitude of war in the early nineteenth century. The pattern for the late twentieth century was just the opposite. And, at the same time, when we examine the relationship between the occurrence of war and the structure of the international system, we should always keep it in mind that their relationship varies depending upon the way in which the international system is classified by researchers. For example, is the international system in the early 21st century unipolar or multipolar?

Thirdly, we may have to pay attention also to the transition of one polarity type to another rather than to the types themselves. The issue of transition will be taken up later in 4.3.2.

To conclude, what we saw was not a clear or illuminating research achievements, but only rather unrewarding research efforts. War occurs frequently in any type of polarity. None can be credited with making a significant contribution to peace.

In the following chapters, we will first take up systemic or structural factors with special reference to the so-called great wars. After the discussion of great wars, we will proceed to the examination of arms race which has been considered one of the most important causes of war. Last in order but not least in significance, we will take up the issue of internal conflict.

4 Studies on Great Wars

4.1 General Introduction

In this and the following chapters, we will limit our concept of peace to the traditional category of organized armed conflicts. More concretely, we will address two types of war. First we will deal, in this chapter, with great interstate wars among major powers. Secondly, we will discuss, in Chapter 6, smaller wars which are usually referred to as "local conflict" or "local war" and fought in the very limited geographical area or largely within the territory of a state.

With the collection of data on wars, the time span of research was expanded. To be sure, judging from the previous research results, the arms race is the most important single factor leading to war in the short-term perspective. But the arms race is obviously not the only cause of war. Especially when one takes a long-term view, other factors emerge as more important causes. What we will discuss here is studies and theories of great wars from a long-term perspective, sometimes with a time span of several centuries. Most of these long-term studies were marked by strong interest in the cyclicity or regularity of major wars. Theories of long wave or long cycle of major wars are typical examples.

Wars on a very large, global scale have been variously labeled by different researchers reflecting their diverse interests and perspectives. To mention a few, "global war," "world war," "extensive war," "systemic war," and "hyper war" are the names given to them. Though with minor differences, however, most of them refer to essentially the same phenomena (Levy 1985a: 344 note 1). Great wars can be defined as wars (1) fought over large expanses of territory, by many actors, for a number of years, and (2) with profound implications for the winners, the losers, and even neutral bystanders.

These wars are regarded as a distinctive set of wars that are a critical part of the functioning of global political economy. They are fought to determine whose policy preferences are most likely to influence the way (and for whose benefit) the global political economy operates. They usually lead to a new phase of significant re-concentration of power and a global military-political and economic leadership. In sum, they are instrumental in determining how the world is structured. These wars are significant "cogs" in the political economy "machinery" that structure global politics and economics (Rasler and Thompson 2000: 301, 302, 309).

Studies on these great wars are commonly marked by two characteristics.

First, they assume that the world constitutes a single system.
Secondly, they ascribe the occurrences of great wars to the systemic factors, or the properties of the system, on the basis of the long-term political and economic data.

These studies on great wars can be viewed as systemic theories of war, or macroscopic theories of the causes of war, in that they emphasize the structure of the international system as an important cause of war. In addition, they are also characterized by the common insistence upon (or assumption of) the cyclical or recurrent nature of great wars, with or without a regular interval of, say, fifty or hundred years. As typical theories of great wars, we will examine the following three approaches: theory of lateral pressure, theory of economic cycle, and theory of long cycle or long wave.

4.2 Lateral Pressure

As a typical example of a combination of a classical systemic approach and a statistical methodology, we will first take up the "lateral pressure" approach. The concept of "lateral pressure" was first proposed in the joint research by Nazli Choucri and Robert North. Starting with the very basic data such as population and national income, they showed, through the application of highly sophisticated mathematical procedures, the complex process in which these variables are combined and linked with other variables, leading finally to the First World War. Theirs may be one of the most successful of the long-term studies which try to show the complex process leading to a great war.

Choucri and North first define "master variables," that is, basic variables which constitute the basis and starting point of their research These are population, resources, and technology. Next, they hypothesize that the population increase will become the basic cause of war when it is combined with other master variables (Choucri and North 1987: 205, 206).

Using the data on European major powers from 1870 to 1914, they explain the process leading to the outbreak of the First World War in the following way. Figure 11 schematically illustrates this process.

Figure 11 Lateral Pressure and the Process Leading to War
source: Choucri and North (1975), 245

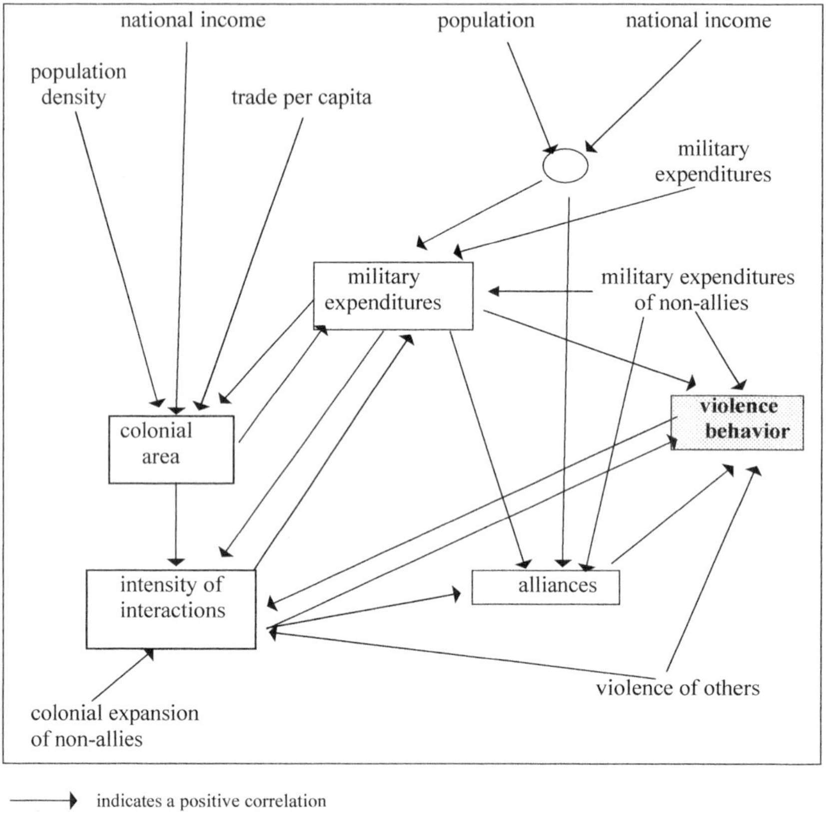

⟶ indicates a positive correlation

First, the domestic growth pressure through the increases in population and

60

income (especially in the population density and per capita national income) produced pressures for external expansion such as the expansion of colonies, intensification of external economic activities, and increase in military activities and military expenditures. "Lateral pressure" is the name given to this outward pressure of expansion. The increased lateral pressure heightened the possibility of conflict of interests among major powers, and the heightened possibility of conflict in turn increased military expenditures and intensified military alliances and coalitions among the powers. The process culminated in the outbreak of the war.

As is observed in the figure, Choucri and North employed a great number of variables, and the mutual relationships between those variables are very complicated. The process can be reiterated in an oversimplified way as follows.

When the increase of population is combined or accompanied with technological progress or industrialization, the existing resource base, that is, the limited resources and environment of one country or one region, may not be capable of supporting or sustaining it. Then, it must perforce be transformed into the pressure toward external expansion. And it is this pressure for external expansion that lies at the socioeconomic root of the violence of war. They conclude that, through the mediation of several variables, specific combination of master variables underlies the lateral pressure, and, mediated by several variables, the lateral pressure lies at the root of a modern international crisis (Choucri and North 1987: 207-211). The dynamic of lateral pressure that the authors show was actually that of colonial expansion in the age of imperialism, and some called the approach "a study of imperialism with mathematical equations."

Of course, wars are not the only solution of lateral pressure. Choucri and North mention various "solutions" such as immigration, migrant labor, trade and overseas investment, expansion of territory (the cases of the United States and the Imperial Russia) etc, and combination of any of these. The feasibility of these solutions depends upon the levels of technologies and resources available (Choucri and North 1987: 208-211).

Needless to say, one cannot explain the occurrence of war directly by the master variables like population and technologies. One cannot claim that the master variables are the direct causes of war. In the long term, however, these variables heighten the lateral pressure and thus pave the way leading to war (Choucri and North 1987: 211).

The work has been highly praised because it elegantly treated long-term historical data with a sophisticated mathematical methodology, and more importantly because it demonstrated that combinations of domestic factors like population, technology and resources produced the lateral pressure which in the long term led ultimately to the outbreak of war.

This kind of studies raises the question of what historical factors cause great war in the long run. Studies focusing upon great wars are one of the attempts at answering this question.

4.3 Cycles of Great Wars

As part of the efforts to identify causes of war, a considerable number of scholars have been interested in exploring long-term historical conditions or patterns leading to war, especially to great war. These studies have tried to understand great wars and their causes in terms of the development of the world system or long-term economic or other cycles.

The research interest in the long-term causes of war was a part of a broader interest in the long-term trends of world order or world system especially among the American scholars. And the interest was motivated against the background of the alleged decline of the US hegemony, namely, the decline of the US leadership and system-sustaining capability in the international system (Yamakage 1994: 12) in the 1980s. Of course, even at that time, some still argued that the decline of the US hegemony is simply a myth (Strange 1987: 574).

The research interest necessitated a reexamination of the post-war world order and produced a considerable number of studies on long-term historical changes and transformations such as the rise and fall of great powers or civilizations, or very long-term economic cycles. One strand of the studies attempted to advance a variety of long cycle theories and explain the development and expansion of the modern international system since its inception in terms of the change of hegemony in the system. Economic and military factors are the two most important variables in the explanation proposed by the theories. Though some argue that most of the long cycle or long wave theories are now viewed as "nothing but a plausible tale" (Yamakage 1994: 14), long cycle theories have provided us with many important insights concerning the causes of great wars. We will take up two major approaches here: economic cycles and politico-military cycles.

4.3.1 Economic Cycles and Great Wars

Several long-term studies on the historical development of world system or world order are interested in the relationship of great war with the long-term economic fluctuations or economic cycles. Most of the studies have focused upon the Kondratieff's long wave.

In the 1920s, a Russian economist, Nikolai Kondratieff pointed out the existence of long term economic cycles with an interval of some fifty years. The economic cycle has now come to be called "Kondratieff's long wave (K-wave)." Many economists today doubt if the Kondratieff waves exist at all. The long wave has, however, recently been given a renewed attention after many years of neglect in connection with the rise and fall of great powers or the onsets of great wars. So-called long-cyclists insist that the Kondratieff's waves operate parallel to world leadership cycles. Usually, one-hundred-year world leadership cycles are linked to a pair of K-waves. Some argue that, while it is difficult to say either that K-waves cause major wars or that majors wars cause K-waves, a relationship between them does exist. It seems that global wars and K-waves reflect a common underlying process (Cashman 2000: 267).

Kondratieff himself argued that economic upswing periods of the wave coincided with the intensification of wars as Figure 12 shows, though some may oppose that the selection of the wars is problematic.

Figure 12 Kondratieff's Long Waves and Wars
source: adapted from Shindo (1988), 66

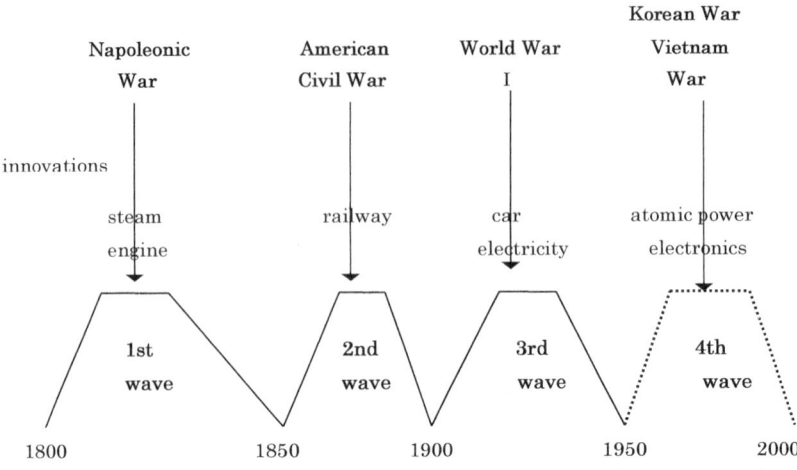

```
                                                    Korean War
        Napoleonic        American        World War    Vietnam
           War            Civil War           I          War
            │                │                │           │
innovations │                │                │           │
            ▼                ▼                ▼           ▼
          steam           railway            car      atomic power
          engine                          electricity  electronics

           /\              /\              /\          ,·······.
          /  \            /  \            /  \       ,'         ',
         / 1st\          / 2nd\          / 3rd\     /   4th       ',
        /  wave\        /  wave\        /  wave\  /    wave        ',
       /        \      /        \      /        \/                   ',

      1800            1850            1900          1950            2000
```
Note: The first to third waves are from Kondratieff, and the fourth is Shindo's extraporation.

Joshua Goldstein demonstrated a clear relationship of the Kondratieff's long wave with wars since the early sixteenth century. Goldstein calculated yearly war casualties and compared the number of deaths in the upswing and downswing periods in the long wave. The results are shown in Figure 13.

As is clear from the figure, the battle fatalities in the economic upswing are much greater than those in the economic downswing. Since the vertical axis which indicates the number of casualties is in the logarithmic scale, the actual differences are far greater than we can see in the figure. The long term economic upswings were periods in which great wars intensified. We should take note, however, that Goldstein's data in Figure 13 says nothing about the frequency (of onset) of wars. In fact, the number of wars is roughly equal in upswing and downswing periods. What Goldstein uncovers is a clear association between K-waves and war severity measured by the average battle deaths per year.

Figure 13 Economic Cycles and Battle Fatalities
source: adapted from Goldstein (1985), 422

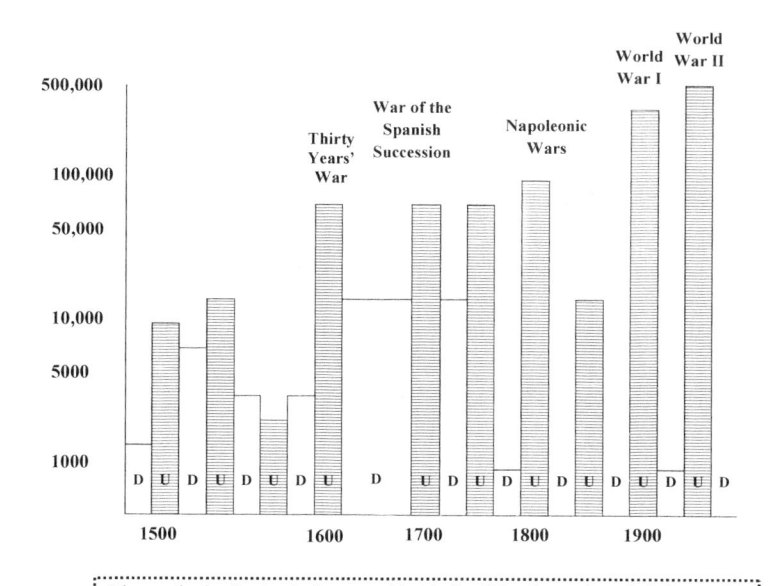

The vertical axis stands for annual battle fatalities for each period (log scale).
U = economic upswing, D = economic downswing
Wars with over one million total fatalities are named.

Jack Levy reexamined the issue, matching Goldstein's data on economic production cycle against the ten "general" wars of the last five centuries. He found that many of the wars broke out near the transition from downswing to upswing, so that the casualties were mainly associated with the upswing phase even though the wars might have begun in the downswing. It explains why Goldstein found an association between K-waves and severity of war, but not between K-waves and war initiation (Cashman 2000: 268).

The correspondence between economic upswings and war severity is causally ascribed to two factors at least. For one thing, an economic upswing or economic expansion intensified competition for raw materials and markets in the modern world development. For another, the economic prosperity made the increase of military expenditures and military buildups easier. This kind of the relationship between the economic expansion and the intensification of war endorses the same conclusion as that of the lateral pressure thesis above.

Incidentally, Figure 13 mentions five wars: Thirty Years War (1618-1648), Wars of Spanish Succession (1702-1713), (the French Revolution and) Napoleonic Wars (1792-1815), and two World Wars. These wars are regarded as cases of great wars by most of the researchers. There are some who go so far as to argue that the two world wars in the twentieth century should be considered to be two parts of a single war, perhaps, a second thirty years war, beginning in 1914 and ending in 1945.

4.3.2 Cycles of Great Wars

Many studies have been done on the regularity or cyclicity of great wars. In what follows, we will examine four models of long cycles of great wars: Toynbee's model, Wallerstein's world-system model, Gilpin's hegemonic model and Modelski's naval power model.

Arnold Toynbee made an early attempt at exploring the cyclicity of great wars. He postulated the following cycle (Modelski and Thompson 1989: 28-29).

- → general war
- → breathing space
- → supplementary war
- → general peace

This model by Toynbee was perhaps the first important attempt at the construction of a cyclic theory of great wars. And it is clearly based upon the balance of power theory. According to Toynbee, the opposition between the dominant state seeking the world hegemony on the one hand, and the alliance of other states seeking the maintenance of the balance of power on the other, brings about what he calls "general war." The general war usually ends in the defeat of the challenging state and in the short "breathing peace." But this peace is unstable and lasts only for a short time, because the main challenger is only temporarily defeated and the issue producing the general war has not yet been solved. Consequently, this short peace is followed by a relatively short and mild "supplementary war." The war finally resolves important issues and brings about the enduring "general peace." The cycle is repeated roughly with an interval of one century (Levy 1985a: 345-346).

Toynbee's theory is different from other models of great wars in that the general war neither decides the future of the system nor establishes a new system or new leadership. The general war functions as the build-in stabilizer of the existing system. The general war works to maintain the present system. It is because his model is based on the balance of power theory. Toynbee argues that a general war is waged in order to prevent the increase of the power of a dominant state who challenges the system. As we saw in 3.3, the most important goal of the balance of power is to prevent the emergence of a dominant state (hegemon) which poses a threat to the survival of other states in the international system.

However, this model does not say anything explicit about how the cycle is repeated, or why a general war occurs again after the general enduring peace. The model does not incorporate anything which moves the cycle from within, except for the implicit assumption of the logic of balance of power. Something outside the cycle seems to move and hence repeat the cycle.

Except for the early attempt by Toynbee, it is only recently that studies on the cyclicity or regularity of great wars have begun in earnest. And in this respect, Immanuel Wallerstein's world-systems theory was very influential. Wallerstein's cycle consists of four phases given below. And the cycle of hegemony and great war corresponds to the two cycles of the Kondratieff waves.

→ ascending hegemony
→ hegemonic victory (in a World War)
→ hegemonic maturity
→ declining hegemony
  (Modelski and Thompson 1989: 32).

When the system of production and exchange of goods and services meeting human physical and mental needs is expanded and extended on a global scale, it is called "world system." According to Wallerstein, the modern capitalist world system came into existence around 1500. And, in the development of the modern world system since the sixteenth century, there emerged three hegemons, namely, the Netherlands in the seventeenth century, the British Empire in the nineteenth century, and the United States in the twentieth century. More importantly, in each of the processes of the establishment of the new hegemony, a great war, called "world war" occurred: The Thirty Years War ("World War Alpha," 1618-1648), the French Revolution and the subsequent Napoleonic Wars ("World War Beta," 1792-1815), the First and Second World Wars ("World War Gamma," 1914-1945). According to the naming, the next, probably, nuclear war would be World War Delta, if it ever happened (Schaeffer 1989: 2).

World-systems theorists place war in the framework of the development and expansion of the capitalist world system. Accordingly, in this model, the cycle of great war is part of the development of world economy (Modelski and Thompson 1989: 31). Changes in the distribution of power are rooted in the underlying economic order and in uneven rates of capitalist development. Shifts in political-military power may be important, but they are brought about by economic processes. According to the theory, world wars can be seen as a struggle to shape the institutional structures of the capitalist world economy so as to construct the world market whose operation would favor particular economic actors. World wars are essentially attempts to reconfigure the interstate political structure so as to reflect the changing economic realities (Cashman 2000: 264,265).

The world war establishes the hegemony of the core state or hegemonic power. Here, hegemony means the power of imposing the norms and preferences upon the system through the dominant positions in the world market in agricultural and industrial production, trade and finance (Levy 1985a: 348).

With respect to the military power, the hegemons (the Netherlands, the British Empire and the United States in this case) were primarily naval powers. This point is greatly stressed in Modelski's long cycle theory, as we will see shortly. But, in order to counter the challenging states based on the continent (Germany, France etc), they became land powers as well.

After the establishment of hegemony through a world war, the hegemon enjoys its dominant position. But the position also requires its cost, namely, cost of dominance and leadership. It is because the hegemon is obliged to undertake the task of maintaining the system, especially its security and stability through the provision of the so-called international public goods (for the discussion of public goods, see 7.1). After the maturity of hegemony, the increase in the cost of leadership reduces the productivity in agriculture and industry, and it also leads to the collapse of alliances. The situation is called the "decline of hegemony." The decline in turn gives rise to the emergence of a challenger, and finally to the outbreak of the world war. The result of a "world war" is basically determined not by military factors alone but by economic factors as well (Levy 1985a: 349).

Thus, in Wallerstein's model, unicentricity or unipolarity is associated with relative peace, and multicentricity with relatively higher levels of war. And note here that the challengers in these world wars have always failed. And the winners (Great Britain and the United States) usually were the ones that remained allied with the declining hegemon (Cashman 2000: 265).

Wallerstein's model emphasizes economic factors, especially production, trade and finance, as major causes of great wars. In contrast, other scholars pay more attention to political and military aspects of wars over hegemony. Robert Gilpin's theory of hegemonic transition is a typical example of such an approach. Gilpin argues that a great war occurs when a newly emerging power (challenger state) catches up and confronts the existing hegemon and that the pattern has been repeated roughly with an interval of one hundred years. Figure 14 is a schematic representation of Gilpin's model.

According to Gilpin, the international system is in a state of "equilibrium" as far as the major powers are content with the status quo, especially with the existing conditions of territory, politics, and economy. With the exceptions of minor revisions and adjustments, the equilibrium is the state in which a major power or a group of major powers cannot expect additional benefit which exceeds the cost of changing the system. In the equilibrium, the expected net profit of changing the system is not greater than that of maintaining the system. Only when the expected benefits of changing the system are perceived to exceed the expected costs, there is a possibility of war (Gilpin 1981: 11). In this way, Gilpin's model incorporates a rational choice theory. (For rational choice, see 6.6.2).

Figure 14 Hegemonic Cycle
source: adapted from Gilpin (1981), 12

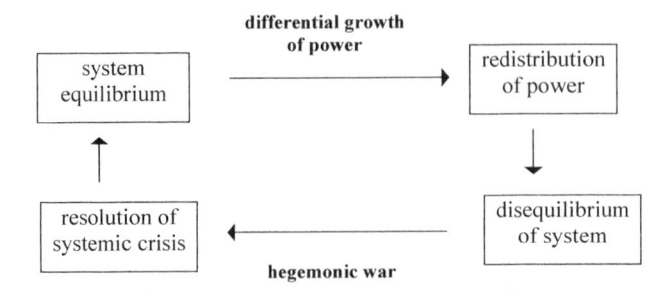

```
                    differential growth
                        of power
   ┌──────────────┐  ──────────────▶  ┌──────────────┐
   │    system    │                    │ redistribution│
   │  equilibrium │                    │   of power    │
   └──────────────┘                    └──────────────┘
          ▲                                    │
          │                                    ▼
   ┌──────────────┐                    ┌──────────────┐
   │ resolution of│  ◀──────────────   │disequilibrium│
   │systemic crisis│                   │  of system   │
   └──────────────┘   hegemonic war    └──────────────┘
```

Gilpin is interested primarily in wars fought for dominance in the international system. "Hegemonic wars" are direct contests between the dominant power(s) and a rising challenger or challengers over the governance and leadership of the international system.

The greatest destabilizing factor in this system of Gilpin is the differential power growth of great powers. In the international system under consideration, powers of the major states change or grow differentially or unequally depending upon their political, economic and technological developments. The differential growth of powers of the states brings about the redistribution of power, that is, the change in the relative power of the states (Gilpin 1981: 13). As a result, the international system moves from the state of equilibrium to the state of "disequilibrium." In the disequilibrium, due to the political, economic, or technological developments, the expected benefit of the system change has significantly increased or the expected cost of the system change has significantly decreased, and, therefore, to some states at least, the expected net profit of the system change has become greater than that of maintaining the system (Gilpin 1981: 14).

This contradiction of the international system in the form of the greater expected profit of the system change leads to the crisis of the system. It is not impossible to solve the crisis through a peaceful means, to be sure. But the primary mechanism of the solution of this crisis is historically a "hegemonic war." A hegemonic war decides which state or states dominate and control the system (Gilpin 1981: 15). In this way, in Gilpin's model, the hegemonic war functions as a stabilizer or stabilizing mechanism to resolve the disequilibrium or the crisis in the international system.

Gilpin's model assumes that the existence of a powerful hegemon maintains the stability of the international system. There is an inverse relationship between the power of the hegemon and the likelihood of war. The unipolar system (system of "hegemonic governance") is seen as the most stable, while instability accompanies the decline of the hegemon's military preponderance (Cashman 2000: 256).

At the same time, Gilpin's model also incorporates a destabilizing factor as is seen in Figure 14, and implies that the hegemony is not permanent or that the establishment of the hegemony does not perpetuate the stability of the system. It is for this dual or contradictory property that his theory can be seen either as hegemonic (or hegemonial) stability theory or as hegemonic cycle theory.

A model which focuses more narrowly on a specific aspect of power is proposed by George Modelski and his colleagues. They advance a theory of long cycle of great war, which they called "global war." Modelski sees global war as a war which decides the structure of the world political system and the allocation of authority in it. Thus, the global war is a struggle for a new leader of the system (Levy 1985a: 347).

In this model, the cycle consists of the following four stages and it is repeated with an interval of roughly one hundred years

→ agenda setting (delegitimation)
→ coalitioning (deconcentration)
→ macrodecision (global war)
→ implementation (establishment of the position as world power)

Global wars (or "macrodecision" above) were fought between the incumbent global system leader and its allies on the one hand, and a principal challenger and its allies on the other. Table 16 lists "great wars" with the changes of the hegemon and challenger(s) which occurred with an interval of roughly one hundred years. And it is said that this cycle began around 1500 (Rasler and Thompson 2000: 309).

Table 16 "Global Wars"
source: Rasler and Thompson 2000, 310-311

global wars	leader coalition	challenger(s)
Italian and Indian Ocean Wars (1495-1516)	Portugal / Spain / England	France
Dutch-Spanish War (1580-1608)	Netherlands / England / France	Spain
Wars of Grand Alliance (1688-1713)	Britain / Netherlands	France
French Revolution and Napoleonic Wars (1792-1815)	Britain / Russia	France
World Wars I and II (1914-1945)	United States/ Britain	Germany / Japan

As Table 16 shows, the challenger never won. At the same time, the incumbent leader might lose its status to one of its allies. The junior partner going into the war emerged as the senior partner and the new system leader (Rasler and Thompson 2000: 310).

As a result of a global war, a new world power emerges. The world power monopolies the military power with a truly global reach (hence the importance of the naval and later air power). The world power also dominates world trade. The world power is therefore capable of creating a new system of world politics and world economy, and maintaining it (Levy 1985a: 346-347). This is the "implementation" phase. The leading position gradually declines mainly due to the cost of the system maintenance, and a new challenger appears on the scene. Then, the system moves to the phases of "delegitimation" and "deconcentration," leading to the next global war (Levy 1985a: 346-347).

Figure 15 schematically shows the long cycles of great war and hegemony. As is clear from the figure, there is an unmistakable correspondence between the global wars and the rises and falls of the (relative) naval power of the hegemons (Portugal, the Netherlands, Great Britain (twice), United States). It was also suggested that the long cycle corresponds to a pair of Kondratieff's waves (Rasler and Thompson 2000: 305).

In this model, the prime mover of the cycle is the naval power (including air power in the twentieth century) because it contributes most to the command of "global reach" (Cashman 1993: 258). A military capability to participate in, and to protect, long-distance, interregional transactions and leading sector industrial production has translated most readily into naval and, more recently, aerospace power, though the naval capability leadership is ascribed to the economic leadership (Rasler and Thompson 2000: 313, 316).

Figure 15 Long Cycles and Naval Power
source: prepared from Modelski and Thompson (1989), 25, 36

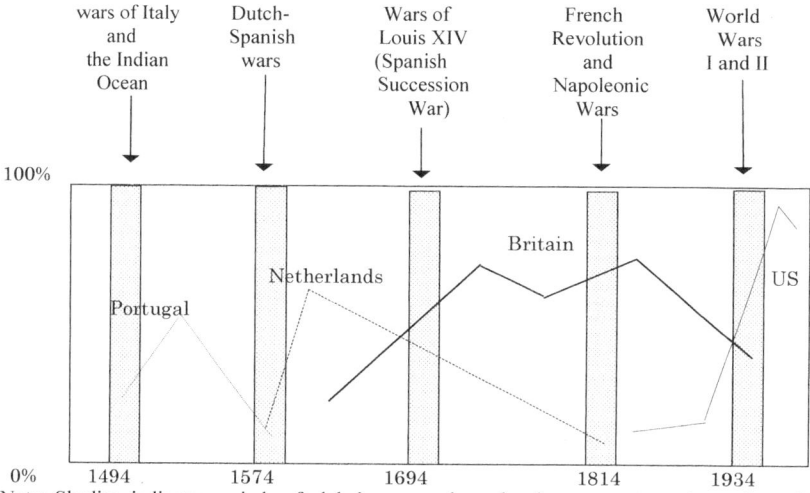

Note: Shading indicates periods of global wars, and graphs show percentage share of naval power

In addition to the studies on great wars we examined in this chapter, we should also mention Charles Doran's model of relative power cycle, which primarily associated with major wars (Cashman 1993: 272-273). The model is actually concerned with the life cycle of the power of a major state, but not with the cycle in the international system. The theory of relative power cycle has, however, an important implication for great wars. A cycle of relative power for a major power consists of four phases: rapid rise, slow rise, slow decline and rapid decline. There are four points of transition from one phase to another. These transition points are called "critical" points because the average magnitude, severity, and duration of wars were much higher during the periods. But the frequency of war is not related to relative power cycle.

A similar view was proposed by A.F.K.Organsky. He and his colleagues emphasize the changes in the distribution of power in the international system. They argue that wars among major powers occur only if a power transition is underway. Power transition is a necessary, if not sufficient, condition for such wars (Cashman 1993: 248, 250).

4.3.3 Retrospect on Studies on Great Wars

These studies on great wars and their alleged cycles have shown that one of the major causes of the past great wars was the struggle for the acquisition and maintenance of the hegemony in the international system. These studies share the following similarities. They

(1) address the issue of major wars rather than all interstate wars,
(2) deal with the modern state system that emerged around 1500, and emphasize long-term causes of war,
(3) emphasize the importance of the changes in power distribution (transition or systemic disequilibrium) mainly brought about by uneven rates of growth among the system members
(4) tend to see a unipolar concentration of power in the hands of a system leader as representing a relatively stable and peaceful situation, though they also agree that this situation cannot last indefinitely (Cashman 1993: 274, Rasler and Thompson 2000: 303, 309)

As these studies have shown, there is no doubt that great wars occurred with some regularity especially in modern Europe characterized by the capitalist development. But note here that the there is nothing inherent in the logic of long-cycles that necessitates great wars. Disequilibria in the international system could be resolved through peaceful change. Alternative mechanisms for the transfer of global leadership may be found. As Cashman argues, the cause of great wars in the past centuries was simply the lack of a nonviolent mechanism of the global decision-making about political leadership (Cashman 1993: 262).

There are many criticisms against long cycle theories of great wars. First, there is no agreement on the definition or selection of great wars. If we take a cynical view, we can go so far as to say that there were so many great wars that we can find one with any interval we like. For example, compare wars listed in figures 12 and 13 and table 16.

Secondly, there is a serious anomaly in most of the theories. Let us take up one example. It is generally agreed that, prior to World War I (and World War II, for that matter), Great Britain was the hegemonic power and Germany was the primary challenger. What, then, are we to do with the fact that by 1914 the United States had already passed both Great Britain and Germany in terms of industrial production, leading sector position, and gross national product? The statistics for the pre-World War II period are even more lopsided in favor of the United States. In either case, was the German challenge directed at the United States? If the United States is neither the initiator nor the chief defender, how can these wars be about global leadership? The wars did indeed result in a change of global leadership. And, as we pointed out above, a junior partner often became the leader. Results and causes should not be confused (Cashman 1993: 266).

Thirdly, another serious problem with these studies on great wars is that of prediction or future extrapolation. It is true, we cannot learn too much from the past history. But, will the past regularity of great wars be repeated in future? If the cycle of great war repeats itself with an interval of one hundred years, then we will soon have another world war perhaps early in the twenty-first century. The studies cannot answer the question.

In this connection, John Mueller has recently put forth an argument for the "obsolescence of major wars" (Mueller 1990). The most important factors for his argument seem to be the spread of democracy and the spread of peaceful norms. Mueller believes, however, that the connection between the spread of democracy and peace is spurious. He contends that the primary causal factor is simply the geographic spread of the idea that interstate war is unacceptable, though it should be emphasized that the trend is not yet global in scope. The two (democracy and peace norm) are associated geographically, but not causally, contrary to the democratic peace theory (Cashman 1993: 285-286).

Fourthly, one of the most serious defects of these studies on great wars is that they are too much concerned with the great wars and hegemonic wars and too blinded by the glorious rise and fall of the great powers, to be concerned either with other types of wars or with the human and material costs and sacrifices of these wars. But, to be a little more theoretical, there are two issues to be considered.

First, to be sure, no one can deny that studies on great wars are a legitimate research area. No one can deny the significance of great wars to the whole world, or to world politics and world economy. However, studies on great wars have not explored empirically or theoretically the relations of these great wars with other kinds of wars, for example local wars prevalent in our world. If we want to explore the nature and causes of wars in order to finally prevent or "eliminate" them, then a broader theoretical framework will be required in which both great wars and other wars are analyzed in a systematic way, which, to the regret of the author, this book cannot attain at present.

Next, we must not forget the vast human and material costs and sacrifices these wars brought about. Peace studies seeks to abolish war primarily because of its costs, sacrifices and disastrous consequences. If war does not demand any cost or sacrifice from an individual, a family, a group or community, a society, or a state, then war is not much worth studying.

Lastly, these studies are too Euro-centric as well. Most of them are too much concerned about great wars in modern Europe with no interest in other areas of the world, for example, developing countries.

5 Arms Race

5.1 Introduction: Significance of Arms Race

One of the most quoted definitions of arms race is: "a progressive, competitive peacetime increase in armaments by two states or coalitions of states."

For the outbreak of war, there should be "belligerents," namely parties to the war. In addition, parties to the war should be equipped with the war-fighting capabilities, or with human and material resources necessary to wage a war. Among the parties' capabilities and resources, the most important is the armaments or weapons. For this reason, unilateral or bilateral (and sometimes multilateral) increase of armaments is one of the most important issues when we study causes of war. To say the least, researchers have believed that arms race somehow plays an important role in the outbreak of war. In fact, arms race is one of the most discussed major causes of war in general. And most of the empirical and theoretical studies on arms race have addressed primarily the arms races between and among states, especially major powers.

Let us first glance at two set of data which seem to show the significance of arms race in the outbreak of war. According to Singer and others, from 1816 to 1965, only 13% of the disputes or conflicts between major powers resulted in war as is shown in Table 17.

Table 17 Arms Race and the Outbreak of War (1816-1965)
source: Singer (1981), 11

	percentage escalating to war
major power militarized disputes	13
+ approximately equal in military terms	20
+ arms race during the three years prior to the disputes	75

When the military capabilities or military power of the major powers concerned were roughly on a par, the percentage rose to 20%. And, what is more important, if the parties were increasing their armaments for some years, that is, if they were engaged in an arms race, the percentage rose quickly to as much as 75% (Singer 1981: 11).

Similarly, in one of the most cited articles, Wallace demonstrated that, of all the arms races between great powers during the period, only 18% never led to war as the following Table 18 shows.

Table 18 Escalation from Arms Race to War (1816-1965)
Source: Wallace (1979), 15

	arms race	no arms race
leads to war	23 (82%)	3 (4%)
not leads to war	5 (18%)	68 (96%)

Figures indicate the number of disputes for each category.

In addition, though they are not arms races in the strict sense of word, in the case of semi-peripheral or middle-income countries, these countries' involvement in armed conflicts is closely correlated with the growth rate of their military expenditures (Väyrynen 1983: 180).

Though they are not meant to deny the importance of arms race in studying war causes, there have been many criticisms of the findings given tables 17 and 18. We will take up these issues later again after the examination of theories and models of arms race itself.

When we examine arms race as one of the causes of war, we should not confuse causes and effects. It is because the arms race can be both a cause and an effect of the war intention of the parties concerned. The intention or prospect of war may accelerate armaments expansion, or the arms race may precipitate the parties into war. Even if it may not be a causal relationship, the above data have made clear that there is a very strong correlation relationship between the outbreak of war and arms race.

In this chapter, we will first discuss theories and models which try to explain why arms races occur. And then we will proceed to the discussion of the relationship between arms race and war.

Studies on arms race vary greatly in their emphasis on the structural constraints, dyadic relationships and domestic/internal factors. Of various theories and models, we will take up only three models: that is, security dilemma, the Richardson model, and autistic (or self-propagating) model of arms race. A fourth model, the game of prisoner's dilemma, is also frequently used to explain an arms race. But we will examine prisoner's dilemma later in a broader context of cooperation and conflict among states.

The four models or explanations can be summarized in the way given in Table 19. The first two models in the table, security dilemma and the Richardson model, are rather similar in their focus. Both focus primarily upon the dyadic relation between states, and view security or fear as the main motive of the state behavior in the arms race. They differ only in the relative emphasis on domestic or international factors. While the security dilemma model takes systemic factors into consideration, the Richardson model views domestic factors mainly as a constraint on the arms race.

Table 19 Models of the Arms Race

	\multicolumn{3}{c	}{causes/causal factors}	motives
	domestic factors	interaction between states	systemic factors	motives
security dilemma		main	some	security
Richardson model	some	main	none	security
Autistic model	main	none	none	interests
Prisoner's Dilemma		main	some	interests

The other two models regard interests, rather than security, as the prime mover of the arms race. The autistic/self-propagating model is peculiar in that it exclusively focuses upon the domestic factors, especially so-called military-industrial complex. The prisoner's dilemma model pays attention mainly to the interaction of states, assuming that the systemic property of anarchy is given.

5.2 Security Dilemma

The concept of "security dilemma" is usually ascribed to John H. Herz (1950). Anarchy in the international system is said to give rise to the dilemma (Evans and Newnham 1992: 296). According to Herz, "[g]roups or individuals living in such a constellation must be, and usually are, concerned about their security from being attacked, subjected, dominated, or annihilated by other groups or individuals." (Herz 1950: 157). "[W]herever such anarchic society has existed, [...] there has arisen what may be called the "security dilemma" of men, or groups, or their leaders." They are, therefore, driven to the efforts toward enhancing their security. And, in many cases, here begins the security dilemma. "Striving to attain security from such attack, they are driven to acquire more and more power. [...]. This, in turn, renders the others more insecure and compels them to prepare for the worst. Since none can ever feel entirely secure in such a world of competing units, power competition ensues, and the vicious circle of security and power accumulation is on" (Herz 1950: 157). The security dilemma may, therefore, be regarded as a structural attribute (Evans and Newnham 1992: 296).

Similarly, Robert Jervis defined the security dilemma as follows: "many of the means which a state tries to increase its security decrease the security of others" or "[i]n international politics, [...], one state's gain in security often inadvertently threatens others" (Jervis 1978: 169-170).

We should distinguish three closely related definitions of the security dilemma. First of all, as Jervis defined the concept, the term refers to the tragic nature of one's efforts to enhance one's own security resulting in making others less secure under anarchy in the international system.

But the problem does not end here. As Herz' use of "vicious circle" suggests, the property of the security enhancement given in the first definition above triggers a series of action-reaction behaviors. The second definition arises here. To illustrate, suppose that "State A acquires weapons in order to ensure its security. State B feels threatened by State A's weapons acquisition and decides that it requires more firepower itself." And this process has often resulted in arms races (Spear 1997: 121). The process is referred to as the "spiral model" of the security dilemma. The process is illustrated in Figure 16. As can be seen from the figure, this definition focuses upon the interactive process, typically arms race, and the cumulative amount of armaments. It says nothing about how much the security of the parties concerned is increased or decreased.

However, Cashman (and many others) adopts the third definition, by focusing explicitly on the resultant amount of security. "Attempts to create greater security for oneself may, unfortunately, result in even *less security*. [...] The result of attempts by each state to create greater security for itself is that *no one is more secure*" (Cashman 1993: 185, emphasis added).

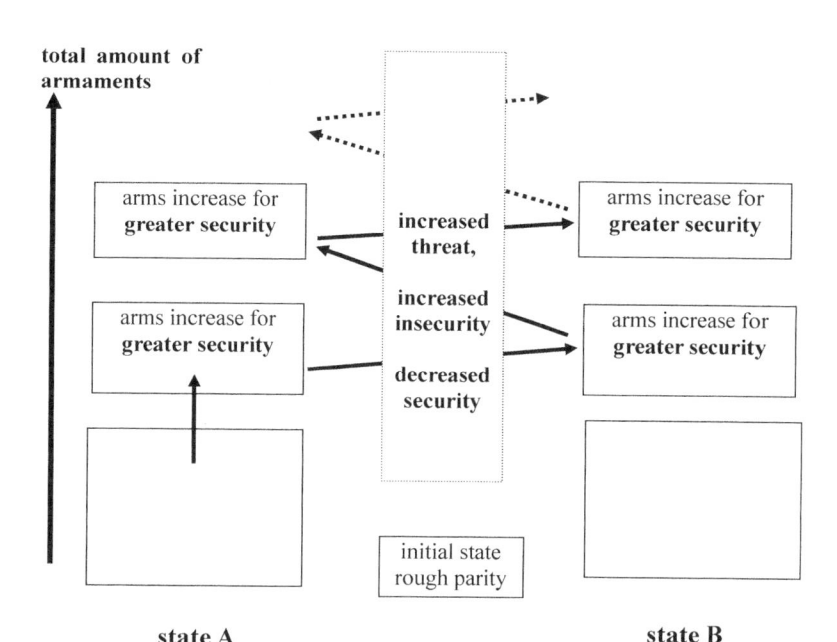

Figure 16 Security Dilemma: Spiral Model

```
total amount of
armaments
    ↑
                    ┌─────────────┐
                ╱╲  ┊             ┊  ╌╌▶
               ╱  ╲ ┊             ┊
        ┌──────────┐┊             ┊┌──────────┐
        │arms increase for│ increased │arms increase for│
        │greater security│◀─ threat, ─▶│greater security│
        └──────────┘┊             ┊└──────────┘
                    ┊ increased   ┊
        ┌──────────┐┊ insecurity  ┊┌──────────┐
        │arms increase for│        │arms increase for│
        │greater security│◀────   ────▶│greater security│
        └──────────┘┊ decreased   ┊└──────────┘
               ↑    ┊ security    ┊
        ┌──────────┐┊             ┊┌──────────┐
        │          │┊             ┊│          │
        │          │└─────────────┘│          │
        │          │  initial state │          │
        │          │  rough parity  │          │
        └──────────┘                └──────────┘

        state A                         state B
```

The relationship between the total amount of security and the total amount of armaments or weapons is not linear. two factors are involved. First, the amount of security is relative to the amount of armaments of others, especially that of real or imagined enemy or enemies. Moreover, it depends largely upon the perception as in the case of the spiral model. Secondly, as one can easily see, an excessive amount of weapons does not give us surplus security. Even if the United States adds millions of missiles, it does not necessarily mean that its security increases by the amount. The third interpretation of security dilemma may be accounted for by these factors.

When some vested interests are involved, security dilemma means quite a different thing from their perspective. We will take up the issue shortly below.

As we saw above, the security dilemma may cause an arms race. But, not always. As both Herz and Jervis argue, the security dilemma does not preclude cooperation (Herz 1950: 157). Remember the title of Jervis's article, "Cooperation under the Security Dilemma." We will later enlarge upon the possibility of cooperation in an anarchic international system in chapter 7..

5.3 Richardson Model

Lewis Richardson advanced the first formal mathematical (and perhaps the most famous) model of arms race, which came to be known as Richardson model or Richardson equations. The model was intended to show the change in the military budgets of the two states. Richardson equations are the following simultaneous equations given in Table 20.

Table 20 Richardson Model of Arms Race (Richardson Equations)

$dx/dt = ky - ax + g$ (State A)
$dy/dt = lx - by + h$ (State B)

where
- x, y : military expenditures of A and B, respectively
- k, l : defense coefficients
- a, b : fatigue coefficients
- g, h : grievance coefficients (constant)

> The equation shows that the increment of the military expenditure of a given state at a given time is decided by a positive reaction to the military expenditure of the other state, a negative reaction to its own military expenditure, and the constant.

The left sides of the equations stand for the increase or decrease of the military budgets of the two states in question, at a certain point of time, $time_t$ in this formula. In other words, the left side of the equation indicates how much the arms race is promoted or reduced.

The variables X and Y stand respectively for the military expenditures (of the immediately previous year) of the two states A and B in the absolute values.

The two coefficients, "k" and "l," are called "defence coefficients." The defence coefficient indicates the extent to which one state is concerned about the military budget of the other, or the military buildup of the other represented by the annual military budget. The values of defence coefficients were assumed to be in the positive by Richardson for an obvious reason. According to the equation, the greater the military expenditure of the other state and the greater the value of the defence coefficient, the greater the increase in the military budget of the state in question will be. This promotes the arms race.

The other set of coefficients, "a" and "b," are called "fatigue coefficients." The coefficients stand for the degree to which the state in question feels dissatisfied or burdened with its own military budget. The coefficients were assumed to be in the negative. In a word, the coefficients represent the "defence burden."

The constants, "g" and "h," are called "grievance coefficients." The coefficients are usually considered to stand for the extent of hostility or hatred toward the other state irrespective of the amount of armament or military budget.

According to the Richardson equations, the amount of change in the military budget of a state at a certain point of time responds positively to the military budget (of the previous year) of the other state and, at the same time, responds negatively to its own military budget of the previous year. Moreover, the actual amount of change in the military budget also depends upon the values of defence and fatigue coefficients. The model assumes that an arms race is an interactive process, or a stimulus-response process, in which each party responds mutually to the military budget, and hence armament, of the other. Richardson's is a typical interaction model of arms race. And such an interactive process as suggested by the model has come to be generally referred to as Richardson process after his name.

Richardson demonstrated convincingly that, though with several assumptions, the approximation by the equations fitted very well with the actual process of the arms race among the great powers before the Second World War. The result is shown in Figure 17 below. The figure shows that there is an evident linear relationship between the actual military budgets and their increase or increments, as the model predicts.

Figure 17 Arms race leading to World War II based on the Richardson Model
source: Alcock and Lowe (1969), 105

increment of
military expenditure

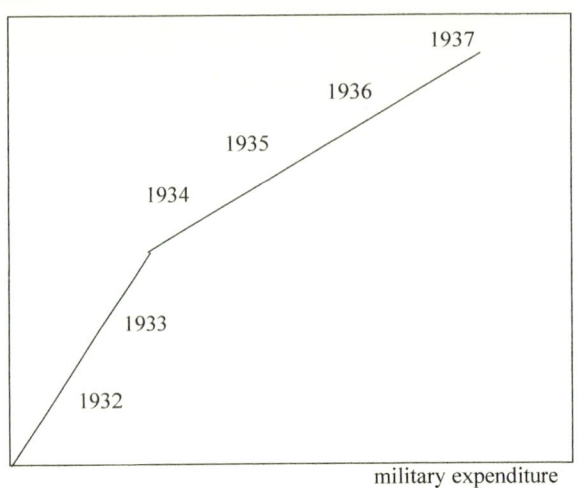

[Figure: graph with x-axis labeled "military expenditure" showing a line plot through data points labeled 1932, 1933, 1934, 1935, 1936, 1937]

military expenditure

> The procedure employed in the figure can be described in the following way. Suppose that $k = 1$ and $a = b$ in the Richardson equations. Then the sum of the two equations will be:
>
> $d(x + y)/dt = (g + h) + (k - a)(x + y)$
>
> Here, let $d(x+y)/dt = Y$ and $x + y = X$. Then we obtain:
>
> $Y = (g+h) + (k - a)X$
>
> This is a line with the slope of $(k-a)$ and the intercept of $(g+h)$ (on the Y axis).
> (Alcock and Lowe 1969: 110-111).

The Richardson model has been highly praised as the first attempt at the mathematical expression of the dynamics of arms race. And even today there are still many attempts at a revision, expansion or sophistication of the original model. There are, however, two important problems with this model.

First, according to the model, the outcome of the arms race between the two states is determined completely by the relationship defined in the model. The model does not admit of the influence of all the other possible variables upon the outcome of the arms race. If an arms race actually develops as the model predicts, then the result will be automatically determined given the initial values of the military budgets and the values of coefficients. The developments and outcomes of an arms race are automatically determined beyond any human effort. The model seems to imply that arms races obey scientific law, and, therefore, they are beyond human efforts or intentions. It seems that, once the process has started, no country is at fault, the escalation is a consequence of systemic interaction rather than aggression (Dunne et al 2003: 178), if no human efforts are made or no other factors work upon the process. In short, the Richardson model is too deterministic (Matelly 2003: 160). Perhaps the model is, by intention, deterministic enough to "describe what happens when people do not stop to think" (Rapoport 1974: 172).

Secondly, there is rather a technical problem. As is clear from Figure 17 above, the degree of fitness between observed and theoretically expected values will be greatly reduced unless the values of the coefficients are changed, though the values of the coefficients are normally assumed to be constant by definition. But in Figure 17, the linear model can describe the arms race only for a few years. This difficulty is presumably due to the fact that the model assumes a linear relationship between the variables. For this reason, many attempts have been made at the revision of the equations, such as the introduction of new variables, change into the quadratic equations and so on.

Thirdly, Richardson's model uses the flow of military expenditures. Some ask whether it is better to consider the stock or the accumulated amount of armaments as a determinant of the arms race (Matelly 2003: 160).

Despite the criticisms, Richardson's model has been applied to various actual arms races. But, many of these attempts were less than successful. For example, Dunne et al (2003) analyses two cases of apparent arms races: that between Greece and Turkey, and that between India and Pakistan (Dunne et al 2003: 178). They found that the arms race between India and Pakistan takes the classical Richardson form but the arms race between Greece and Turkey does not (Dunne et al 2003: 185-186).

In order to remedy the failures of the Richardson model, various extensions and sophistications were proposed and applied to real data. For example, Figure 18 shows the actual arms race between the United States and the Soviet Union during the Cold War. And the arms race can be very well approximated by the following model, which is a small extension of the original Richardson model. Specifically, if the original model is changed in the time lag for the military expenditures of the other party in the following way,

$$dX/dt = \alpha Y(t-2) + \beta X(t-1) + \gamma$$

> where X and Y are military expenditures of US and USSR, respectively. Note that the equation is different in the time lag, (t-2) instead of (t-1), from the original.

then the modified model fits very well with the arms race between the two superpowers during the Cold War. But, the model cannot be applied to the data after the end of the Cold War because it cannot predict the sharp fall of the military expenditures of the Soviet Union/Russia in this period (Matelly 2003: 166-169).

Figure 18 The Arms Race between the Two Superpowers during the Cold War
source: Matelly 2003, 164

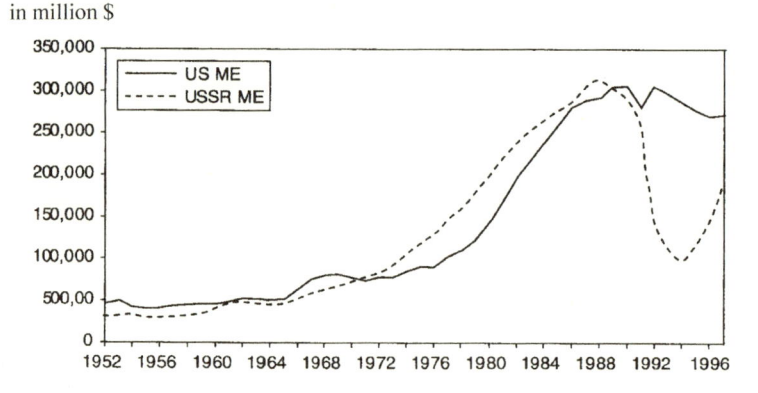

In connection with this, in one of the "most-cited articles in *Journal of Peace Research* (Gleditsch 1993: 446)," Paul Smoker applied the Richardson model to the superpower arms race in the 1950s. He found the curve (actually a straight line) suddenly changed in 1952 in the same way as Figure 17. The growth rate of military budgets of the two superpowers clearly decreased after 1952 (Smoker 1964: 59-62).

Note here that the arms race data which we saw above in Figure 18 began in 1952, the very year when the slope changed.

Smoker argued that the nuclear weapons accounted for this change, since they introduced a new dimension of fear (called "submissiveness" by Richardson) into world politics (Smoker 1964: 55). If such fear existed as Smoker argued, it can endorse the argument partially at least that the superpowers perceived the Cold War as the game of "chicken" which may end in the devastation of both. We will touch upon the issue again in 7.3.2.

From these applications, we can see that the Richardson model has not yet lost its validity. And, besides arms races, the Richardson model has been applied to other similar interaction processes as well. For example, if the battle deaths in the Vietnam War are used in place of military budgets, the escalation process of the war can be approximated as a Richardson process at least in term of battle casualties (Alcock and Lowe 1969).

In the Richardson model of arms race, two states are engaged in the arms race by responding to, or interacting with, the other's military expenditure as a stimulus. The Richardson model is an interaction model of arms race. But, we can imagine a situation in which the expansion or increase of armament seems to advance of itself, independently of the level of armament of the other state. In this case, the increase or expansion (or, decrease or reduction, for that matter) of armaments reproduces itself.

In addition to an interactive arms race, there are cases of self-propagating (or unilateral) expansion of armaments. And, in order to explain such cases of self-reproducing armament increase, several theories have been proposed which emphasize the domestic factors of armament. The "autistic" model of arms race of Dieter Senghaas is a typical example.

5.4 Unilateral Model

In contrast to the emphasis on the interactive factors of the arms race in the early peace studies, peace studies in the 1970s is characterized by the increased interest in the internal factors of the arms race, especially in the domestic interest groups, autistic tendency, military industrial complex and so on (Wiberg 1981: 119).

In the 1970s, the détente between the United States and the Soviet Union advanced. Quite contrary to the expectations, however, the armaments of the superpowers continued to increase (for example, see Figure 18 above). In the 1970s, while the détente advanced, the expansion of military expenditures continued. The détente and the expansion of armaments went side by side.

The Richardson model could not explain this curious, apparently contradictory phenomenon. Even if the model fitted well with actual increase, as we saw in Figure 18, the Richardson model could not explain why the arms race advanced in an era of detente. It is because the Richardson model was based on the assumption that one of the major causes of the arms race is the sense of insecurity and hostility of the parties toward each other. The assumption was expressed as defence coefficient in the model. If the détente reduced the sense of insecurity and hostility, then the growth rate of the military budget (if not the total military budget) should have been reduced accordingly through the decrease of the value of the defence coefficient.

In this way, new models or theories gained ground which argued that the US-USSR arms race was not an interactive process, but rather reproduced itself due to the domestic factors. Among them, Dieter Senghaas' "autistic model" was the most influential (Takayanagi 1989: 308ff). Though one may wonder whether such a unilateral arms increase should be termed arms race, we will take it up here because both superpowers expanded their arms buildups during the era of détente.

The expansion of armaments is usually justified by the real or imagined threats from a (hypothetical) enemy, the Soviet Union in the case of the United States. If this is true, there was no reason for the expansion of armaments in the détente period because the threats from the archenemy were diminishing, as the word détente suggested. But, in reality, the armaments of the two superpowers were expanded. It was for this reason that instead of the logic of threats from the enemy, a different logic of justification (or another ideology) was required and actually employed. With the decreased threats in the détente period, this logic or ideology played a more and more important role in justifying the expansion of armaments. For this reason, the ideology which justified the arms expansion occupied an important place in the mechanism of the expansion of armaments in the détente period.

It was the nuclear deterrence theory which played the key role in the superpower arms race in the détente period. It was argued that the nuclear deterrence theory functioned as a crucial ideology for justifying the armament expansion. The deterrence theory in general and the nuclear deterrence theory in particular requires the possession of superior or much greater military force, rather than the military force equal to the enemy's military force. Such superior military capabilities are necessary to deter the first strike of the opponent, because such capabilities alone make the second strike or retaliation possible and it is actually this second strike capability that deters the enemy from the preemptive strike in the first place. The issue of nuclear deterrence will be touched upon again in 7.3.2.

In short, the nuclear deterrence theory requires additional (second strike) armaments. It is a very convenient theory for the expansion of armaments, and it is natural that it should have been adopted and employed to justify further expansion of armaments.

It is true that the nuclear deterrence theory functioned as an ideology justifying the expansion of armaments in the United States. But, such an ideology alone did not and could not promote the expansion of armaments. There was a much more important factor for the armament expansion during the period. And actually, the deterrence theory was just a means for justification employed by those who wanted the armament expansion.

There was an interest group who had vested interests in, and gained vast amount of profit from, the expansion of armaments. The interest group is often called "military-industrial complex," or in extended versions, "military - industrial - bureaucratic - academic-…complex." The expansion of armaments has now become the vested interests to this group. And, importantly, the group has a very strong influence in the decision making and resource allocation in the domestic politics in United States. The autistic theory does not, however, intend to explain why such interest groups have so great an influence upon domestic politics (Møller 1999: 87).

Other factors of the self-reproducing expansion of armaments can be found in the nature of modern military technologies. It is often pointed out that, in the developed countries, the expansion of armaments has now changed its nature form the quantity to the quality. In both the United States and the Soviet Union, the question of armament expansion was actually the question of developing newest high technology weapons. Consequently, military research institutions compete bitterly for the research and development of the new high technology weapons. it was a competition for an increased government budget.

The rapid rise of the military budgets was also due to the costs of the development of new weapons. Some pointed out that the development of new weapons costs twice as much as that of the existing weapons, and argued that such an expansion of armaments functions as a mechanism to maintain and develop the capitalist economy. What is important here is the fact that the expansion of armaments always brings increased profit to a certain interest group, whether the expansion is profitable or beneficial to the state or society as a whole.

5.5 Arms Race and War Revisited

In this chapter, we assumed that arms race is one of the important causes of war, and examined three models of arms race. Now, let us more critically *re*-examine the relations between arms race and war. There are two reasons for this. One is a broader question about the relationship between arms expansion (of which arms race is only a part) and war. The other is a methodological issue.

First, Paul Diehl and Jean Kingston consider three theoretical possibilities of the relationship between arms buildups including arms races, and armed conflicts. They categorically reject the classical deterrence theory as the forth possibility, contrary to the conclusion drawn by Frank Zagare and D. Mark Kilgour which we will examine below. A classical expression of the theory is the *para bellum* doctrine ("if you want peace, prepare for war"), which claims that military buildups lessen the likelihood of conflict occurring (Diehl and Kingston 1987: 801-804).

The first possibility is that military buildups are an early warning indicator of impending military conflict. In this case, an increase in armaments does not promote conflict, but rather is a by-product of the tension underlying it. The second possibility is that arms buildups make military confrontations more likely. In this scenario, military buildups produce the tension and competition that result in armed confrontation and war. Finally, a possible third outcome is the absence of a causal relationship between military buildups and conflict. In that case, arms races may not be quite so important as to justify the scholarly attention and journal space they have received (Diehl and Kingston 1987: 801-804).

On the basis of various statistical analyses, they conclude that a state's "military spending exhibited little or no impact on its propensity to initiate or become involved in militarized conflict in the short run" and "one nation's military spending behavior is apparently unrelated to its subsequent conflict involvement." An arms race or unilateral arms buildup neither reflects hostility or conflict, nor increases the likelihood of conflict involvement (Diehl and Kingston 1987: 808-809, 811).

For this absence of the relationship between military buildup and war (either escalation or initiation), they suggest two reasons. First, states may choose alternate means, beside military buildups, when reacting to impending conflict. An external threat may generate a variety of different responses: alliance formation, retreat to isolationism, or a military buildup. Secondly, a state's military spending may primarily be a product of domestic concerns as well as a reaction to an opponent's spending behavior (Diehl and Kingston 1987: 811). This lends some empirical support to the self-propagation model we discussed above.

Zagare and Kilgour, however, propose an analysis which supports the relevance of arms buildups to the issue of war. They argue that there are actually two apparently opposing theories on the role of military buildups in the outbreak or escalation of war: what they call "classical deterrence theory" and the "spiral model." A fundamental tenet of classical deterrence theory is that credible and capable threats can prevent the initiation, and contain the escalation, of conflict. By contrast, proponents of the spiral model claim that military buildups frequently lead to vicious cycles of reciprocal armament expansion (Zagare and Kilgour 1998: 59-60).

According to Zagare and Kilgour's game-theoretic analysis, both theories are partially correct, because they are valid under very different sets of circumstances, and the two theories complement each other rather than substitute the other. They conclude that the dichotomy is false and that "empirical attempts to validate either theoretical framework at the expense of the other are doomed to failure" (Zagare and Kilgour 1998:

85).

So far, we have focused upon the latter theory, and we examined only a small part of it, that is, arms race.

The second reason for the reexamination of the relationship between arms race and war is that there have been many criticisms even of the apparently very convincing findings which we saw in the Tables 17 and 18 (Diehl and Kingston 1987: 801). Thus, the role of arms races must be examined in more detail, and in a much broader context.

Let us take up Wallace's findings given in Table 17 as an example. Wallace chose to treat all arms races and all wars as dyadic (bilateral, that is between two states, and not between alliances). This meant that, instead of World War I being represented by a single case, it was represented by nine cases, and, instead of World War II being represented by one or two cases, it was represented by seven cases. Overall, twenty-six distinct wars of dyads were created where only seven or eight integrated wars occurred. The effect of this was to vastly overemphasize the statistical importance of the arms races that preceded the two World Wars. It is said that what Wallace in fact had attempted was to test his "tinderbox hypothesis" and suggest that while arms races don't necessarily lead to wars directly, they may play an important intervening role in the escalation of disputes to war (Cashman 1993: 180-181).

Wallace's study thus stimulated a number of reexamination studies on the relationship between arms race and war using similar data. Table 21 below lists some of the results. As the table shows, many wars were preceded by an arms race, it is true. But there are also many wars which were not preceded by an arms race.

Table 21 Arms Race and War: Varying Results
source: Cashman 1993, 181

	Wallace		Weede		Diehl		Altfeld	
	war	no war	war	no war	war	no war	war	no war
arms race	23	3	6	5	3	9	11	0
no arms race	5	68	2	68	10	64	15	73

Figures indicate the numbers of cases.

Perhaps, it is too early to conclude from these data that "arms races play only a modest, subsidiary role in the general causation of war," though "they are neither necessary nor a sufficient condition for the outbreak of [war]" (Cashman 1993: 182). It is because various later tests showed that "there is a significant positive link between arming and dispute escalation [into war]" (Sample 2000: 168).

A more fundamental question needs to be asked: Does arms race lead to war or does expectation of war lead to arms race? Is arms race a cause or an effect? It may be that men do not fight because they have arms, but rather they have arms because it is necessary to fight. These questions imply that arms race ought not to be considered as a root cause of war, but rather as a manifestation of other underlying causes of war (Cashman 1993: 184, Diehl and Kingston 1987: 802, Møller 1999: 88-89).

So far, we examined the relationship between arms race and war in a very simple way as if there were a direct relationship between them. But, these days, many researchers use a three-stage escalation model from conflict or dispute to war. Such a three-stage model can be illustrated in Figure 19. Though distinctions between stages or phases are rather blurred (cf. Brecher and Harvey 1988: 7-10, Wilkenfeld and Brecher 2000: 272-273), the path of escalation is clear. Conflicts may escalate into crises, and crises into wars. Of the three stages, "crisis" can be regarded as the same as what is called "militarized dispute." A militarized dispute is defined as "a set of interactions between or among states involving threats to use military force, displays of military force, or actual use of military force ... explicit, overt, non-accidental, and government sanctioned" (cited in Diehl and Kingston 1987: 804).

Figure 19 Conflict, Crisis and War
source: Brecher and Harvey (1998), 10 / Wilkenfeld and Brecher (2000), 273

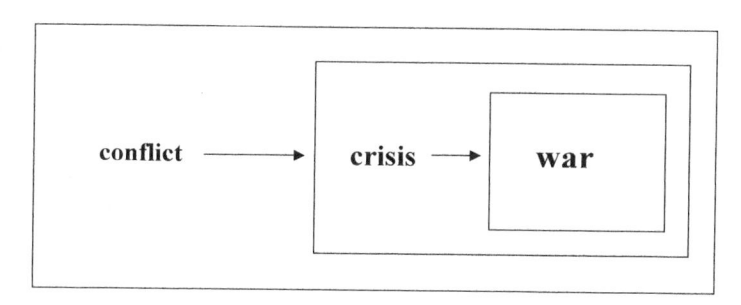

conflict ⟶ crisis ⟶ war

If we adopt this kind of framework, we should examine the role(s) of arms buildups or arms races not only at each stage but also in the escalation from one stage to the next.

In this chapter, we examined arms race as one of the major causes of war. But arms race is only a part of a broader dynamics of arms buildups. And if we broaden our perspective to include local or internal conflict, we should pay attention to such issues as military expenditures and arms transfer. Though we will examine the former briefly in 6.6.3, the limitation of space does not allow us to examine the latter issue of arms transfer and arms trade. Yearbooks such as *World Military Expenditures and Arms Transfers* (U.S. Department of State Bureau of Verification and Compliance) and *SIPRI Yearbook*: (Stockholm International Peace Research Institute) are good guidebooks.

5.6 Disarmament Efforts

5.6.1 Disarmament and Arms Control

We briefly examined the issue of arms race. The international society has not looked idly on the aggravating state of affairs. Though the achievements were rather meager so far, efforts have been made to stop and reverse the trend of global expansion of armaments. (For the expansion of the world military expenditures during the Cold War, see Sivard 1993: 42, and for later trends, see the Yearbook of the U.S. Department of State Bureau of Verification and Compliance, *World Military Expenditures and Arms Transfers*).

Here, focusing upon the weapons of mass destruction, particularly upon nuclear weapons, let us briefly examine the history of disarmament, especially of nuclear disarmament.

In the discussion of disarmament in general and nuclear disarmament in particular, some preliminary sorting out of terms is in order. It is because there are such terms as 'arms control' 'arms regulation', 'arms limitation', 'arms reduction' or 'disarmament,' which are often used interchangeably with each other (Goldblat 2002: 3). In discussing nuclear disarmament, probably the most important conceptual distinction is that between the concepts of arms control and disarmament.

The two terms are frequently used in the same sense. But, to be precise, the terms may sometimes contradict each other. The concept of disarmament is rather straightforward. It simply means the reduction or abolition of weapons and armed forces. On the contrary, the concept of arms control has many meanings depending on the contexts and the users. Arms control is usually defined as measures for the restraints on the acquisition, procurement, deployment and use of military capabilities, especially weapons and armaments (Evans and Newnham 1992: 19). Arms control can also be defined as any agreement among states to regulate some aspects of their military capabilities or potential. The agreement may apply to the location, amount, readiness, and types of military forces, weapons, and facilities (Larsen 2002: 1). If we borrow the words of Thomas Schelling, founder of the United States' arms control theory, "not acquiring," "not deploying," and "not using" certain types of weapons and armaments are the focus of arms control (Schelling 2000: xiv). Josef Goldblat mentions a much wider range of measures such as: (a) to freeze, limit, reduce or abolish certain categories of weapons; (b) to ban the testing of certain weapons; (c) to prevent certain military activities; (d) to regulate the deployment of armed forces; (e) to proscribe transfers of some militarily important items; (f) to reduce the risk of accidental war; (g) to constrain or prohibit the use of certain weapons or methods of war; and (h) to build up confidence among states through greater openness in military matters (Goldblat 2002: 3).

Irrespective of the definition(s), the critical difference of arms control from disarmament is that it does not always reduce or abolish exiting weaponry, but it may sometimes increase it as when an arms control agreement sets the future upper bound on the amount of a certain type of weapons. Arms control does not necessary mean the reduction or abolition of weapons and armaments. As we will see shortly, such cases are found in the earlier arms control negotiations between the United States and the Soviet Union.

When we discuss nuclear arms control between the two superpowers, we should also examine how arms control was conceived in the United States. Around 1960, the theoretical basis of arms control was established in the United States. Its basic objectives were threefold;

(1)　　reducing the likelihood of war
(2)　　reducing the political and economic costs of preparing for war
(3)　　and minimizing the scope and violence of war if it occurred. (Larsen 2002: 2)

There were, and still are, in the United States, two important goals attained by these measures. First, arms control was conceived as a way to enhance national security. The dominant goal of arms control was national security, not the reduction of arms per se. In fact it was understood that not all reductions were necessarily useful for that purpose. Secondly, the foremost goal of arms control was the prevention of war, especially nuclear war (Larsen 2002: 3, 5-6). It was the same with the Soviet Union. The superpowers shared a common interest in avoiding nuclear war (Larsen 2002: 7, Schelling 2000: xiv). Accordingly, arms control during the Cold War was in fact nuclear arms control, and the term arms control referred rather to measures of maintaining strategic stability between the United States and the Soviet Union. This is why the negotiations between the two superpowers began as arms control talks.

Let us briefly follow the major developments of these negotiations. Table 22 gives the rough outline of the history of negotiations and treaties between them, and Table 23 gives details of the later disarmament agreements concerning strategic weapons.

Table 22 Major Bilateral Arms Control and Disarmament Negotiations between US and USSR (or Russia)

Strategic Arms Limitation Talk (SALT I)
    1972　Treaty on the Limitation of Anti-Ballistic Missile Systems
        (ABM Treaty)
Strategic Arms Limitation Talk (SALT II)
    1979 Strategic Arms Limitation Treaty
        Set the upper limits on the number of ICBMs, SLBMs, and Strategic Bombers (not entered into effect)
1987　Treaty of the Elimination of Intermediate-Range and Short-Range Missiles (INF Treaty)
1993　Treaty on the Reduction and Limitation of Strategic Offensive Arms (START I Treaty)
1993　Treaty on Further Reduction and Limitation of Strategic Offensive Arms (START II Treaty)

Table 23 Strategic Nuclear Disarmament Agreements between the United States and the Soviet Union/Russia
source: *Arms Control Today* 32(5) (June, 2002), 13

	START I	START II	START III	SORT
deployed warhead limit	6,000	3,000 – 3,500	2,000 – 2,500	1,700 – 2,200
deployed delivery vehicle limit	1,600	--	--	--
Status	in force	never entered into force	never negotiated	signed, awaits ratification
date signed	July 31, 91	Jan. 3, 93	--	May 24, 02
date entered into force	Dec. 5, 94	--	--	?
implementation deadline	Dec,. 5, 01	Dec. 31, 07	Dec. 31, 07	Dec. 31, 12
expiration date	Dec. 5, 09	Dec. 5, 09	--	Dec. 31, 12

In the earlier period, the arms control agreements between the two superpowers placed a certain upper limit on the present or future number of strategic nuclear weapons possessed by each party. The two rounds of Strategic Arms Limitation Talk (SALT), SALT I and SALT II, were instances of this. The final agreements put the upper limits on the future number of nuclear weapons, but did not reduce the existing nuclear weapons.

It was virtually not until the end of the Cold War that the arms control efforts were changed to disarmament efforts. Among the bilateral agreements between the United States and the Soviet Union, the first disarmament agreement was the INF Treaty (Treaty of the Elimination of Intermediate-Range and Short-Range Missiles) in 1987. For the first time, the superpowers agreed to reduce nuclear weapons, particularly intermediate nuclear weapons (sometimes called "theater" nuclear weapons).

The INF Treaty, as well as the end of Cold War, paved the way to the bilateral disarmament negotiations between the United States and the Soviet Union (later its successor Russia). After the end of the Cold War, two bilateral treaties, START I and START II (Treaty on the Reduction and Limitation of Strategic Offensive Arms: START I, Treaty on Further Reduction and Limitation of Strategic Offensive Arms: START II), agreed to reduce the existing strategic weapons.

Recently the Bush administration announced its opposition to the ABM Treaty, and withdrew from it. The administration then proposed a Strategic Offensive Reductions Treaty (SORT) to Russia, and concluded it in May, 2002. But it was criticized that it accomplishes little more than misleading the public into thinking that some progress is being made toward nuclear disarmament.

Usually, however, the two concepts, arms control and disarmament, cannot be so clearly distinguished both in practice and in theory as in case of the bilateral negotiations between the United States and the Soviet Union (or Russia). For arms control is normally conceptualized as a precondition for the reduction and abolition of weapons and armaments. Arms control efforts for nuclear non-proliferation and nuclear free zones (or nuclear weapon-free zones) are of significance only under this assumption. And, apart from the bilateral agreements between the United States and the Soviet Union, developments in these two areas are the most significant achievements in the nuclear disarmament process. Table 24 shows major nuclear disarmament treaties together with other treaties on weapons of mass destruction (WMD).

Table 24 Major Arms Control and Disarmament Treaties concerning Weapons of Mass Destruction

Name (Abbreviation etc)	signed
Antarctic Treaty	1959
Partial Test Ban Treaty (PTBT)	1963
Outer Space Treaty	1967
Treaty for the Prohibition of Nuclear Weapons in Latin America and the Caribbean (Treaty of Tlatelolco)	1967
Non-Proliferation Treaty (NPT)	1968
Seabed Treaty	1972
Biological and Toxin Weapons Convention	1972
South Pacific Nuclear Free Zone Treaty (Treaty of Rarotonga)	1985
Chemical Weapons Convention	1993
Treaty on the Southeast Asia Nuclear Weapon-Free Zone (Treaty of Bangkok)	1995
African Nuclear Weapon-Free Zone Treaty (Treaty of Pelindaba)	1996
Comprehensive Nuclear Test-Ban Treaty (CTBT)	1996

Most of the treaties concerning nuclear weapons were based on the above assumption. In principle, they were intended to reduce and ultimately abolish nuclear weapons by making them unusable weapons. Anyway, most of the international or multilateral treaties were attempts to promote nuclear disarmament by making nuclear weapons unusable or useless weapons. Proposals for declarations of "non-use" or "no first use" of nuclear weapons, especially against non-nuclear states are essentially the same attempts at arms control in that they restrict the use of nuclear weapons. In this way, nuclear arms control has been regarded as a precondition for, or a first step to nuclear disarmament. In this respect, nuclear free zones and nuclear non-proliferation regime are of particular importance.

5.6.2 Nuclear (Weapon) Free Zones

A nuclear weapon-free zone bans the use, possession, or deployment of nuclear weapons in a given geographical area(s) called "zone." The nuclear weapon-free zone is an attempt to make nuclear weapons unusable or useless in a certain geographical area. As is clear from Table 24, the nuclear free zones were first established in places which belonged to no state's territory and which did not affect strategies of nuclear states, such as the Antarctic (Antarctic Treaty, 1959), outer space (Outer Space Treaty, 1967), and ocean bed (Seabed Treaty, 1972).

The Treaty for the Prohibition of Nuclear Weapons in Latin America and the Caribbean (Treaty of Tlatelolco) concluded in 1967 was the first nuclear weapon-free zone. However, this kind of nuclear free zones which covered territories of states and international waters did not spread smoothly. It was partly due to the opposition of nuclear states which wanted freedom of the movement of their nuclear warships, and partly due to the nonparticipation of potential nuclear states which wanted to keep an "open option" to retain the right to the possession of nuclear weapons. It was only in 1985, nearly twenty years after the Treaty of Tlatelolco, that the next nuclear free zone was established in the South Pacific (South Pacific Nuclear Free Zone Treaty: Treaty of Rarotonga). The subsequent spread of nuclear free zones was slow for the same reasons. But, both the atmosphere favorable to nuclear disarmament after the end of the Cold

War and the intention of nuclear powers to maintain the non-proliferation regime facilitated the conclusion of new nuclear free zone treaties in Southeast Asia and Africa, Treaty on the Southeast Asia Nuclear Weapon-Free Zone: Treaty of Bangkok in 1995 and African Nuclear-Weapon-Free Zone Treaty: Treaty of Pelindaba in 1996, respectively. With these two treaties, the Southern Hemisphere has now become mostly nuclear weapon-free area. At present, nuclear free zones in Central Asia and in Central Europe are envisaged. But, there are other regions like the Middle East, South Asia and Northeast Asia which face a great difficulty. Moreover, nuclear weapon-free zones in Europe (or Eurasia) or North America will be impossible unless nuclear weapons are totally eliminated.

5.6.3 Nuclear Non-Proliferation Regime

Another pillar of nuclear arms control is the so-called nuclear non-proliferation regime. A regime (or an international regime) is a formal and informal institution of cooperation among states. The core of the non-proliferation regime is treaties which ban nuclear tests and the acquisition and/or possession of nuclear weapons. While nuclear free zones restrict nuclear weapons in a certain geographical area, non-proliferation regime aims to restrict or ban the testing or possession of nuclear weapons.

As is shown in Table 24, the Partial Test Ban Treaty (PTBT) was signed as early as 1963. The treaty banned all the nuclear tests except underground tests. Banning (surface) nuclear tests was an effective measure for preventing the emergence of a new nuclear state, as far as the parties to the treaty were concerned. But it also had its own loophole of permitting underground tests. At that time, all the nuclear states like the United States, the Soviet Union and the United Kingdom, had established the technology of underground nuclear tests.

More than thirty years after the PTBT, the Comprehensive Test Ban Treaty (CTBT) was concluded in 1996. The treaty banned all the nuclear tests including underground ones. But the treaty left some problems unresolved. Three issues can be mentioned.

First, while it can be a preventive measure for the proliferation of nuclear weapons, especially for the emergence of new nuclear states, the treaty does not reduce or abolish existing nuclear weapons. Nor does it ban their production and deployment. Secondly, the treaty bans nuclear explosion tests, but it does not ban so-called "sub-critical" tests, those tests which stop just short of explosion. Both the United States and Russia made several sub-critical tests even after the conclusion of the treaty. Thirdly, though the treaty is not the only case, there are states which refuse to join the treaty. In the case of CTBT, India and Pakistan have refused to join the treaty, in order to keep their open options. Both performed nuclear tests in 1998.

The most important foundation on which the non-proliferation regime has been based is the Non-Proliferation Treaty (NPT) concluded in 1968. The treaty prohibits any country except the five nuclear states specified in it from possessing nuclear weapons, though the five nuclear states were not obliged to reduce or eliminate their nuclear arsenals. In return for the banning, non-nuclear parties to the treaty were to be accorded the greatest facility for the peaceful use of nuclear energy, especially for nuclear power generation. These two purposes were accomplished through International Atomic Energy Agency (IAEA). Non-nuclear member states were placed under a very strict inspection and the development of nuclear weapons was impossible theoretically at least. But even the strict inspection by IAEA could not detect clandestine projects of nuclear development, as in the cases of Iraq and North Korea, and, recently, of South Korea and Iran. Of course, the treaty was quite ineffective when non-party states like South Africa tried to develop nuclear capability. South Africa was a non-member when it produced atomic bombs and disposed of them later. In 1995, NPT was extended indefinitely.

It is said that the non-proliferation regime has two serious problems. One is the problem of the monopolization of nuclear weapons by the nuclear states. The other is the existence of non-member states.

In the 1995 negotiations for the extension of NPT, one of the greatest issues was that, if the treaty was to be extended indefinitely, non-nuclear member states would be banned permanently from possessing nuclear weapons, while the five nuclear states specified in the treaty were only under moral obligation to pursue complete and comprehensive nuclear disarmament in earnest. The permanent extension of the treaty would assure them of the privileged status of nuclear states. It is for this reason that NPT has often been regarded as an "unequal," one-sided treaty. Though, of course, the "equal" possession of nuclear weapons would be by no means desirable. (For the debate about nuclear proliferation, see Sagan and Waltz (1995)).

Nuclear states have created and maintained the non-proliferation regime in the way which will do virtually no harm to their possession and production of nuclear weapons. While the regime sought to prevent the further emergence of nuclear weapon states or the horizontal proliferation of nuclear weapons, it also guaranteed the monopoly of nuclear weapons by the existing nuclear weapon states. Nuclear arms control and international institutions for that purpose like the non-proliferation regime are originally intended to be a step toward achieving the end of nuclear disarmament. But now the non-proliferation has turned into an end itself and has been reduced to a means to perpetuate the monopoly on nuclear weapons by the nuclear states.

5.6.4 Nuclear Disarmament as a Process Utopia

We discussed the concept of "process Utopia" in the first chapter (1.1). The concept has its own drawbacks. It is because a process Utopia contains an inherent tension or dilemma between what is possible and what is desirable, or between what is realistic and what is idealistic. Recent nuclear disarmament process clearly shows this dilemma of the process Utopia (Matsuo 2001).

A famous classical paradox or fable of Achilles and Turtle may be illustrative here. Achilles, the hero in the Greek Myth, is famous for his fast running as well as his bravery. According to the paradox, in spite of his speed, he cannot overtake a turtle which moves very slowly. The paradox goes like this. Suppose that Achilles is in now at the point called P_0, and the turtle is at the point P_1. When Achilles reaches the point P_1, where the turtle initially was, the turtle has made a little advance, and it is now at the point P_2. Similarly, when Achilles reaches P_2, the turtle will be at the point P_3, a little away from P_2. Thus, in spite of his fast running, Achilles can never overtake the turtle.

As we can see easily, the paradox is due to the way in which the short-term goal of Achilles at each run is set. The goal is set at the point where the turtle is. If we change the goal or set the destination differently, the paradox will disappear. If the process Utopia sets its goal wrongly, it will be trapped in a similar pitfall.

Recent nuclear disarmament proposals and their implementation processes have certainly followed the process Utopian approach. Not only activists and diplomats but also scholars have recommended and/or adopted the approach. For example, Sverre Lodgaard argues that the immediate and comprehensive elimination of nuclear weapons will be unrealistic and counter-productive, and that nuclear disarmament process should be staged (Lodgaard 2000: 17-18.)

Perhaps due to the favorable atmosphere after the end of the Cold War, many nuclear disarmament proposals were made in the late 1990s. The most striking feature of the nuclear elimination proposals is that all of them adopt a staged approach, or a process utopian approach, to the reduction and elimination of nuclear weapons. Henry Stimson Center published *An Evolving US Nuclear Posture,* which proposed staged reduction and elimination of nuclear weapons. The Canberra Commission and The New Agenda Coalition followed suit. But in these and other proposals, the path leading to the ultimate goal of the elimination of nuclear weapons seems to be divided into too many steps or "process Utopias." For example, it is argued that after the conclusion of CTBT, the next task will be the so-called Cutoff Treaty. The treaty aims to reduce the amount of production of nuclear material as a step toward the final stopping of the production itself. It may take several years for negotiation, signature, and ratification and so on. And only then the next step will begin which aims at the termination of the production of nuclear fissile material. Even a small step like the prohibition of the production of nuclear material is actually divided into steps. Thus the path to the final goal has been and will be divided, or we should say sliced, into perhaps too great a number of short-term goals. Such a division may have the same effect of postponing the achievement of the final goal considerably, if not endlessly. If we put the "depleted Uranium weapons" issue on the agenda, it may have the same effect.

In cannot be denied that, in nuclear disarmament process, selected process goals should be realizable and, therefore, emphasis should be placed on the feasibility and the formation of agreement among the parties involved, especially the five nuclear powers. But if we place too much emphasis on the feasibility at the expense of desirability and set the intermediate goal too near, then, as the paradox of Achilles teaches us, we may not be able to achieve our final goal forever. In recent nuclear disarmament process, the intermediate goals seem to be set too near.

In this way, the notion of process Utopia may have its own pitfalls. It is perhaps because it is very difficult to keep a tension and balance between what is possible and what is desirable, and it is much easier to tilt the balance toward what is possible, as in the case of nuclear disarmament. As Ramesh Thakur says, "[A] step-by-step is the best policy: But such caution can be fatal if the need is to cross a chasm" (Thakur 2000: 38).

6 Internal Conflict

6.1 General Introduction: What Is Internal Conflict?

We discussed studies on great wars in chapter 4. Now, we will examine wars on a smaller scale, which we call "local wars/conflicts." Compared with nuclear wars or great wars between major powers, local conflicts are rather small in their scope and geographical extent. Hence the name "local." They pose, however, one of the most serious problems to our world. In spite of the smaller scale of these wars when viewed separately, since the end of the Second World War, the total casualties of these wars have exceeded 20 millions by the end of the Cold War, as Table 25 shows. Note also that the casualties were overwhelmingly concentrated in developing countries.

Table 25 Wars and Conflicts after the World War Two (1945-1989)
(Wars, Civil Wars, Invasions, Interventions)
source: adapted from Sivard (1989), 22

area	numbers	deaths (1.000s)
Latin America	23	668
Europe	4	176
Middle East	18	1,613
Asia	46	13,748
Africa	36	5,604
Total	127	21,809

In addition, the number of refugees and so-called internally displaced persons (IDP) mainly due to these conflicts exceeded 20 millions at its peak (UNHCR 1997: 2). Table 26 gives recent statistics.

The developed Western states have enjoyed "a long peace" and its dividend, and seem to be moving toward a "non-war community." In stark contrast, as tables 25 and 26 suggest, developing countries have been war-stricken as well as poverty-stricken. In this sense, the relevance and importance of local wars cannot be overemphasized, especially to developing countries.

Table 26 Number of Refugees and Internally Displaced Persons
(estimate as of January 1, 2001)
source: UNHCR home page

	in 1,000s
Asia	8,450
Africa	6,073
Europe	5,572
North America	1,047
Latin America and the Caribbean	576
Oceania	76
Total	**21,273**

To reiterate, the importance and urgency of local wars are due to the recognition of the vastness of human costs as we saw in tables 25 and 26, though recently a group of economists have begun to pay attention to economic and developmental costs (for example, see Collier et al 2003). And as we will see shortly, the international society has increasingly come to the recognition that they constitute the threat to "international peace and security."

The term local war or local conflict may be the most generic and comprehensive term for the kind of armed conflicts we have in mind. There are actually a great variety of names and labels for similar kinds of wars. Some are intended to be generic names, covering the whole range of the phenomena, while others are intended to be specific, paying attention to, and trying to capture, some specific subset of conflicts. To mention a few, we have such terms as "local war," "domestic conflict," "civil war," "internal conflict," "internal war," and so on. Some prefer the term "strife" to "war" or "conflict." Of course, there are many other terms and our list may continue apparently without end; "communal conflict," "ethnic conflict," "anti-regime conflict," "national liberation war," "guerrilla warfare," "protracted conflict," and so on. They are usually subcategories or special types of what we may call "local war," which seek to characterize specific types of conflict in terms of parties to the conflict, nature or issue of the conflict and so on.

The abundance of names and labels (for example, see Beaumont 1995: 21-23) is due to the fact that local wars vary greatly in their scale, duration, severity, causes and issues, parties, domestic and international implications etc.

In this connection, we must mention two other terms of recent origin. The one is "low intensity conflict (LIC)." The term is frequently used, especially in everyday non-technical sense, to mean roughly the same thing as local war. As a technical term, however, it was originally coined as part of the American military strategy and intended to mean, and still means, informal military operations not involving formal armies and lying outside the formal military operations or campaign. Typical examples are usually secret operations like counterinsurgency and pro-insurgency operations for or against anti-government revolts and so on (Klare 1989: 114).

Recently some scholars have begun to use the term "complex emergency" or "complex political emergency." The term is aimed to capture the complex political, economic and social implications of local war as well as the war itself. It is a reflection of the fact that local war, especially when it is prolonged and protracted, severely affects both the whole structure of the state in question and the entire population living in it. For example, local wars may result, in an extreme case, in the internal and international displacement of people as in many parts of Africa, and in the collapse and fragmentation of the state as in Somalia. The urgency of the solution of local war actually lies not only in the losses of human lives and material resources brought about by local war, but also in the vast and lasting damages of its ramifications.

"Protracted duration," "profound human suffering," "political (power struggle) origin," "social cleavage between groups," and "crisis of state" are among the major characteristics of a complex (political) emergency (Goodhand and Hulme 1999: 16-17, Pearce 1999: 51). We can add other effects to the list such as general impoverishment, destruction or deterioration of social and economic infrastructures and social capital, and many more (Cliffe and Luckham 1999: 31). Since the issue is often discussed in connection of "state failure," we will examine the issue in some detail later again 6.6.3 (1). Here, however, we will focus our attention rather narrowly on the wars and conflicts themselves.

In this connection, we should also mention the concept of "new wars." The term tries to capture the distinct characteristics of local wars since the 1980s. (For details, see Kaldor 1999: 1-10).

As we saw above, there is no consensus, at present, on the name of what we refer to as "local war" or "conflict," though the name of "local conflict" is the most common. In addition, there is no agreement upon the definition of local conflict. So, let us provisionally define local conflict very broadly as any wars excluding world wars and major wars. However we may define world war and major war, this definition includes all other wars and armed conflicts between or among sovereign states such as the Falkland Conflict, India-Pakistani Wars, the Iran-Iraqi War, the Middle East wars, and it may include even the Korean War and the Vietnam War. In view of the prevalence of domestic or intrastate war instead of interstate war, we need another category to distinguish intrastate war from local war in general so defined. We can define internal conflict (or intrastate war) much more narrowly as local war fought primarily by internal parties largely within the territory of a state. In this chapter, we will mainly, if not exclusively, focus upon internal conflict. And, in refereeing to this category of war, we will follow the majority practice of "internal conflict" rather than "internal war" or "intrastate war."

6.2 Realities of the "Local Wars" in the Postwar World

Until the end of the 1970s, local conflicts were not a major research theme of peace studies and international relations research. Consequently, a pioneering work in the study of local conflicts was born rather on the periphery than at the center of peace studies and international relations research. It is ascribed to a Hungarian researcher, Istvan Kende. The significance of Kende's pioneering work does not lie in the detailed descriptions and analyses of individual local conflicts. Such case studies of individual conflicts actually abounded. But, the significance of his work lies in his comprehensive and systematic treatment of local conflicts which he calls "local wars." He clarified their nature, and demonstrated their importance in our world on the basis of quantitative analysis. In this, he rightfully inherited the spirits of Wright and Richardson. His use of the term "local war" instead of "local conflict" was to emphasize the importance of the issue.

Kende amassed data on local wars during the 30 years after 1945. While there was no world war or major war, Kende showed that there were as many as 120 local wars in the period. According to Kende, the average of 11.5 local wars was fought every day throughout the period. Kende classified local wars into three categories shown in Table 27. The first category is "internal anti-regime war," fought between the government and a party aiming at the overthrow of the government for various reasons. The second category is "internal tribal war," fought between ethnic and religious groups or between them and the government. This category corresponds to what we now call "ethnic" or "communal" conflict. The third category is "border war." The term does not mean war over the territory or over the state border. It simply means "interstate" war between the states. Of all the three, only the third category is a war in the traditional sense. Each of the three types can be further subdivided in terms of the presence or absence of foreign intervention or interference.

Table 27 Local Wars (1945-1976)
source: Kende (1978), 231-232

	intervention	no intervention	total
internal anti-regime wars	56	17	73
internal tribal wars	12	17	29
border wars	6	12	18
Total	74	46	120

Even this simple classification is sufficient to clearly reveal the characteristics of modern local wars. We can point out three characteristics.

First of all, the modern local wars are predominantly internal or intrastate wars fought mainly within the territory of a state, whether they are anti-regime wars or ethnic wars. In contrast, the traditional interstate wars (called "border wars") are distinctly a minority. Secondly, local wars are characterized by the intervention of a third foreign party, especially a great power. This gave rise the name of "proxy wars." Thirdly, the regional distribution of local wars given in Table 28 shows clearly that local wars are concentrated in developing countries. It is true also of the casualties or victims, as we saw above in Table 25. With no great war among major military powers in the postwar period, modern wars are local wars in developing countries, especially those local wars fought mainly within the territory of a single state.

Table 28 Regional Distribution of Local Wars (1945-1976)
source: Kende (1978), 229

Region	number of local wars
Europe	5
Asia	35
Middle East	36
Africa	21
Latin America	23
Total	120

But all the developing countries are not necessarily war-stricken to the same extent. Some are afflicted by local wars more, and others less. For example, Timberlake and Williams (1987) argues that, when we take into consideration various forms of political violence such as terrorism and assassination together with local wars, they are concentrated in a certain group of states, in those states in the semi-periphery of the world system. We will discuss the issue also in 6.6.3 (2).

Kende dealt with local wars which occurred from 1945 to 1976. Nearly 50 new local wars occurred after 1977. These wars had the same characteristics. In 1988, in the last days of the Cold War, there were 33 armed conflicts with more than one thousand cumulative deaths. Of the 33 local wars, all occurred in developing countries with the only exception of Northern Ireland. 17 of the 33 wars were fought over the control of the government, 11 were fought over the issues of autonomy or independence. Only 5 of them were interstate wars. The above characteristics of modern local wars pointed out by Kende still persisted until the end of the Cold War.

6.3 Local Conflicts in the Post-Cold War Era

Table 29 gives the incidence of local wars which continued or emerged since the end of the Cold War. We can safely conclude from the table that there were few interstate wars in the post-Cold War period. At the same time, the tendency pointed out earlier by

Kende has now been amplified. In the 1990s after the Cold War, local wars are overwhelmingly internal or intrastate wars, though foreign interventions decreased sharply.

Table 29 Post-Cold War Armed Conflicts, 1989-2000
source: adapted from Wallensteen and Sollenberg (2001), 632

	intrastate conflict	intrastate conflict with foreign intervention	interstate conflict	all wars
1989	43	1	3	47
1990	44	2	3	49
1991	49	1	1	51
1992	52	2	1	55
1993	42	4	0	46
1994	42	0	0	42
1995	34	0	1	35
1996	33	1	2	36
1997	30	3	1	34
1998	33	2	2	37
1999	33	2	2	37
2000	30	1	2	33
all years	95	9	7	111

A further comparison of the data after the end of the Cold War with those of Kende reveals that ethnic conflicts which Kende called "internal tribal wars" greatly increased in number relative to the "anti-regime" wars which are fought over the control or the type of government or regime. Local conflicts in the post-Cold War era are marked by the prominence of ethnic conflicts.

To be sure, ethnic (or communal) conflicts are one of the urgent problems facing the contemporary world. Take note, however, that ethnic conflicts are not unique to the post-Cold War period, though their number increased during the period as Table 30 below shows. Ethnic conflicts frequently occurred even during the Cold War and many outlived it. The average duration of the ethnic conflicts still continuing in 1996 is 22.4 years and 10 of the total of the 77 ethnic conflicts after the Second World War lasted for more than 30 years (Ayres 2000: 110). This accounts for the prevalence of ethnic conflicts which outlived the Cold War, and persisted well into the new century. As the table shows, however, the post-Cold War era is characterized rather by the termination of ethnic conflicts than by the onset of new conflicts (Ayres 2000: 113). We will discuss the termination of conflict shortly below.

Table 30 Ethnic Conflicts: Beginnings and Endings
source: adapted from Ayres (2000), 112

Year	Beginnings	Endings
1945-49	16	5
1950-54	0	7
1955-59	5	1
1960-64	9	3
1965-69	7	0
1970-74	1	6
1975-79	8	1
1980-84	8	2
1985-89	8	5
1990-96	14	20

It is true that, after the end of the Cold War, ethnic conflicts came to attract much greater popular and academic attention. It is perhaps due to the fact that new ethnic conflicts erupted very close to Western Europe, for example, in the Balkans and in Caucasus. But ethnic conflicts are not "new wars." The end of the Cold War did not "[change] all the answers and the questions," (Kennedy-Pipe 2000: 2, 7-8).

Table 31 shows the regional distribution of armed conflicts which occurred from 1989 to 1996.

Table 31 Regional Distribution of Armed Conflicts after the End of the Cold War
source: adapted from Wallensteen and Sorenberg (1997), 341

	1989	1990	1991	1992	1993	1994	1995	1996
Europe	2	3	6	9	10	5	5	1
Middle East	4	6	7	7	7	5	4	5
Asia	19	18	16	20	15	15	13	14
Africa	14	17	17	15	11	13	9	14
Americas	8	5	5	4	3	4	4	2
World Total	47	49	51	55	46	42	35	36

In this table, the armed conflicts are classified into the following three categories. And the table gives the total of all three categories.

> minor armed conflict
> > 25 or more annual average battle deaths and less than 1,000 in total
>
> intermediate armed conflict
> > annual average battle deaths between 25 and 1,000,
> > and 1,000 or more in total.
>
> war
> > 1,000 or more annual battle deaths
>
> (Wallensteen and Axell 1993: 343-344)

As is clear from Table 31, the post-Cold War era is marked by the emergence of new armed conflicts in the broader Europe, in Eastern Europe and the former Soviet Union. When we consider local conflicts as a whole, however, the basic trends during the Cold War still continue. Local armed conflicts are concentrated in developing countries, especially in Asia and Africa. It is clear that local conflicts were not "new" after the end of the Cold War.

As far as the number is concerned, armed conflicts reached the peak in 1992, but after the peak the number of armed conflicts began to decrease as is seen in Table 31. In 2003, however, such many countries were afflicted by internal conflict as: Algeria, Burundi, Liberia, Sudan, Colombia, Peru, India (Kashmir), Indonesia (Aceh), Myanmar (Karen), Nepal, Philippines, Sri Lanka, Israel (Palestine), Turkey, Russia (Chechnya) (Eriksson and Wallensteen 2004: 140-142). The details of the current armed conflicts and their histories and natures can be obtained, for example, from the works by Peter Wallensteen and his colleagues which are usually annually printed in *Journal of Peace Research* (some of which are given in the references) or Stockholm International Peace Research Institute's yearbook, *SIPRI Yearbook: Armaments, Disarmament and International Security*.

The decrease is due to the fact that a considerable number of armed conflicts were terminated after the end of the Cold War. Indeed, as we saw above in Table 30, the post-Cold War era is marked rather by the termination of old armed conflicts than by the emergence of new conflicts. Table 32 shows how these conflicts end. Of course, the termination of an armed conflict is nothing more than the stopping or suspension of the fighting. It is not by any means a permanent or desirable solution of root causes of conflicts

Table 32 Conflict Termination in the Post-Cold War Era, 1989-1996
source: adapted from Walensteen and Sollenberg (1997), 342

All Conflicts	99
conflicts terminated	66
peace agreement	19
Victory	23
Others	24

Armed conflicts terminate in many different ways. Wallensteen and Sollenberg (1997: 342) proposes the following typology:

> "peace agreement": explicit agreement by the warring parties to end the conflict, including partial peace agreement and agreement on the negotiation for a peace agreement
> "victory"
> "other outcomes": cease-fire agreement, that is, agreement to stop (but not always end) fighting among the warring parties.

As is clear from the table, the termination of conflicts can be seen as one of characteristics of the post-Cold War era. For example, we saw peace agreements or cease-fire agreements in Angola, Mozambique, Myanmar, Ethiopia, Georgia, the Philippines and so on. It is needless to say that conflicts are not always terminated in a desirable way, but any kind of termination is better than fighting and killing in most of the cases.

In spite of the termination of many armed conflicts, the picture is not particularly rosy. On the one hand, though the number of armed conflicts decreased substantially, there are still more than 30 ongoing armed conflicts throughout the world. Some conflicts get bogged down and protracted. On the other, cease-fire or peace agreements are very fragile and they are often broken soon after the conclusion. And in addition, old conflicts suddenly resume after some period of cease-fire as in Rwanda, Burundi and so on. Still others may be only latent. These latter situations have given rise to the notion of "post-conflict conflict prevention" as part of post-conflict reconstruction efforts.

6.4 New Trends in the Post-Cold War Era

Concerning local conflicts in the post-Cold War era, we can point out a few new trends, not existent during the Cold War. Probably, the most important of the new trends in the post-Cold War era is the change in the attitude of the international society toward local conflicts and its responses to them.

First of all, the international society, especially the United Nations, have become involved more and more in these conflicts. In fact, the United Nations had been engaged in the so-called peacekeeping activities even during the Cold War. But after the end of the Cold War, the United Nations began an active engagement in a new, more ambitious kind of peacekeeping activities. The original peacekeeping activities of the United Nations were intended to maintain peace reached by the parties to the conflicts, and followed the four principles:

(1) the existence of peace agreement or cease-fire agreement among the parties to the conflict,
(2) the acceptance of the UN peacekeeping by all the parties concerned,
(3) the maintenance of neutrality of the peacekeeping UN troops, and
(4) the ban of the use of force except for the self-defence.

This type of peacekeeping is called "first generation" or "traditional" peacekeeping. But with the end of the Cold War, the United Nations embarked upon the so-called second generation peacekeeping, an extended and more ambitious one. The then secretary-general of the United Nations, Boutros Boutros-Ghali's *Agenda for Peace* published in 1992 was a conceptual watershed. The new concept of peacekeeping was aimed to enlarge the missions of the peacekeeping in order to prevent or stop serious humanitarian crises even with the use of force when there is no peace agreement. It was because many conflicts brought about the state of "complex emergency."

The new peacekeeping activities of the United Nations were successful in Namibia and perhaps in Cambodia, but they were nearly complete failures in Somalia and the former Yugoslavia. Consequently, though the new interventions of the United

Nations were hailed as a panacea at first, they were later severely criticized as useless and harmful (Weiss 1995: 3).

Besides the issue of the United Nations' new kind of peacekeeping, we should also mention the concept of humanitarian (military) intervention in passing. The proponents of humanitarian intervention argue that for humanitarian purposes, for example, in order to stop or prevent gross human rights violations, the international society has the obligation and right to intervene in the local conflict, even with the use of force and at the expense of the sovereignty of states concerned which is the very basis of the traditional international relations (Weiss 1995: 5). They argue that collective use of force is permitted in order to prevent and stop the humanitarian crises. Proponents of intervention often evoke the cause of "international peace and security" expressed in the Charter of the United Nations as well.

Probably stimulated by the increased attention of the international society, new ways of looking at, and coping with, local conflicts and their devastating effects have emerged. We will very briefly take up three of them: early warning, preventive diplomacy, and peace-building.

The solution of local conflicts is one of the urgent problems facing the world. But once an armed conflict breaks out, it is very difficult to stop it, not to speak of solving the root causes. Conflicts often become prolonged and protracted, and accumulate fear and hostility among the people involved. It is for this reason that the prevention rather than solution of the conflict has come to be stressed. In this connection, two trends are worth mentioning. One is the concept of "early warning" (for example, see Davies and Gurr (eds.) (1998)) and the other is that of "preventive diplomacy" advanced by Boutros-Ghali in his *Agenda for Peace*.

With the prevalence of local conflict, the international society faces another difficult task. It is increasingly recognized that in order to consolidate the fragile peace reached by the parties to the conflict and prevent the resumption of a conflict, the restoration of a stable and peaceful society after the destruction and hatred of a conflict and the establishment and maintenance of an effective and democratic government, peace-building in a word, are an essential task. This task of post-conflict reconstruction including the economic restoration is perhaps the most difficult because it involves the solution of the root causes of conflict.

After the end of the Cold War, the international society made various new efforts ranging from the prevention and solution of local conflict to peacekeeping and post-conflict reconstruction as Figure 20 schematically illustrates. The international society has tried to prevent, solve, or reconstruct at each of the phases of conflict.

Figure 20 Processes of Conflict and the International Community

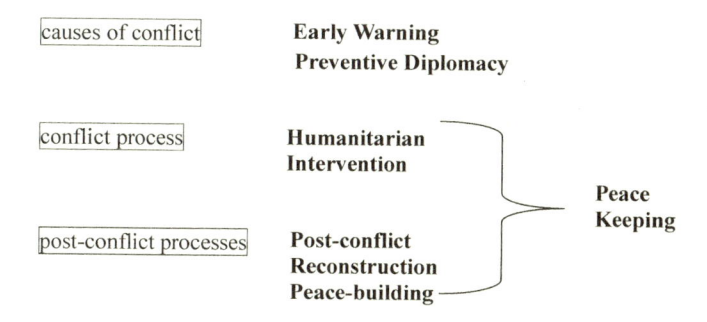

causes of conflict	**Early Warning**
	Preventive Diplomacy
conflict process	**Humanitarian Intervention**
	Peace Keeping
post-conflict processes	**Post-conflict Reconstruction**
	Peace-building

So far, we have discussed local conflict in general, but, as was pointed out above, the majority of local conflicts today are internal/intrastate conflicts. In what follows, therefore, we will narrow our attention to internal conflicts, and examine their nature and causes.

6.5 Nature of Internal Conflict

Internal conflicts are fought mainly within the territory of the state and fought by internal parties like government, commual groups, anti-governmental guerrilla groups and so on. As was stated above, there are a great variety of terms referring to internal conflicts. This is partly due to the diversity and complexity of internal conflicts. So, instead of proceeding directly to the examination of their causes, it is better to have some rough idea of what internal conflicts are like and what they involve.

There are, of course, various attempts at the clarification of the nature of internal conflicts in terms of the parties to the conflict, issues, and demands advanced by the parties etc. The model of internal conflict advanced by Kalevi Holsti is among the most universally applicable ones. The model is illustrated in Figure 21.

Figure 21 Two Types of Internal Conflict
source: Holsti (1998), 124

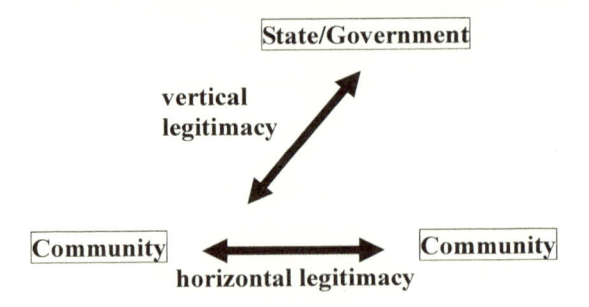

```
                    State/Government
                         ↗↙
         vertical
         legitimacy


   Community  ←——————→  Community
              horizontal legitimacy
```

Holsti ascribes the cause of internal conflict either to the loss of the legitimacy of the state (or government), which he calls the loss of the vertical legitimacy, or to the loss of the legitimacy of other domestic community or communities, which he calls the loss of the horizontal legitimacy. This brings about two basic types of internal conflicts. On the one hand, there are conflicts between the state/national government and an internal group or groups. On the other, there are conflicts between internal groups like ethnic groups without the involvement of the government of the state in question (Henderson and Singer 2000: 276, Holsti 1998: 124). In fact, however, the loss of the horizontal legitimacy among internal communities or groups, especially the collapse of mutual trust among internal groups, and the loss or decline of the vertical state/government legitimacy, frequently go together. As a result, internal conflicts often take on a dual character. They can be conflicts between the state or government and community group(s) or anti-government "rebellious" group(s), and at the same time, they can also be conflicts between internal groups. The dual character can be ascribed to the following factors.

As Ted Robert Gurr and Barbara Harff point out, a community group like an ethnic group advances a variety of demands to the central government, ranging, from domestic reforms for the improvement or promotion of their status and rights, to autonomy or even secession (Gurr and Harff 1994: 15-24). Whatever the demand is, the conflict involves a confrontation with the national government on the one hand, and, in a multiethnic state, it may also involve a competition or struggle with other communities or communal groups.

To complicate the matter, as many others pointed out, it is often the case that the central government is not a neutral arbiter or mediator between conflicting domestic forces and interest groups. It often takes side, or is (mis)perceived to take side, with one of the parties to the conflict. And, more often than not, the central government represents the interests of a particular community, usually a dominant community, or it is perceived to be so. This results in the loss of the state legitimacy.

The loss of state legitimacy may also due to the collapse of the central government brought about by the conflict. Such a situation is often referred to as "state failure." State failure is one of the salient features of "complex political emergency," which we discussed above. Which of the two, internal conflict and state failure, causes the other is a difficult question to answer. But we will take up the issue of state failure as one of the factors of internal conflict in the next section.

6.6 Causes of Internal Conflict

6.6.1 General Introduction

When we examine causes of internal conflicts, we must keep in mind that they vary greatly in nature and character depending upon the parties, goals and issues, geopolitical location, and international and domestic contexts. And history and culture may have to be added to this list of explanatory factors. Accordingly, causes of conflicts also vary greatly. But we will try to answer whether there is some common cause or causes and whether some generalization is possible or not.

In examining causes of internal conflict, we should also take heed of which kind of a cause-effect relationship we will assume. Studies on causes of internal conflict can be divided into three types of approach in terms of the causal relationship employed. First, in a "simple causal relationship," one or more causes (with due weight of emphasis) are assumed to bring the effect, usually the onset of internal conflict. Holsti's argument above can be included in this category, though the cause is of very high abstraction.

Secondly, instead of the direct causation, we can think of the "factors which heighten the likelihood of war" (Henderson and Singer 2000: 280). At the root of the concept lies the following assumption. There are many factors which heighten the likelihood of war in general and internal conflict in particular. Each of them may not directly cause a particular conflict by itself. But a combination of some of them, or the simultaneous existence of some of them, can cause a conflict.

Thirdly, in trying to explain the occurrence of local conflict, some researchers propose to establish the "causal chains" of factors or "causal path" which lead finally to the onset of local conflict. Homer-Dixon and his colleagues' research on "environmental conflict" is a typical example. They have focused upon the conflicts caused by "scarcities" of vital renewable resources such as soil, water, forests, fish, and so on (Homer-Dixon 1994: 290), and have proposed a causal chain of factors leading to local conflict as is given in Figure 22.

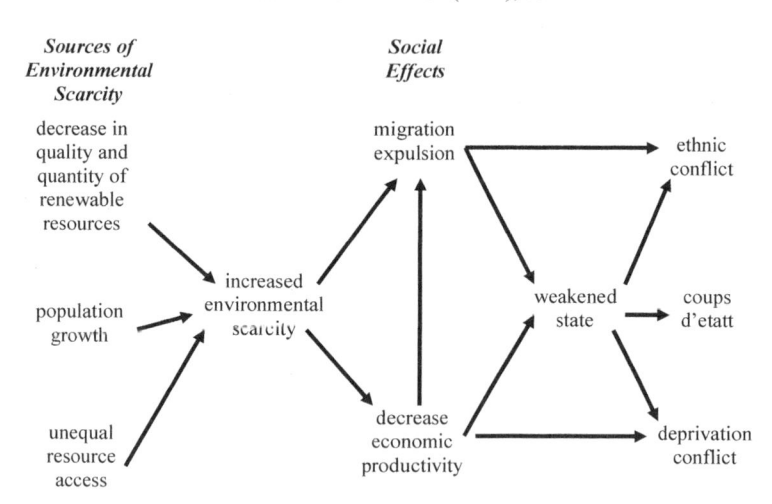

Figure 22 Environmental Scarcity and Armed Conflicts
source: Homer-Dixon (1994), 302

Sources of Environmental Scarcity

- decrease in quality and quantity of renewable resources
- population growth
- unequal resource access

Social Effects

- increased environmental scarcity
- migration expulsion
- decrease economic productivity
- weakened state
- ethnic conflict
- coups d'etatt
- deprivation conflict

According to them, excessive or unequal use of renewable resources combined with population growth produces "environmental scarcity." This in turn brings about

120

population movement or migration on the one hand, and the decrease in economic productivity (especially in land etc) on the other. These socioeconomic effects of environmental scarcity cause the weakening of states and/or directly cause certain kinds of internal conflict. Population growth in Bangladesh caused millions of in-migration of Bengalis into Assam and neighboring areas, finally causing bloodshed. The case of Mauritania and Senegal along the Senegal River basin is essentially the same (Homer-Dixon 1994: 302-304).

As this simplified explanation shows, local conflicts (especially ethnic conflicts and "deprivation" conflicts) are caused by a long causal chain of factors through the existence of intermediate factors or variables. (Remember the thesis of lateral pressure which postulates a similar process for the occurrence of war.) This kind of "path analysis" is one of the typical explanations of complex relationships among causal factors.

While the above approach tries to arrange factors or causes in a causal order, a more frequent way of sorting various causes is to divide them into long-term and short-term causes, or into "underlying and proximate" causes (Brown 1997: 4). On the review of literature on causes of local conflict, Michael Brown proposes the following four major categories of underlying causes and divides them into several subcategories (Brown 1997: 5-13).

> structural factors
> political factors
> economic/social factors
> cultural/perceptual factors (Brown 1997: 5)

Compared with the exploration of underlying causes, previous research has rather neglected proximate causes, that is, catalytic (acting as catalyst) or triggering causes. As to the proximate causes, Brown proposes to categorize internal conflicts according to two criteria: whether they are triggered by elite-level or mass-level factors, and whether they are triggered by internal or external factors (Brown 1997: 4, 13, 15). But we will not discuss proximate causes here. It is partly because the presence of these proximate factors does not necessarily lead to internal conflict. The presence of these factors is rather the necessary conditions for the occurrence of internal conflict, than the sufficient conditions. They heighten the likelihood of internal conflict separately or in combination. But each one of them or the combination of them do not necessarily lead to the outbreak of internal conflict.

In addition to underlying and proximate causes, we may need another concept, that of "tipping event" which triggers the onset of conflict. Tipping events cannot be considered direct causes of internal conflict in any sense. For example, the assassination of the Austrian prince in Sarajevo in 1914 triggered the First World War and was a typical example of a tipping event, but it did not, in any significant sense, cause the war.

So far, we have reviewed several approaches to the causes of internal conflict. It is obvious that, in view of the enormous number of candidates, we cannot deal with all the possible causes of internal conflict, whether separately or in combination. In what follows, we must limit our attention in some way or other. First, we will focus rather upon the long-term or underlying causes than on the short-term direct ones. Secondly, since many scholars argue that internal conflict largely results from internal factors rather than external or international factors (Henderson and Singer 2000: 278), in what follows, we will concentrate on the internal or domestic factors to the exclusion of external or international factors. External or outside factors may be proximate cause of internal conflict, as Brown argued. But we will concentrate upon the internal factors.

6.6.2 General Theories of Conflict

In the discussion of causes of local conflict, we will first take up two general theories of conflict, which are intended to be a theory of conflict in general. They are relative deprivation theory and rational actor (rational choice) theory. Both focus upon the perceptual or cognitive factors rather than upon material or physical factors. After the examination of these general theories, we will proceed to examine individual factors, separate political, economic, or cultural factors as possible candidates for heightening the likelihood of internal conflict.

Ted Robert Gurr argues that when an individual gets less than he or she believes they are rightfully entitled to, the result is frustration leading to violence

(David 1998: 80-81). The relative deprivation theory argues that the potential of collective violence depends on the discontent of members of a society. The discontent or frustration is a result of a "perceived" gap between what they have and what they think they should have. This gap is called "relative deprivation" (Brush 1996: 527). The theory is intended to explain collective violence in general, and not internal conflict alone. However, relative deprivation is no longer considered the primary cause of collective violence, though it may be a significant factor contributing to the outbreak of internal conflict in some circumstances. The failure of the theory is due to the fact that, "given the ubiquity of grievance [that is, relative deprivation], problematique is to explain why people *do not* rebel" (Lichbach 1995: 13, emphasis added).

Though it can account for only a small part of causes of internal conflict, relative deprivation, (or frustration or discontent for that matter), borne from the gap between what one has and the expectation(s) for what one should have, is still an important factor increasing the likelihood of internal conflict. For example, see Brown's list of causes in Table 33 below.

If we take the risk of oversimplification, the rational choice theory is based on two assumptions. First, an individual actor has a set of preferences or utility values ranked and ordered (preference order) under a particular circumstance. Second, the individual actor seeks to maximize his or her utility under the constraints of the circumstance. Hence, the name "rational actor." The term "rational" here means to be rational in maximizing one's profit, or simply to be seeking the maximization of one's profit. There are, of course, many doubts raised concerning the applicability of the basic assumptions of the rational choice theory. Yet, the theory has been applied to many diverse research field including peace studies and international relations as we shall see later. The theory has been also applied to the issues of collective violence and internal conflict.

A simple example can best illustrate the main points of the theory and its application to internal conflict. Our example here is what Mark Irving Lichbach calls "rebel's dilemma." Suppose that Jane wants to abolish sexual and racial discrimination. Her friends, many of them active members of a movement against discrimination, plan to stage a massive demonstration next day. Suppose further that, if the demonstration is successful, many discriminatory rules and regulations will be abolished. Now the question is what she should do. Suppose there are two options for her: to join the demonstration, and to stay home. And suppose that everyone else has the same two options and makes the same choice as a whole.

If everyone else chooses to join the demonstration, the result will be a success. Then, if Jane joins, she loses, we assume, her precious time. But if she stays home she will not lose her time. Irrespective of her choice, Jane can enjoy the result. If Jane stays home, however, she can enjoy the result without paying any cost. So it is better or more profitable to stay home. It is better to be a "free rider."

Now suppose that everyone else chooses to stay home. Then the result will be a failure and the current discrimination continues. Whether Jane participates or not, the demonstration will not be successful. But if Jane stays home, she can avoid the loss of her time. In this case again, it is better or more profitable to stay home (Lichbach 1995: 5-6).

In conclusion, if Jane is a rational actor, she will stay home. And if everyone else is also rational, he or she will stay home with the result that no demonstration will be staged. And this is the serious dilemma facing those who wish to mobilize fellow citizens for collective action in general and internal conflict in particular.

The rational choice theory was originally employed to explain the collective violence as the result of the rational choice of actors, but it now faces this rebel's dilemma. Rational potential rebels will not voluntarily contribute to the planned activities whether they are violent or not. Instead, they will choose to be free riders. Unless free riding like Jane's is overcome, there will be no violent conflict. Given the ubiquity of free riding, the rational choice theory is to explain why people do rebel (Lichbach 1995: xii, 13). This problem is a special case of so-called public goods dilemma. We will discuss it in 7.1, in a more generalized form and in a broader context of conflict and cooperation.

6.6.3 Major Factors of Internal Conflict

Previous studies on internal conflict advanced a great number of general or individual causes. Here, however, we will focus upon major factors, following mainly four recent studies: Auvinen (1997), Brown (1977), Collier and Hoeffler (2001), and Henderson and Singer (2000). Of the four, only Auvinen (1997) focus on the intensity of war (182).

Major factors of internal conflict so far examined can be divided, in a similar way as Brown (1997) proposes, roughly into four groups: structural factors, political factors, economic factors and ethnic or cultural factors. The following table, Table 33, gives a classification of major underlying causes of internal conflict proposed by Brown (1997).

Table 33 Underlying Causes of Internal Conflict
source: adapted from Brown (1997), 5-13

structural factors	weak states (lack of legitimacy, lack of well-functioning institutions)
	intrastate security dilemma
	ethnic heterogeneity/contentious minority / geographic concentration
political factors	discriminatory political institutions (state favors a particular group at the expense of others)
	exclusionary national ideologies (nation based on citizenship or ethnicity/religion?)
	intergroup politics (intergroup competition for power)
	elite politics (leaders' policy toward other domestic/foreign groups)
economic/social factors	economic problems (unemployment, inflation, poverty, resource competition)
	discriminatory economic systems (economic inequalities, especially apparently based on such criteria as ethnicity, class, region etc.)
	economic development and modernization (strain on the existing social and political systems and the rise of expectations)
cultural/perceptual factors	patterns of cultural discrimination (education, religion, language, attempt at assimilation)
	problematic group histories (clash of ethnic myths)

Since we cannot examine all the subcategorical factors listed in the table, we will have to limit our attention to one or two of the subcategories. At the same time, we should also take up factors which have attracted much attention, though not explicitly mentioned in the list. The issue of military expenditures is one such example. In short, we will take up the flowing issues as major causes of internal conflict:

(1) "weak state" or "failed state" as structural factors,
(2) "regime type" together with "military regime" as politico-military factors,
(3) "level of economic development" and "military expenditure" as economic factors and
(4) "ethnicity" as ethnic / cultural factors.

Let us examine the impact of these groups one by one.

(1) Structural Factors

In Table 33, three structural factors are listed: "weak states (lack of legitimacy, lack of well-functioning institutions)," "intrastate security dilemma," and "ethnic heterogeneity/contentious minority/geographic concentration." We will examine the first two factors here, but deal with the third later in connection with cultural / perceptual factors because it involves ethnicity and/or minority issues.

As we saw above in Holsti's model, Home-Dixson's conflict path, and Brown's underlying causes, "weak or collapsed states" occupy an important place in the causal chain or causal configuration leading to local conflict. However, internal conflict can be both causes and effects of the state failure in many of developing countries. On the one hand, when the state or the government cannot function properly or sometimes at all, it may lead to internal conflict. On the other, an internal conflict may lead to the weakening of the state or the government. It is still an open question whether the weak state causes a conflict or a conflict brings about the weak state. But, as far as the state or government is concerned, the outcome is the same collapse of the central authority. It is tantamount to the absence of the central authority which arbitrates and mediates between conflicting domestic groups, or which can accommodate various demands of internal groups. These states are often called "quasi-states." or "failed states."

The "weak state" factor gives rise to two issues. One is the issue of state-building or nation-building, and the other is that of internal anarchy and "intrastate security dilemma."

After independence, many developing countries have coped with, and have not been successful in, the difficult tasks of state-building and nation-building. Many post-colonial states had very short time compared with the developed countries in which to build effective state structures and institutions and cohesive overarching national loyalties and identities (Henderson and Singer 2000: 278). In many states, political elites have faced what Holsti calls the "state-strength dilemma." Their attempts to create a strong state actually create the resistance from heterogeneous groups, which will further weaken the state (Holsti 1998: 128). It is because internal conflict is partly ascribed to the failure of nation-building that post-conflict reconstruction efforts pay special attention to this issue.

The mainstream theory of international relations assumes that the most important characteristic of the international society is what is called "anarchy." Anarchy means the absence of central authority or the central government. As for the domestic society, we cannot think of any modern society without a central government. Therefore, the anarchy has been considered to be the property unique to the international system. It has been assumed that it is true only of the international system consisting of sovereign independent states. Consequently, until very recently, especially until the end of 1980s, international relations research showed very little interest in internal conflict. Indeed, in retrospect, "the wars and violent confrontations that were ongoing were ignored in most of the mainstream literature" (Kennedy-Pipe 2000: 1-2) As we saw above, this negligence of internal war is perhaps best exemplified by the Correlates of War Project of University of Michigan. It was largely the case with peace studies as well.

Recently, however, there emerged many states which seemed virtually without any central government, though the nominal entities called government may exist. The condition of anarchy seems now to be true also of the situations of these failed states. If the condition of anarchy holds internally in the state, then other concepts regarded as proper to the international system can also be applied to the domestic situation, especially of war-torn states. The concept of "security dilemma" is the most frequently employed example. Security dilemma has been applied to explain several of internal ethnic conflicts (Kaufman 1996, Posen 1993, Roe 1999). In these studies, it is argued that the anarchy in the domestic political system primarily account for the armed confrontation of internal groups.

Peter Wallensteen advances a similar view which finds similarities between internal conflict and traditional interstate war. He argues that intrastate and interstate wars are caused by largely the same factors. The ultimate goals of security and survival of the parties in question are common both to intrastate and interstate wars (Wallensteen 1985: 220-222, 228).

(2) Politico-Military Factors

Most of the studies pay particular attention to the two of the factors in this group: regime type and military expenditure. We will first discuss the issue of regime type. Since the issue of military expenditure is often investigated in close connection with the issue of economic development, we will take it up later as one of economic factors.

There are findings which demonstrate that the type of regime or the political system of a state has a great impact on the onset of internal conflict. The regime type is usually divided into three categories in terms of the degree of democratization: autocracy, semi-democracy or authoritarian regime, and democracy. Though there are some studies concluding a monotonic relationship between the degree of democratization and internal conflict (Auvinen 1997: 181, Henderson and Singer 2000: 279), most research results support the inverted U-relationship, like that of the famous Kuznets' curve (Kuznets 1963), between them (Auvinen 1997: 181, Mousseau 2001: 561). The non-linear relationship is schematically illustrated in Figure 23.

Figure 23 Regime Types and Internal Conflict

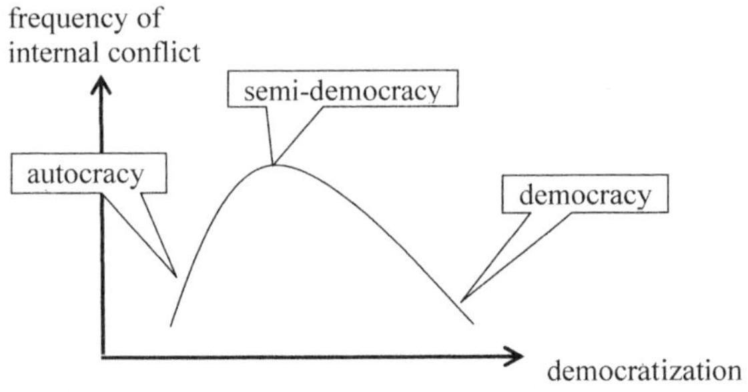

The non-linear relationship in the figure between internal conflict and democratization is explained in the following way. First, autocracies, the least democratized type of regime, can stifle insurgency and rebellion through the use of repressive means, while democracies have enough channels of expressing demands and grievances in the form of well-developed institutions. Therefore, the intermediate type of regime, which Henderson and Singer (2000) calls "semi-democracy" and which is more often referred to as "authoritarian regime," is most prone to internal conflict. It is because semi-democracies have neither the potential for resolving conflict peacefully nor the adequate means of repression (Henderson and Singer 2000: 279). In most studies, semi-democracy or authoritarian regime is significantly associated with an increased likelihood of internal conflict (Auvinen 1997: 188, Henderson and Singer 2000: 289, 295). In addition, recent research suggests that the inverted U-relationship between regime type and internal conflict is not symmetric because democracies experience less violence than autocracies (Henderson and Singer 2000: 289).

Semi-democracies or authoritarian regimes are usually regarded as intermediate stage lying between autocracies and democracies on the path toward democratization. Such regimes are most prone to internal conflict. Then, the question arises whether the change or transition of regime type accounts for the conflict-proneness of semi-democracies. There is an argument that "democratizing states were more likely to fight wars than were states that had undergone no regime change" (Mansfield and Snyder 1995: 12). The conclusion is true both of internal conflict and interstate war. Though the argument does not focus exclusively on internal conflict, it partially corroborates the inverted U-relationship between democratization and internal conflict.

Some have opposed to this conclusion that regime change clearly cannot serve as an explanation for the higher level of internal conflict in semi-democracies. They argue that there is something about semi-democracies which makes them more prone to violent domestic conflict, even when they have had time to stabilize from the regime change (Henderson and Singer 2000: 193). This argument emphasizes the intrinsic property of semi-democracies rather than their transitional nature, as an important factor of internal conflict. Strictly speaking, semi-democracies or authoritarian regimes are not the same as democratizing states, but the debates are still unsolved and open. In addition, we should also take into consideration experiences in other places. For example, democratization processes in the Iberian Peninsula in the 1970s and in Central and Eastern Europe around 1990 were quite peaceful with the only exception of Romania.

We will postpone the examination of military expenditure (or spending) to the next subsection. But the issue has a serious implication for political situations, especially in developing countries. Though most of the developing countries are resource-strained, they often divert to the military their limited resources which could be distributed to disaffected people, as is clear from the following table, Table 34. The table compares social expenditures such as education health care expenditures with military expenditures, and it is clear that developing countries allocate their resources much more favorably to the military.

Table 34 Military and Social Expenditures (1991)
source : Sivard (1993), 42
Figures are the ratios to the military expenditures.

	developed	developing
education	1.46	1.02
health	1.49	0.41

Because of such privileged resource allocation, the military often become stronger and more effective than the civilian government and become quite able and eager to usurp political authority which has fed them, as the frequency of coups d'etat in developing countries exemplifies (Auvinen 1997: 182, Henderson and Singer 2000: 281).

The frequency of coups d'etat brings us to the issue of "militarization" in developing countries. Some trace the origin of the concept of militarization to that of "garrison state" proposed by Harold Lasswell (Lasswell 1941). The core of the concept of garrison state is the predominance of the military over the civilian (Regan 1994: 2, 6). At present, however, there is no consensus among scholars on the definition of the term. For example, scholars are divided over the question whether militarization involves actual military activities or not (Szentes 1984: 46, Wallensteen 1985: 220, Wallensteen et al 1985: xii-xiii). Some scholars such as Patrick M. Regan stress the importance of the mobilization of citizens for the preparation of war as an important element of militarization (Regan 1994: 4, 6). Still others stress the penetration of the military into the society, especially the military values and perspectives and military ways of behavior, into the norms and values of the society. The penetration can become so pervasive that it sometimes transforms the culture of the society into an "armament culture" (Luckham 1984: 1, 2). But the following is among the most important operational indicators of militarization. (For other indicators, see Szentes 1984: 46 as well).

    size of the military force
    presence of military regime
    frequency of internal conflict
    frequency of external war   (chosen from Davis et al 1989: 33).

Thus, militarization can be seen, among others, as the increase or increased level of armaments and military activities. The presence of military regime is one of the important indicators of militarization.

Table 35 shows the number (and the prevalence) of military regimes in developing countries. In the 1980s and in the early 1990s, more than half of developing countries were under military or military-controlled regimes (Sivard 1993: 22).

Table 35 Number of Military-Controlled Regimes
source: Sivard (1993), 22

	number of states military-controlled
1960	26
1982	52
1992	61[1]

1)   number of developing countries = 112

If we adopt a broader perspective of peace like "positive peace," military regimes are characterized also by serious human rights abuses (Sivard 1987: 26, Sivard 1993: 23). We will, however, confine our attention to internal conflict. Table 36 gives an indication of their nature as viewed from the perspective of armed conflict. The table compares developing countries under military regime and other developing countries.

It is clear from the comparison in the table that:

(1) military regimes tend to be lasting and perpetuated,
(2) whether military regimes are more war-prone by nature or not, they are clearly engaged in internal or external war much longer than other countries,
(3) as is expected, the size of the military and military expenditure is obviously greater in military regimes,
(4) as a corollary of high war involvement, cumulative war casualties is much greater in countries under military regimes.

Table 36 Characteristics of Military Regimes
source: Sivard (1993), 23 and Sivard (1989), 20

	military controlled	other developing countries
Years of Military Rule (1960-1992) (cumulative)	22.4	8.1
Years at War (1960—1992)(cumulative)	6.9	1.2
Armed Forces per 1,000 population (1992)	4.5	2.5
Per capita Military Budget (US$)(average)	53	29
Deaths in Wars (in 1,000s)(1960-1992) (cumulative total)	13,924	1,924

It is obvious that military regimes tend to be much more deeply involved in armed conflict, whether it is internal or external. The greater involvement in armed conflict of military regimes seems to be descriptively correct. But some scholars argue that military regimes (or authoritarian regimes, for that matter) should not be regarded as one of the causes of armed conflict, but that they should be regarded rather an intervening or intermediate variable than an independent or explanatory variable, because other more fundamental factors, such as the capitalist world system, for example, brought about the prevalence of military regime and shaped its basic characters (Albrecht et al 1974: 174, Väyrynen 1983: 165-166, 179).

(3) Economic Factors

Let us first examine the relationship of (the level of) economic development with internal conflict. As far as developing countries are concerned, empirical studies largely support the view that economic development provides a prophylactic against internal conflict. In other words, increased development is associated with a decreased likelihood of internal conflict (Henderson and Singer 2000: 282, 289-290). "Male secondary education enrollment, per capita income and the growth rate all have statistically significant and substantial effects that reduce conflict risk" (Collier and Hoefller 2001: 16)

There are, however, studies which draw the opposite conclusion. For example, as we saw above, Timberlake and Williams (1987) argues that internal conflict (together with other kinds of political violence) is concentrated in those states in the semi-periphery of the world system (see also Mousseau 2001: 563, Väyrynen 1983: 179).

The contradictory results can be accounted for by the difference in the outcome (or dependent) variable. If one focuses on the onset or outbreak of internal conflict, its likelihood decreases with economic development. But if one focuses on the magnitude or severity (operationalized in terms of the number of deaths), then it may increase with economic development (Henderson and Singer 2000: 289-290). The question is, however, still open.

In addition to the level of economic development, there are other economic issues apparently closely connected with internal conflict. For example, the issue of income distribution within the state, especially the inequality between the poor and the rich, has been studied extensively. Researchers have asked "Does Economic Inequality Breed Political Conflict?" (Lichbach 1989) or "Does Grievance Breed Political Conflict?" Though economic inequality (represented, for example, by income inequality) seems to be closely related with the occurrence of internal conflict (Lichbach 1989: 431-432), there is no consensus at present. Some even deny the significant relationship of economic inequality with internal conflict (Collier and Hoeffler 2001: 16 and Zwicky 1898: 85). We will leave this issue open.

The next economic factor of internal conflict we consider is military expenditure (or spending). In most of the studies, military expenditure is significantly associated with the increased likelihood of internal conflict (Auvinen 1997: 188, Henderson and Singer 2000: 290). But, it is not clear whether military expenditure is an independent variable or not. It is because relevance of military expenditure as a factor of internal conflict can be viewed in the following two ways.

First, as we saw above, the privileged resource allocation to the military breeds militarization leading to coups d'état and military control of government. Secondly, n view of the limited resources of developing countries, such excesses of military expenditures wastes scarce human and material resources to be directed toward desirable social and economic development, and hampers development. Since we have already briefly touched upon the first issue, we will only discuss the second issue.

When we discuss military expenditures, however, it is necessary to keep in mind the caution of many scholars. Figures of military expenditures of many countries are often quite unreliable due to the unreliability of the country data, differences in the definitions of "military expenditure," and the conversion (or exchange rate) problem (Brzoska 1981: 262, 264, 270-271). Michael Brzoska recommends us to admit of 10 % errors for their comparison (ibid: 268).

Many studies agree that the burden of military expenditures has a negative effect upon economic development (for example, Ball 1983: 52, Szentes 1984: 50). We should distinguish two types, the strong and weak versions, of the proposition "the burden of military expenditures has a negative effect upon economic development." The strong proposition asserts that it hold *everywhere and every time*. On the contrary, the weak proposition asserts that it holds *usually, butt not always*. As the weak proposition is corroborated by most studies, let us examine whether the strong proposition holds or not, or whether there are really exceptional cases.

Emile Benoit's research in the late 1960s on 44 countries has been frequently cited as an instance of the argument that military expenditures can have a positive effect on development. But Benoit himself admits that we cannot conclude that the military expenditures have a positive economic effect. And in fact, in most of the cases, the military burden has a negative effect on economic development (Ball 1983: 39-40, 52). Though most agree on this weak proposition, we have not been able to demonstrate the stronger version. It is because we cannot completely deny the possibility that, in some circumstances at least, a goal of "rich country and strong army" can be pursued successfully.

A long-term perspective will present us a little different picture. For example, from a long-term historical perspective, A. Mullins, Jr. argues that in West European cases military capability and development required and promoted each other (Mullins 1987: 14). On the basis of historical examination, he proposes the four categories of relationship between military capability and development, as is given in Table 37. The matrix in Table 37 is prepared by two criteria: first, whether or not military capability is necessary for development, and secondly, whether or not development is necessary for military capability. The combination of the answers to the two questions produces four categories in the table. The combinations in cells 1 and 3 (left cells) have quite negative implications for restraining arms buildups, since states must acquire military power to promote development. The history of most West European states went through the path given in cell 1. On the contrary, the third one is especially dangerous, because, as in many developing states, states seeking development must arm first, and may not be successful in development. Cells 2 and 4 (right cells) are more positive for restraining military expansion, because military growth is not required for development as in the case of post-war Germany and Japan and its level is rather limited by the level of economic development.

Table 37 Development and Military Capability
source: Mullins (1987), 13

	military capability **required for** development	military capability **not required for** development
development **necessary for** military capability	1 development and military capability accompany, and are accompanied, by each other ("Rich Country, Strong Army": Western experience)	2 development is a necessary but not sufficient condition of military capability growth, and is not always accompanied by military capability growth. (post-War Japan and Germany)
development **not necessary for** military capability	3 military capability growth is a necessary but not sufficient conditions of development and is not always accompanied by development. (Third World)	4 There is no positive relationship between military capability and development. They are independent and unrelated.

There is no category showing explicitly that military expenditures are detrimental to development. The category is perhaps subsumed under the fourth. But we can say that we are moving from the historical case of the first cell toward the second and the third, and perhaps toward the fourth since the latter half of the 20th century.

(4) Ethnic or Cultural Factors

Most, if not all, developing countries, (and developed countries as well, for that matter), contain a number of communal groups or cultural groups, be it racial, ethnic, religious or otherwise. Here, we will concentrate our focus upon ethnic groups, and examine the relationship between their existence and internal conflict. As the question what an ethnic group is will take a lengthy examination, let us just mention two books by Anthony D. Smith for definition (Smith, 1986, and Smith, 1991).

Many authors have argued that the existence of multiple ethnic groups and inequalities among them are frequently an important cause of internal conflict, especially of so-called communal or ethnic conflict. Relations between these ethnic groups contribute to internal conflict in two ways. First, the dominance of one group over others breeds discontent and relative (and absolute) deprivation among the subordinated group(s), and facilitates the mobilization of members of these groups against the dominant group. Let us call this "dominance-subordination or inequality thesis." Secondly, in some cases, there are two or more powerful ethnic groups. They compete for power, status and resources. The competition or rivalry may cause an internal conflict. Let us call this "rivalry or competition thesis" (Auvinen 1997: 178-179). The distinction roughly corresponds to that of "grievance" and "greed."

In addition to the two theses, there are some who argue that the plurality of ethnic groups itself is an important factor of internal conflict, in some circumstances at least (Rummel 1997: 167). Though multiethnicity itself in a state should not be neglected as a factor of internal conflict, we will not discuss it.

Ethnicity or more precisely the plurality, rivalry, or inequality of ethnic groups has been considered a fertile breeding ground for internal conflict. For example, many argued that ethnic dominance often brought about coups d'etat in Africa. In fact, many scholars argue that ethnicity, especially dominance and competition, is an important factor of internal conflict (Auvinen 1997: 178, 187, 188). There is, however, no agreement about the role of ethnicity as a causal or aggravating factor of internal conflict.

Contrary to the majority argument, Henderson and Singer do not find support for the importance of ethnic polarization or ethnic mobilization in the form of "ethnopolitical groups" as defined by Gurr and Harff (1994: 190). They conclude that post-colonial states are not doomed to be cauldrons of inter-ethnic conflicts (Henderson and Singer 2000: 293). In the same vein, Lake and Rothschild assert that even ethnic conflict is not caused directly by ethnicity or ethnic differences (Lake and Rothschild 1998: 4, 7).

Perhaps, the most decisive refutation of these "ethnic thesis" comes from Fearon and Laitin (1996). On the basis of statistical analysis of African data, they conclude that "[d]espite the conventional wisdom that ethnic violence is ubiquitous under conditions of cultural pluralism and weak states, the actual violent communal events as a percentage of potential events hovers around zero." From around 1960 to 1979, communal violence, though horrifying, was extremely rare [compared to the totality of logical possibility] in Africa. According to them, the error of the conventional wisdom is due to the fact that scholars have "select[ed] on the dependent variable," that is, "scholars have focused their attention overwhelmingly on cases of significant ethnic violence" (Fearon and Laitin 1996: 716, 717).

Here, however, we should make two reservations. First, their conclusion does not necessarily imply that ethnicity is a negligible factor of internal conflict, if it is not a major factor. Secondly, if we admit the small relevance of ethnicity as a causal factor of internal conflict, the question still remains why today the majority of internal conflicts are ethnic conflicts, or why the majority of internal conflicts are fought along the ethnic fault lines.

So far we examined major factors of internal conflict. After a lengthy examination, we seem to find ourselves where we started. And it is the state of art, as far as studies of international and internal conflict are concerned. We have uncovered many factors and some of them may account for the outbreak of a particular war. But we have a long way to go before we arrive at some kind of generalization.

7 Conflict and Cooperation in International Society

We have examined various realities and causes of armed conflict. In this chapter, we will adopt a broader and more abstract perspective, and examine the general issue of conflict and cooperation in the international society from that perspective. As we saw above, the current mainstream of international relations research holds the view that the most important property of the international society is anarchy. Anarchy means the lack of central government or central authority which assures states of (the advantage of) cooperation or peace. According to the mainstream international relations theory, every state seeks to maximize its national gain whether it is national interest or survival possibility. Given the condition of anarchy, where every state is obliged to seek maximization of its gain, how is cooperation among states possible? This is the question we will try to answer in this chapter. If the cooperation among states were impossible, then peace studies would surely lose its raison d'être.

To answer this question, we will adopt game theory as our tool. It is mainly because we assume that state actors are "rational" in the sense of "profit maximizing" as they were defined in 6.6.2. Under this assumption, games can show in very clear and simple form how the cooperation among state actors is possible or impossible in an international system where every state actor is engaged in the maximization of its gain under anarchy. Though at the highly abstract and simplified level, games can provide us with important insights to our understanding of the issue. It is also because, in the investigation into the issue of conflict and cooperation, game theory was employed early in peace studies, and it has attracted the renewed attention of international relations researchers.

7.1 Collective Action Dilemmas

Among the games, the greatest attention has been paid to a group of games called "collective action dilemma" (Goetze 1994: 58-59). Though they can be formulated in the terms of game theory, let us examine these dilemmas first in more general forms.

Such situations as "prisoner's dilemma," "tragedy of the commons," and "public goods problem" are among the best known of the collective action dilemmas (Goetze 1994). Collective action dilemmas attract great attention of social scientists because, as we shall see in many later examples, rational (profit-maximizing) behaviors of individual actors may result in "irrational" consequences, which do not maximize either the profit for individual actors or for the whole. Generally speaking, in these dilemmas, individual rationality is not enough for collective rationality. This proposition is quite the opposite of the thesis ascribed to Adam Smith that the pursuit of individual rationality, that is, the maximization of the profit, always automatically guarantees the achievement of the collective rationality, or the collective maximization of profit (Olson 1992: vii-viii). In Adam Smith's world, the invisible hand of God always assures individual profit maximizers of such a happy result.

In international relations and peace studies, such dilemmas represent a situation in which an undesirable result for the whole human kind, say, total nuclear war, may result from rational or profit-maximizing behaviors of states.

Collective action dilemmas are often called mixed motive games as well, because they involve both common interests and contradictory interests of the actors (Snyder 1971: 84). In mixed motive games, while there is a possibility of mutual gains by the cooperation of the actors, there is always an incentive and temptation for a possibility of greater gains by the pursuit of non-cooperative individual rationality. Collective action dilemmas (and mixed motive games) represent situations in the real world in which rational, profit-maximizing behaviors of individual actors cannot necessarily guarantee either the rationality or profit maximization of the collectivity of actors as a whole, or the intended rationality or profit maximization of individual actors. The game of prisoner's dilemma is probably the best known model of these situations. But before discussing the games proper, we will briefly examine two famous collective action dilemmas: tragedy of the commons and free ride in public goods.

Suppose that there is a common land suitable for grazing cows (commons). Each farmer has a right to put a single cow on the commons. And suppose further that there is sufficient grassland to provide good feed for more cows in total. Under such a circumstance, a farmer can gain an additional profit by putting another cow on the commons. Putting aside ethical or moral consideration, rationality requires a farmer to put more cows on the common pasture. From an individual perspective, it is a perfectly rational choice.

However, the tragedy of the commons is caused by the very rational behaviors of all or most of the farmers. It is a tragedy precisely because it is caused by rational action. What will happen when all or most of the farmers act rationally? At first, addition of cows may bring about greater profit or income both to individual farmers and to the whole farmers as Figure 24 suggests. But further addition of cows will exceed the grazing capacity of the commons. Then, the total income of farmers will begin to decrease, and the income of each of the individual farmers will begin to decline. In an extreme hypothetical case, when farmers are foolish and egoistic enough, the total income of the farmers will be smaller than the initial state, or all the cows will be starved to death from the shortage of grass (Nicholson 1992: 193-195). Figure 24 shows the tragedy schematically.

Figure 24 The Tragedy of the Commons
source: Nicholson (1992), 195

Total profit of the cow holders

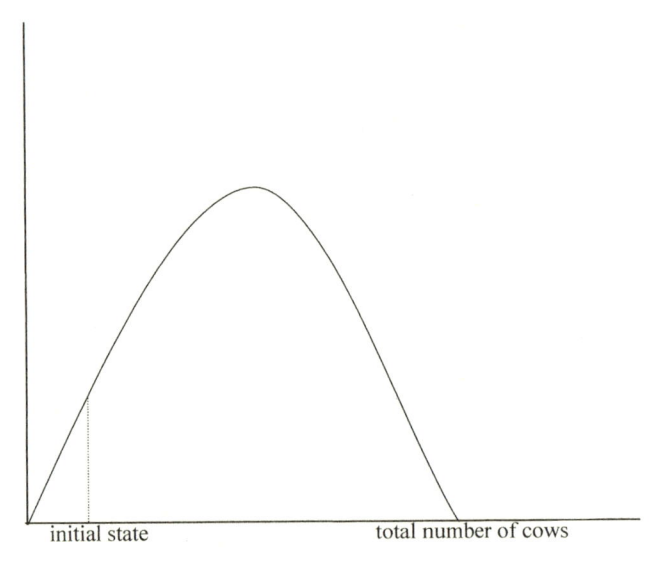

        initial state   total number of cows

In the tragedy of the commons, even though it is possible to achieve greater gains by some kind of cooperation, every actor pursues the rational maximization of one's profit. Such non-cooperative rational behaviors of individual actors result not only in the failure in maximizing one's gains but also in the failure in maximizing the gains of the whole society.

Our next issue is the "free ride" problem in public goods. Pure public goods are defined as goods and services characterized by two criteria: nonexcludability and nonsubtractability in consumption. Public goods are nonexcludable in that, once the goods or services are provided, no one can be excluded from their consumption. In other words, every one can enjoy them. And public goods are nonsubtractable in that no consumption of the goods by any one will subtract the benefit of the goods. In everyday language, the goods or services will never diminish by the use of any one. In the real world, however, there are few pure public goods in the strict sense of the term which satisfy these two conditions. But, security and safety in the domestic society, common infrastructure like roads, and international peace etc, are usually regarded as public goods. We can include clean air and clean water. In connection with this, a distinction is sometimes made between public goods and common-pool resources (CPRs). For example, air or the oxygen in the air is so abundant that its consumption by any individuals or groups does not affect others' consumption at all. Therefore it is public goods in a broader sense. But clean water is in short supply in many parts of the world, and its consumption by individuals affects the consumption by others. Accordingly, it should be regarded as common-pool resources rather than public goods. Public goods and common-pool resources are two ends of the same spectrum and the actual situation lies and moves between the two (Keohane and Ostrom 1995: 15). In addition to this distinction, there are "collective goods." The concept of "collective goods" is a subcategory of public goods and refers to goods and services which satisfy the above two conditions as far as a given group is concerned. Even an illegal institutionalized collusion can be collective goods for a particular group of business firms (Olson 1992: viii, Stein 1990: 32-33).

When the public goods must be provided by some one, it matters who should pay the initial cost of provision. For, once the public goods are provided, by definition, everyone can consume them even if he or she has not paid the initial cost. Every one can be a free rider and enjoy the consumption of the public goods without paying the initial cost at all. This is the famous "free ride" problem of the public goods (Goetze 1994: 66, Ordeshook 1986: 211-212, Sandler 1992: 17).

In public goods provision, actors face the temptation of free ride. Free riders expect that they can enjoy the benefit of public goods without paying the cost after others pay for the provision. Their behaviors of free riding are based on the assumption that all the others who provide public goods behave on motives other than free ride, but the assumption is not necessarily valid (Rosecrance 1986: 235-236).

What we discussed as a rebel's dilemma concerning rational choice theory as one of the causes of internal conflict in 6.6.2 above was a case of public goods dilemma (Lichbach 1995: xii). We will give another example of the problem when we discuss prisoner's dilemma.

Of course, in the real world, there are many institutions for avoiding such undesirable results (Olson 1992: ix). But we will not go into the details here.

There are many other cases in which rational behaviors of individual actors defeat themselves. The game of prisoner's dilemma is the best known of them. But, before discussing the prisoner's dilemma, it is necessary to have an idea of what a game is.

7.2 Game Theory

Game theory was first formulated by John von Neuman and Oskar Morgenstern (von Neuman and Morgenstern 1944). The theory was originally intended to explain the rational economic behavior of an actor. The rational choice model of game theory attempts to explain the behavior of an actor on the assumption that he or she intends to maximize his or her utility or profit in the very abstract sense. From a viewpoint of the political science, it partially answers the classical question of the discipline formulated by Harold Lasswell, "Who gets what, how and when."

Let us begin with the rules of the game as a starting point of the following discussions. The following table, Table 38, shows the simplest game. First of all, a game refers to a hypothetical situation in which profits or utilities are explicitly specified for every choice. The hypothetical situation is represented by a "payoff matrix" given in the table. The form of the game depends upon various factors.

Table 38 A Sample Payoff Matrix of a Game

		player (actor) B	
		option 1	option 2
Player (actor) A	option 1	P_{A1B1}, P_{B1A1}	P_{A1B2}, P_{B2A1}
	option 2	P_{A2B1}, P_{B1A2}	P_{A2B2}, P_{B2A2}

The first factor is the number of the parties to the game called "player" or actor. The game is divided into two types according to the number of the parties: two person game and "n-person" game. Each player has a fixed number of two or more predetermined options. In the game in Table 38, each player has two options. The number and kind of the options can vary from one player to another. From these two conditions, the simplest game is played by two actors each with two options (2 by 2 game) like that in Table 38.

Only after each player has made a choice, a fixed amount of utility called "payoff" for each player is decided. Here payoff is defined as a net profit, that is, benefit minus cost. In the above table, P_{A1B1} and P_{B1A1} in the upper left cell are the payoffs for the player A and the player B respectively, when both A and B choose option 1. In a two person game, the payoff (P_{A1B1}) of the row player (A) is put on the left side according to the conventional notation. Note here that even if the options are the same for different players, it does not necessarily mean that the payoffs are the same. The payoff may be different. In the above example, P_{A1B1} and P_{B1A1} are not necessarily the same.

There is another factor. While there are games played only once, other games are played more than once. These are called "iterated game." Iterated games can be further divided into two categories: those played by a fixed or finite number of times, and those played by infinite number of times. In the latter case, the game will be played without end theoretically at least.

There are two important points to be stressed here. First, the outcome (or solution) of the game is determined only after all the players have made a choice. It means that the outcome of the game and the payoff for each player cannot be decided by a single choice of a given player and, more importantly, that a player's payoff (or how much one gets) always depends upon the choice of others. Secondly, as we saw above, each player is assumed to choose an option which will maximize his/her payoff. This is the assumption of rationality.

7.3 Prisoner's Dilemma

7.3.1 Prisoner's Dilemma

Prisoner's dilemma is the game most frequently invoked and discussed in international relations research today. The game became well known when Anatol Rapoport applied it to the nuclear arms race between the United States and the Soviet Union, and showed that, according to the logic of nuclear strategists, a nuclear arms race is a logical necessity. In fact, the game was applied most extensively to the issues of arms race and disarmament (Snyder 1971: 68). The dilemma of the game lies in the fact that, in spite of the possibility of greater gains by cooperation, rational actors are obliged not to cooperate, to the dismay of all the actors in the game. It is because the game can express the dilemma very clearly that the game has been invoked so frequently (Olson 1992: xv).

In the original form of the game, there are two prisoners (legally suspects) who are accomplices in the same crime. They are detained in separate cells and have no means of communicating with each other. Now suppose that each of them has two options: to confess or to keep silent. If both prisoners keep silent, they can be set free or released, for example, on the ground of insufficient evidence. Suppose that the payoff matrix will be that which is given in Table 39. If they both keep silent, they can obtain mutual gains as is shown in Table 39. Now, the question is: which choice will be a rational behavior to them, or which choice will give them the greatest payoff?

First, let us consider the question from the viewpoint of prisoner A. If the prisoner B keeps silent from friendship, solidarity or from any other motive, the prisoner A should confess. For, if A confesses in this case, A will gain 10 units of payoff (lower left cell) compared with one unit when he or she keeps silent (upper right cell). Next if the prisoner B confesses, the prisoner A should confess this time again. For, as the payoffs show, prisoner A will suffer from the loss of only one units when he or she confesses (lower right cell), but A will suffer from the loss of ten units when he or she keeps silent (upper right cell). Therefore, from the viewpoint of the prisoner A, it is always rational to confess irrespective of the choices of the other prisoner, prisoner B. In this game, confession is a dominant strategy for prisoner A, a choice which brings the greatest payoff irrespective of the choices of the other player (Sandler 1992: 4-5).

Table 39 Prisoner's Dilemma: Original Model

		prisoner B	
		silence	confess
prisoner A	Silence	1, 1	-10, 10
	Confess	10, -10	-1, -1

The same is true of prisoner B. Accordingly, both prisoners should confess in order to be rational or to maximize the payoff. The outcome (or solution) of the game is, therefore, represented by the lower right cell. However, here lies the irony of the game. When both confess, both of them suffer from the loss of one unit, while each of them could gain one unit if they both kept silent. The prisoners miss the chance of being set free because they act rationally.

The lesson of prisoner's dilemma is that, though there is a chance of mutual gains by cooperation, the parties suffer from losses because of rational choice (Snyder 1971: 67). And it provides a clear case in which rational behaviors of individual actors does neither guarantee the rational result for individual actors nor for the whole. It was to emphasize this point that Anatol Rapoport applied the game to the nuclear arms race between the United States and the Soviet Union.

Now let us apply the game of prisoner's dilemma to the arms race between the two superpowers. As we saw above, there is an option which brings profit to both actors. Here, let us assume that disarmament is such an option which will bring profit to both superpowers. The payoff distribution of the prisoner's dilemma model of the US-USSR arms race is given in Table 40. It is the same as the original model in Table 39.

Table 40 Prisoner's Dilemma: US-USSR Arms Race
source : Rapoport (1969), 70

		USSR	
		disarmament	arms race
United States	disarmament	1, 1	-10, 10
	arms race	10, -10	-1, -1

In this game, both United States and the Soviet Union can gain greater profits if they both "disarm" (both gain 1) than if they both "arm" (actually expand their armaments) (they both gain –1 in this case). Under such a condition, the question is why they both expand armaments or why neither of them chooses disarmament.

Let us explore the reason by following the logic of the game. One of the rational choices in a game is a "maximin (or minimax)" solution. The solution minimizes the worst consequence, and chooses an option which maximizes the possible minimum payoff. If the player follows the maximin solution in the prisoner's dilemma game here, both parties will have to choose the "arms race" option. By the maximin criterion, the United States will choose "arms race," through the following process.

When the United States chooses "disarmament,"
    its payoff will be 1 if the Soviet Union chooses "disarmament," and
    its payoff will be –10 if the Soviet Union chooses "arms race."
        (There will be a great military gap with the US left behind.)
Thus, when the United States chooses "disarm," the minimum payoff will be –10.

On the other hand, when the United States chooses "arms race,"
    its payoff will be 10 if the Soviet Union chooses "disarmament," and
    its payoff will be –1 if the Soviet Union chooses "arms race."
Accordingly, when the United States chooses "arms race," the minimum payoff will be –1.

The minimum for "disarmament" is –10 and the minimum for "armament" is –1. Then the United States should choose "arms race" as a rational choice. The solution chooses the option which gives the maximum of the minimum payoffs. (In this case, we can say that the maximin solution minimizes the loss, but the proposition does not always hold for all the cases).

By the same logic, the rational maximin solution for the Soviet Union is to choose "arms race."

We can reach the same conclusion in a little different way. When the Soviet Union chooses "disarmament," "arms race" gives a greater payoff to the United States than "disarmament" (10 > 1). And, when the Soviet Union chooses "arms race," "arms race" brings a greater payoff than "disarmament" (-1 > -10). Thus, the option "arms race" brings a greater payoff in both cases. It is also the case with the Soviet Union. For both players, "arms race" is a rational option.

Needless to say, the rationality in choosing "armament" or "arms race" in the game cannot be regarded as rational or desirable from the common sense viewpoint. Nevertheless, as we saw in 5.4, arms race is very profitable for some interest groups within the superpowers. The game shows that, even if we were to accept the logic of arms expansion as a thought experiment, the apparently rational logic advocated by nuclear strategists actually would produce an irrational and terrible result of endless nuclear arms race. By showing clearly how irrational result would be produced as a result of an individual rational choice, the game exposes the essential contradiction of the logic of armament expansion.

Prisoner's dilemma is frequently applied to many important issues of war and peace. For example, the issue of international cooperation for the reduction of carbon dioxide (CO_2) can be understood as prisoner's dilemma as is given in Table 41 (Soroos 1994: 326-327).

Table 41 Prisoner's Dilemma: Environmental Cooperation
source : adapted from Soroos (1994), 326

		all other states	
		CO2 reduction	free ride
state in question	CO2 reduction	3, 3	1, 4
	free ride	4, 1	2, 2

Suppose that there are two options in this case again: to join international cooperation for the reduction of the CO_2 emission or to free ride, that is, do not pay any cost and enjoy the fruit of the international cooperation of other states for the CO2 reduction. In this case again, the rational choice of a state is to choose "free ride" as can be easily seen from the payoff matrix given in Table 41.

Incidentally, prisoner's dilemma has been interpreted not as a model of rational choice among states but as a model of domination and control. As the original model of prisoner's dilemma suggests, two prisoners are detained in separate cells without any means of communication and hence of cooperation. It is a conventional tactics for domination to keep the subordinated separate and segregated. Thus, prisoner's dilemma can be seen as a model of traditional "divide and rule" policies (Burns and Buckley 1974: 222-224).

The choice in the prisoner's dilemma is quite rational from the perspective of individual actors. But the rational choice produces quite an irrational result of arms race or non-reduction of CO2. Here lies the dilemma of the situation represented by this simple game. Generally speaking, prisoner's dilemma represents situations in which the result of individual rational choice does neither guarantee the individual rationality itself nor the rationality of the whole.

Then, our question is if there is any possibility of disarmament or cooperation in a prisoner's dilemma situation. We will not consider preaching morals, virtue of cooperation, and love of humanity. To be sure, morals and ethics are the very basis on which peace studies stands. But, in view of the fact that many pacifists' arguments were quite ineffectual and futile during the Cold War, we should rather seek a different way. We should seek to find a way in which disarmament is a rational and stable solution, not rejecting the assumption of payoff maximization. We should seek a way in which ethics and interests meet. What peace studies and international relations research have been striving to achieve is just this, that is, the solution of prisoner's dilemma. We will discuss it in detail below.

7.3.2 Games of Conflict and Cooperation

Besides prisoner's dilemma, there are other mixed motive games. To mention a few well known ones, "chicken," "deadlock," and "stag hunt" are examples (Downs et al 1985: 121-122, 127-128, 134-135).

All these games can be called games of cooperation and non-cooperation (or conflict). The general form of the games is given in Table 42.

Table 42 General Form of Mixed Motive Games
source: Downs, Rocke and Siverson (1985), 121

		B	
		C (cooperation)	D (defect)
A	C(cooperation)	CC	CD
	D (defect))	DC	DD

Payoffs are assumed to be symmetric with A and B, and only A's payoffs are indicated.

According to the order of payoffs (called "preference order"), they are divided into four different games.

DC > CC > DD > CD   prisoner's dilemma
DC > CC > CD > DD   chicken game
CC > DC > DD > CD   stag hunt
DC > DD > CC > CD   deadlock

In all these game, the payoff of the unilateral defection (non-cooperation) (DC) is always greater than that of the unilateral cooperation (CD), while the payoff of mutual cooperation (CC) is always greater than that of unilateral cooperation (CD). This nature of the games means that, in situations the games represent, actors are always tempted to gain the benefit of unilateral defect or non-cooperation (DC), while there is a possibility of gaining a certain amount of gain by mutual cooperation (CC). Hence, the name "mixed motive" game.

Let us briefly examine each of the games here.

In the game of deadlock, the preference order is DC > DD > CC > CD. In deadlock, as the name suggests, cooperation is more difficult than in other games. It is because the payoff for the mutual cooperation (CC) is smaller than the payoff for defection (DC or DD). In the game, the defect option (DC or DD) always brings greater profits, by definition, than the cooperation options (CC or CD) (Axelrod and Keohane 1985: 230). As far as cooperation is concerned, the situation of the game is literally "deadlock."

The game of deadlock has been regarded as representing a handful of exceptional and deviant cases like Hitler's Germany (Downs et al 1985: 122). As Downs and others point out, however, deadlock can describe arms races more suitably than prisoner's dilemma (Axelrod and Keohane 1985: 230). As we discussed in 5.4, from the perspective of some domestic interest groups, mutual defection or unilateral defection (mutual or unilateral expansion of armaments) is always preferable to cooperation (disarmament). And if these interest groups have great influence on domestic politics, the preference order of the state as such will also be the same as that of deadlock. It does not necessarily mean that the preference order reflect the insatiable desire for war or military power (or superiority). Rather the game reflects the interests of the particular domestic groups like military-industrial complexes. In this case, deadlock represents the situation of the self-reproducing arms race which we saw above. Deadlock is not a rare deviant situation. It may be much more prevalent than is commonly thought (Downs et al 1985: 122-123).

If we change the preference order of prisoner's dilemma in such a way that mutual cooperation (CC) is better than unilateral defect (DC), then the preference order will be: CC > DC > DD > CD. The game with this preference order is called "stag hunt." The stag hunt is less conflictual than prisoner's dilemma (Axelrod and Keohane 1985: 229). The sample payoff matrix is given in Table 43.

The original model of the game was proposed first by Jean-Jacques Rousseau as the tale of "the stag and the hare" in his *The Social Contract*. In Rousseau's tale, a group of hunters try to catch a stag, which will give them each sufficient food. To catch a stag, they agree to encircle an area where they expect a stag to be, and close in on this area, and eventually catch the animal. Each hunter is assigned a part of this circle and no hunter can see any of the others. Now suppose a small hare runs by one of the hunters. The hunter is faced with the choice of abandoning his or her place of duty to pursue the hare (in which case the hunter catches the hare, but the stag may escape), or keeping his or her place and foregoing the opportunity to get the hare. Which should the hunter do, to keep the place or to pursue the hare? Which is a rational way to take?

Table 43 Stag Hunt
source: Rosecrance (1986), 237

		B	
		C (cooperation)	D (defect)
A	C(cooperation)	4, 4	1, 3
	D (defect))	3, 1	2, 2

In conclusion, the rational choice depends upon the trust which the hunter puts in the other hunters. This is the reason why the game is sometimes called "assurance" game. If the other hunters can be trusted to keep their places, it is rational to keep the place because it will bring a bigger profit (the stag in this case). But if the other hunters cannot be trusted and may pursue a hare running by, then the stag will escape and it is rational to pursue the hare (Palmer 1989: 178-179). In stag hunt, it is rational to choose the cooperation option if the other side is certain to choose the cooperation option, and to choose the defect option if the other side is certain to choose the defect option. In this game, if each of the parties is assured of the other's cooperation, each one will always choose to cooperate and the solution will be very stable (stable and collectively rational) (Rosecrance 1986: 238). But, in actual situations, actors do not always trust others, and, moreover, they often misperceive the motive of others.

For this reason, the game of stag hunt is often used to illustrate the issue of misperception and mutual confidence in the arms race. The game is often the accurate representation of actual arms race, especially the situation of security dilemma in which one side pursues the arms race, on the misperception that the other side pursues the expansion of armament (Downs et al 1985: 135). In many actual situations, the one party chooses "defect" (expansion of armaments), by misperceiving that the other party chooses "defect" (expansion of armaments).

The next game, chicken game, is another frequently cited game in studies on war and peace because it captures a certain aspect of international relations very succinctly. In the original game, two reckless youths drive their cars at a high speed from the opposite ends on a straight road. The one who first swerves to avoid the direct collision will be the loser. The loser is called "chicken," a coward (Snyder 1971: 82, note 12). Of course, if both are "bold" enough not to swerve, then the result will be catastrophic. Both will be dead or severely injured.

In prisoner's dilemma, mutual defection (DD) is better than unilateral cooperation (CD) as is shown in Table 39 or 40. When players prefer the unilateral cooperation (CD) to mutual defect (DD) (CD > DD), the game of prisoner's dilemma (Tables 39, 40, or 41) becomes that of chicken shown in Table 44.

Table 44 Chicken Game: Nuclear War

		USSR	
		Disarm	Nuclear War
US	Disarm	1,1	-10, 10
	Nuclear War	10, -10	-50, -50

In chicken game, the disarmament option is a rational choice for both the players. Otherwise, the result, perhaps a nuclear war, will be catastrophic, as the collision of the cars in the original game. In any case, the gain of mutual defection (lower right cell in the table) will be smaller than that of unilateral cooperation (upper right cell for the United States and lower left cell for the Soviet Union). In Table 44, the payoff for the mutual defection is rather exaggerated to show the devastation of a nuclear war. Compared with such a catastrophe, defeat in the nuclear arms race is much more preferable or much more bearable.

As we saw above, the difference between prisoner's dilemma and chicken lies in the preference order between mutual defection (DD) and unilateral cooperation (CD). In prisoner's dilemma, the gain of mutual defection (DD) is greater than that of unilateral cooperation (CD), while, in chicken, the gain of unilateral cooperation (CD) is greater than that of mutual defection (DD). It is rational to choose "arms race" or "armament" in prisoner's dilemma, while it is rational to choose "disarm" in chicken.

According to the logic of chicken game, it is a rational choice for both parties to choose the "disarm(ament)" strategy. It is because if the arms race were to lead to a nuclear war, the result would be unbearable as the payoffs of Table 44 show.

Unlike prisoner's dilemma, chicken does not force the parties to a predicament in which they cannot cooperate rationally. The logic of the chicken game does not put the parties to mutual punishment as prisoner's dilemma. In chicken, the punishment for mutual defection or non-cooperation (DD) is severer than the punishment of unilateral cooperation or being taken advantage of one's cooperation (CD). In this game, rational players always choose cooperation or (sometimes surrender) to avoid the worst result (Snyder 1971: 83-83).

In chicken, to disarm, or at least not to expand armaments, is a rational choice which maximizes the profits for both parties. But a horrible strategy lurks in the logic of the game. One of the parties can reason in the following way. If the other player is rational, (or if the party in question is certain that the other is rational), the other party cannot but choose to "disarm." Then one can push the matter to the extreme, by choosing the "nuclear war" option, relying upon the rationality of the other. Even though it may be very small, there is of course a danger of mutual destruction or extinction. But as far as the other party *is* rational, pushing the matter to the brink of war (DC or the lower left cell for the US and upper right cell for the USSR in Table 44) will surely bring a victory without actually fighting a nuclear war and will bring a greatest profit as the payoff matrix suggests (either US or USSR gains 10). In this way, the party in question can gain the greatest profit by adopting the brinkmanship strategy of threat. But, unfortunately, this is true for both parties. If both parties reason in the same way and behave in the same way, relying upon the rationality of the other, it will bring about the worst result of a nuclear war. In prisoner's dilemma, this kind of a strong line satisfies the rational maximin choice. But, in chicken, it is not the rational choice, but it only brings the worst result.

The game of chicken has been drawn upon to account for the absence of direct military clash between the two superpowers (or the so-called "long peace") during the

Cold War era. As some argue, the successful crisis management of the superpowers since 1945 owed greatly to their avoidance of the worst cases and their adoption of cooperation strategies (Rosecrance 1986: 234). According to the arguments, both the United States and the Soviet Union were able to keep rational under the chicken-like crisis situations, though they could not overcome the prisoner's dilemma of the nuclear arms race. Both the United States and the Soviet Union were rational enough to satisfy the maximin requirement or to avoid the worst cases. According to this view, chicken is not so conflictual in real world than in a hypothetical world (Rosecrance 1986: 234), because the game warns against the worst case.

Chicken game is used not only to show the irrationality of some nuclear strategic theories, but also to explore the issue of nuclear deterrence. Many who support the possession of nuclear weapons agree that the most important role of nuclear weapons is to deter nuclear attacks from the (hypothetical) enemy. The most important function of nuclear weapons is to deter the surprise attack or first strike by nuclear or conventional weapons of the enemy by the massive nuclear retaliation. This is the essence of nuclear deterrence (Kamo 1990: 5). Generally speaking, three conditions should be met for effective deterrence.

First, military capabilities of performing the threat of retaliation are required. In the case of nuclear deterrence, capabilities of second strike or retaliatory nuclear attack are required. Secondly, the resolve or determination to carry out threats of retaliation is necessary. The human and material destruction in Hiroshima and Nagasaki surely make leaders to hesitate to carry out such a nuclear attack. Therefore, the resolve or determination matters.

But these two conditions are not enough for deterrence. The third condition should be satisfied. The party (deterred party) which is threatened with retaliation or second strike should be certain of the capabilities and the resolution of the deterring party. This last condition is perhaps the most difficult of the three conditions to attain. If the party to be deterred believes that the other (deterring) party has no capabilities or determination for the second strike or retaliation, then deterrence fails and the party may make a surprise nuclear attack (Takayanagi 1991: 168-169).

Here lies the dilemma of nuclear deterrence. For the deterrence to work, the threat of retaliation or second strike should be credible or believed by the other party. If one party can convince the other of its second strike, the other party will choose to be rational for fear of a catastrophe. Then deterrence works. But if the threat of retaliation is not credible enough, or if the other party thinks that the deterring party lacks either in the capabilities or in the determination of nuclear retaliation, or in both, then the deterring party is obliged to constantly convince the other party that it has the capabilities and determination to carry out a nuclear retaliation in order to convince the other party of its threat. For the well functioning of deterrence, the deterring party should always be prepared for a nuclear war, with a plan or a scenario of it. (This may partially account for the superpower nuclear arms race). In spite of the repeated assertion of the nuclear states that they should never use nuclear weapons, they should be able to use them for their strategic purposes (Kamo 1990: 5-6).

The deterrence theory is faced with another difficulty. For one party's threat to be effective (or, for deterrence to work), the other party must be rational. The other party to be deterred must be rational enough to avoid a great damage. In other words, the deterring party has to rely upon the rationality of the other. But if the deterring party is thought to be rational by the other deterred party, the deterring party's threat of nuclear retaliation will not be credible at all because the other party thinks that the deterring party is rational enough not to carry out its threat into actual practice. This is a serious dilemma inherent in the logic of deterrence. The only but impossible way to get out of this dilemma is to be irrational, that is, to use nuclear weapons (Takayanagi 1991: 189). Thus, according to the logic of deterrence, which is intended to avoid a nuclear war, the only effective way is, paradoxically, not to avoid a nuclear war, or more realistically, to persuade the other party that the party in question has the resolve to actually use nuclear weapons.

Much more catastrophic is what happens when both parties reason along this line. A nuclear war ensues, as the game of chicken predicts.

7.4 Solving Prisoner's Dilemma

The logic of prisoner's dilemma portrays a pessimistic, eschatological picture of the world. According to the logic, it seemed quite impossible that the United States and the

Soviet Union would have pursued the path of disarmament during the Cold War. But is there really no way which satisfies the requirement of individual rationality and choose to disarm?

The issue is critical not only to the issues of arms race and disarmament of the two superpowers, but also to much broader issues in international relations and international politics. As was repeatedly stated, in the situation represented by the game, though actors behave rationally, they can obtain only smaller gains than they could obtain if they cooperated. In the mainstream theories of international relations or international politics, every actor is assumed to be engaged in the pursuit of its gains (national interest or survival possibility). And every state seemed to be engaged in what Thomas Hobbes called "war of all against all." The game of prisoner's dilemma captures this characteristic of international relations. Is it possible in such an international system that actors like sovereign states should be able to cooperate? As far as the logic of prisoner's dilemma dictates, the answer will be "no."

On a little reflection, however, we will be convinced that cooperation among states is not rare but frequent in real world, as many international organizations, laws and treaties suggest. Even in military affairs, we find cases of cooperation among states such as arms control or disarmament negotiations.

Then, how is cooperation among states possible, in an international system like prisoner's dilemma? How is it possible that states should be able to cooperate with each other while they are pursuing the maximization of their own gains under the assumption of rational actors? If we can solve the prisoner's dilemma and find a way of cooperation under prisoner's dilemma, we can answer these questions positively. In this sense, prisoner's dilemma and its solution is of extreme importance in peace studies and in international relations studies.

Generally speaking, to solve prisoner's dilemma is to find a way in which individual rational choices guarantees the collective rationality, or to find a logical space like that of Adam Smith.

As we saw above, the problem with collective action dilemmas, like prisoner's dilemma, is that individual rational choices do not necessarily guarantee the collectively rational choice, as in the case of the tragedy of the commons. One solution of these dilemmas is to establish some kind of institution, for example, some rules concerning the use of the commons. Traditional customs or conventions concerning the use of local commons are typical examples. In the international society, what is called regime is an example of this. A regime is a set of formal and informal rules, norms, and expectations of international actors centered round the core of organizations and treaties. To mention a few, the global environmental regime, the nuclear non-proliferation regime, free trade regimes like GATT and WTO are well-known examples. According to Arthur Stein, institutions arise from the necessity of solving these dilemmas (Stein 1990: 39).The problem is that the institutional solutions restrain the rational choice of individual actors.

The solution of prisoner's dilemma which we will take up below is quite different from the institutional solution in that it never abandons the rationality requirement for actors. It is an attempt to move rationality of interest by one step toward an ideal in which ethics and interests are both satisfied. And, in this sense, it is a process Utopia.

As an initial step, prisoner's dilemma can be represented in the generalized form in Table 45.

Table 45 Prisoner's Dilemma: Generalized Form
source: Yamamoto (1989), 343

		B Cooperate	B defect
A	cooperate	<CC> R, R	<CD> S, T
	defect	<DC> T, S	<DD> P, P

R, S, T, P stand for "reword," "sucker's payoff," "temptation," and "punishment" respectively.
where $DC > CC > DD > CD$, or $T > R > P > S$

According to the notation of Table 45 used by Axelrod, the preference order is:

$T > R > P > S$

Here, T, R, P, and S stand for "temptation to defect," "reward for mutual cooperation," "punishment for mutual defection," and "sucker's payoff," respectively (Axelrod 1984: 8).

Our task is to find a way in which all the actors can cooperate on the basis of their rational choices. If such a way is found, all the actors can both maximize their individual profits and achieve the maximum profit as a whole. In the games we reviewed, individual rational choices are not linked to the collective rational choice. Then, our task comes down to finding a solution in which individual rationality agrees with collective rationality. Moreover, the solution should be stable. It should last for some length of time at least. Otherwise, the solution will be valid only for once or twice and will break down quickly. For example, disarmament should be stable in order to stop and reverse arms races.

In sum, the solution which we are looking for must satisfy the three conditions: (1) Each of actors should be able to maximize his or her profit. In a word, the solution should satisfy the condition of individual rationality. (2) The solution should produce the maximum profit for the entire collectivity. The solution should satisfy the condition of collective or social rationality. (3) The solution should be stable. The solution should be always chosen in many rounds of the game.

As a first step to the search for a solution which satisfies the three conditions, we will examine two kinds of solution in game theory.

One of the solutions is "Nash" solution. It is a completely stable solution. In a Nash solution, "no one player can unilaterally improve one's payoff unless others change their choices." If this condition is met, the solution is automatically stabilized even under a mixed motive game. No one player has incentive to change his or her choice (Ordeshook 1992: 97, Shubik 1984: 240). Mutual defection (DD) in prisoner's dilemma is a Nash solution.

The second solution to be considered is a collectively or socially rational solution. "Pareto optimality" is one of the socially or collectively rational solutions. A

"Pareto optimal" state refers to;

> Social state (outcome in the game) in which no one actor can improve one's payoff without causing losses to others.

If

> at least one actor can improve his or her payoff without damaging the others' payoff,

then the state is not in Pareto optimality, but in a Pareto suboptimal state (Sandler 1992: 13). For example, the outcome of the game is a combination of "arms race" and "arms race" (DD) in Table 40. If it moves to "disarmament" and "disarmament" (CC), then both improve their payoffs without damaging the other's payoffs. Therefore, DD is not Pareto optimal.

The concept of Pareto optimality is an intuitively excellent criterion for social or collective rationality. But, there can be many Pareto optimal states and no comparison among them is possible because there is no criterion by which Pareto optimal states can be compared (Sandler 1992: 14).

Generally speaking, to solve prisoner's dilemma is to find a case in which individual rationality is satisfied, and the Pareto optimal solution agrees with the Nash solution. In such a case, we are assured of a stable and socially or collectively rational solution which maximizes both individual and collective profit. In the case of the prisoner's dilemma game of the arms race between the two superpowers, such a solution will provide a stable policy option which maximizes the profit of each and the whole of them.

In this chapter, we have assumed that the game is played only once, and never repeated. Let us now think of a game which is iterated infinitely. In the context of the US-USSR arms race, such an indefinitely repeated game means that the choice between armament expansion and disarmament is made again and again in infinite times. We introduce the element of time in prisoner's dilemma. The criticism against such an assumption will be briefly touched upon below.

In a game which is iterated infinitely, another concept should be introduced. In an iterated game, future "expected utility" or profit will be calculated and reckoned into the profit at any round of the game. For example, in the first round of the game, expected profit after the second round is calculated and added to the payoff of the first round. In view of the uncertainty of the future, however, expected payoff of the future should be discounted. Let the discount parameter or discount rate be "ω" (Axelrod 1984: 12-13). ω is defined as $0 < \omega < 1$.

If we introduce future expected utility, and if, for example, both the United States and the Soviet Union always choose to disarm in the prisoner's dilemma, then their expected profits will be;

$$CC + \omega CC + \omega^2 CC + \ldots \omega^n CC = CC / (1 - \omega)$$

or in the generalized form

$$R + \omega R + \omega^2 R + \ldots \omega^n R = R / (1 - \omega) \text{ (Axelrod 1984: 13)}$$

Here, let $\alpha = 1 / (1 - \omega)$, then the expected sum of payoffs in this case (where both always choose to disarm or cooperate) will be;

$$\alpha CC \text{ or } \alpha R.$$

In an infinitely repeated prisoner's dilemma, there are three major strategies worth considering. First, the party can choose "cooperation" in all the games. Let us call this "permanent cooperation" and represent it by the symbol $C\infty$. Secondly, the party can choose "defection" all the time. Let us call it "permanent defection" and represent it by $D\infty$. Finally, there is a strategy in which the party chooses cooperation in the first game, and, in all the following game, "chooses the same strategy as the other chose in the immediately preceding game." Let us call this "Tit for Tat" or "TFT" for short (Axelrod 1984: 13). It is a reciprocating strategy and can be called reciprocity strategy.

The expected payoffs of the three strategies are shown in Table 46. Is there an outcome which is both a Pareto optimal and a Nash solution?

The TFT strategy (TFT by TFT) in Table 46 is a Pareto optimal solution because there are other outcomes (D∞ by D∞) which cause losses to the parties when an actor changes the option. In addition, the outcome (TFT by TFT) is a Nash solution if and only if the following condition is met.

$$\omega > (T - R) / (T - P)$$

Since the right side is smaller than 1 (because we assumed that $R > P$), there can be ω which can satisfy the equation.

Table 46 Expected Payoff Matrix for Infinitely Repeated Prisoner's Dilemma
source: adapted form Yamamoto (1989), 343-347

		B		
		C∞	TFT	D∞
A	C∞	$\alpha R, \alpha R$	$\alpha R, \alpha R$	$\alpha S, \alpha T$
	TFT	$\alpha R, \alpha R$	$\alpha R, \alpha R$	$S+\alpha\omega P, T+\alpha\omega P$
	D∞	$\alpha T, \alpha S$	$T+\alpha\omega P, S+\alpha\omega P$	$\alpha P, \alpha P$

where $T > R > P > S$
$\alpha = 1 / (1 - \omega)$
ω is the rate of discount for future payoff: $0 < \omega < 1$

In this way, it is demonstrated that TFT by FT strategy is both a Pareto optimal and a Nash solution. It satisfies both the individual rationality and the collective rationality. The next task is to show that the TFT strategy is the best one among strategies which satisfies both Pareto and Nash conditions.

Needless to say, innumerable other strategies are possible in an infinitely repeated game of prisoner's dilemma. But, it has been mathematically proved that, as far as the following condition;

$$R > (T + S) / 2 \text{ or } CC > (DC + CD) / 2$$

is met, TFT will give the greatest payoff to each of the parties in the long run and give the greatest total payoff to the parties as a whole. TFT is the solution, and it satisfies both collective or social rationality condition and stability condition. Now, prisoner's dilemma is solved at last.

In everyday language, the solution is explained in the following way. When the game is played infinitely, without any end in sight, the profit gained by defection in a given single game will be lost by the prospect that it will cause the other party to defect in the next game. Such a profit gained by a single defection will be negligible compared with the difference between the total profit of repeated mutual cooperation (Downs et al 1985: 128). In sum, the total payoff of long-term cooperation is greater than that of reciprocations and exchanges of unilateral cooperation and defection (Axelrod 1984: 10).

Incidentally, TFT was the strategy adopted by the strongest program in the open computer program contests for the solution prisoner's dilemma organized by Robert Axelrod. The program was the strongest in the sense that it brought the greatest profit. Actually, there were two tournaments at different times and the program won in both. Moreover, it was the shortest program of all. The man who submitted the program was no other than Anatol Rapoport who introduced game theory into peace studies (Axelrod 1984: viii, 31, appendix A).

The solution of prisoner's dilemma only shows that, under some circumstance, it is better in an infinitely repeated game to cooperate than to defect. But, in reality, it is not always possible to convince oneself and others, especially in security or military affairs, that the long-term gains from cooperation are greater than the short-term gains of defection (Downs et al 1985: 129). On the other hand, in view of the fact that the TFT always begins with cooperation, one can argue that unilateral disarmament is an effective initiative because it can open the way to the following cooperation.

7.5 Cooperation under Anarchy

7.5.1. Neoliberal Institutionalism vs. Neorealism

Recently there have been debates between two camps of international relations research about the possibility of cooperation among states in the international society under anarchy. One camp, which emphasizes the possibility of cooperation, has been called "neoliberalism" or "neoliberal institutionalism." The most prominent proponent of this school is Robert Keohane. The other camp, represented by Kenneth Waltz, is called "neorealism" or "structural realism." In sharp contrast to the neoliberal camp, the camp emphasizes the small possibility of cooperation (Baldwin 1993: 4, 13).

Actually, however, the two have many things in common, though their backgrounds are rather different. Indeed, both are frequently referred to simply as "neorealism" or "realism" because of the similarities they share (for example, see Strange 1994: 210). Most importantly, they share many key concepts including the concept of anarchy of the international society (Grieco 1988: 486, Stein 1990: 8-9).

Let us examine these similarities and differences according to Table 47.

Both neoliberalism and neorealism assume that the international society is in "anarchy" and anarchy means the "lack of a common government" (Grieco 1988: 497). Here we must take note that anarchy does not necessarily mean the absence of international society, albeit a fragmented and incomplete one, and it does not mean either that it entirely lacks organization (Axelrod and Keohane 1985: 226). As the title of the famous book by Hedley Bull, *Anarchical Society,* suggests, the international society is a society even though it is characterized by anarchy (Stein 1990: 9).

In addition, both share many other key assumptions. They both assume that states are only major actors in the international system, and they are unitary and rational actors (Grieco 1988: 492). In reality, however, there seem to be many exceptions to these two assumptions. For example, states are not always unitary actors in real world. Policies and behaviors of a state may be quite divided over an issue. Sometimes state behaviors cannot be regarded as rational at all in any sense of the word. With these reservations, we can say that the two schools share many key assumptions.

Table 47 Neoliberalism vs. Neorealism
source: adapted from Grieco (1988), 494、503

	neoliberalism	neorealism
International society	Anarchy: No common government	
Actor	State as only major actor	
State	Unitary rational actor	
Meaning of anarchy	No central agency to enforce cooperation	No central agency to enforce cooperation to provide protection
Constraints of Anarchy	Constrains the preferences and behaviors of the state	Constrains the preferences and behaviors of the state
Main goal of the state	Greatest possible absolute gains	Greatest possibility of survival
Basic character of the state	Atomisitc, Neglect of comparison	Positional, Emphasis of comparison
Gains of state	Independent of the gains of other states	Partially relative to the gains of other states (Partially function of the gains of others)
Gains aimed	Absolute gains	Relative gains
Interstate cooperation	Optimistic	Pessimistic
International institutions	Promote cooperation	Not promote cooperation very much

Shaded parts indicate the differences.

On the other hand, there are important differences as well. Neoliberalists take anarchy as meaning that there is no central agency or common government which enforces states to cooperate with each other. In contrast, neorealists take anarchy as meaning not only the absence of central agency to enforce cooperation, but also the absence of higher authority which prevents states from the use of power which may destroy or dominate a state in question (Grieco 1988: 497-498). In short, to neorealists, anarchy in the international society also means the absence of central authority which provides protection to states. As a result, states have to provide their own protection and survival for themselves. And it is in this sense that the international system is that of self-help.

The difference in the interpretations of anarchy leads to another crucial difference in the goal of state. To neorealists, the main goal of state is the survival or security (Grieco 1988: 498). States should and do seek the greatest possibility of survival. In contrast, neoliberalists argue that the main goal of state is not survival, but maximization of national interest.

When a state seeks the maximization of its national interest, it does not need to compare its own national interest with those of others. The interest or gains of the state are not compared with those of other states, and they are independent of those of others. For this reason, according to the arguments of neoliberalism, a state is interested only in "absolute gains" (Grieco 1988: 496-497).

On the contrary, as long as the survival or security is the main goal, a state cannot ignore comparison with other states. It is because that, in such a world, a state cannot neglect a possibility that other states obtains greater profits and can use them to its disadvantage, for example, to use them for arms buildup to attack it. Accordingly, a state should have serious concern about "relative gains" as well as absolute gains (Grieco 1988: 498-499).

The different views of the state goals and state gains lead to another difference. Neoliberalists are more optimistic about the possibility of cooperation among states. But, neorealists argue, if other states can obtain greater gains by cooperation, then a state may refuse to cooperate because greater relative gains of others may be used in future to its disadvantage, even if cooperation may bring it greater absolute gains than non-cooperation. For this reason, neorealists are more pessimistic about the possibility of interstate cooperation than neoliberalists (Grieco 1988: 499).

Consequently, the differences between the two schools boil down to a single issue of absolute vs. relative gains. This is what is called "gains debate." But it is incorrect to simply conclude that one school emphasizes relative gains exclusively and the other is interested solely in absolute gains. Neorealists normally argue that state should be interested in relative gains as well. And neoliberalists admit that they have underestimated the significance of relative gains under a certain circumstance in world politics. Generally speaking, however, neoliberalists have emphasized absolute gains while neorealists have emphasized relative gains (Baldwin 1993: 5-6).

7.5.2 Possibility of Cooperation

With these differences in mind, let us first examine the neoliberal arguments for the cooperation among states under anarchy.

First of all, cooperation is not harmony. In harmony, interests of the parties concerned completely agree, while in cooperation, both agreement and difference, or harmony and conflict, of interests of the parties are involved. Cooperation arises when actors adjust their choices or behaviors in compliance with real or expected gains. In fact, cooperation in this sense comes very close to compromise. And cooperation defined in this way is not always desirable from an ethical or moral viewpoint (Axelrod and Keohane 1985: 226). There can be cooperation among the powerful to suppress the weak. Not only does cooperation ameliorate injustices in our imperfect world, but instead it may also aggravate them. Remember the discussion about collective goods above. Even collusion among business firms can be called cooperation. Nevertheless, in view of many failures in cooperation resulting in war and economic depression, an increase in cooperation among states is better than a decrease (Axelrod and Keohane 1985: 253 – 254).

In exploring possibility of cooperation among states, neoliberalists usually draw upon game theoretic representations of international relations. They rely especially on mixed motive games. According to neoliberalists, states are placed in situations represented by a prisoner's dilemma model (Grieco 1988: 493). As we saw above, however, cooperation is impossible in prisoner's dilemma game if it is played only once. Only when we extend the time dimension in the form of infinitely iterated game, it has been demonstrated that cooperation among actors is possible when a certain conditions are met. Success of cooperation in prisoner's dilemma requires two conditions among others. These are key factors which greatly influence the success or failure of cooperation among states, especially in military-security affairs and in international political economy. These are "reciprocity" and "shadow of the future" (Axelrod and Keohane 1985: 227、234). The two factors are dependent on each other.

For reciprocity, a reciprocating strategy called Tit for Tat (TFT) should be adopted. The strategy of TFT dictates that actors should begin with cooperation in the first game, and, on all the following games, should answer in kind, that is, answer cooperation with cooperation and defection with defection, reciprocating the previous choice of others. The "shadow of the future" means that future expected utility should be great enough or the cost of imposing sanctions or punishment should be low enough (Grieco 1988: 493、495). If these two conditions are satisfied, cooperation is possible in prisoner's dilemma (Axelrod and Keohane 1985: 235、244).

The success of reciprocity depends upon the possibility of reciprocating defection in terms of punishment or sanctions. Reciprocity requires capability of answering defection with defection (Axelrod and Keohane 1985: 249). The logic reminds us of that of nuclear deterrence theory. As deterrence is effective only when capability of retaliation is assured, reciprocity in cooperation is effective only when capability of defection or retaliation is guaranteed. Anyway, the best policy for cooperation among rational actors requires the ability of defection or non-cooperation. Some may find the logic unpalatable, ethically at least. But we must admit that, in many cases, if not in all the cases, even such cooperation can be much better than a direct military confrontation.

There is another difficulty with reciprocity policy like Tit for Tat. In Tit for Tat, actors begin the game with cooperation and retaliate against defection by defection only once in the next game. But an echo effect may take on, and the strategy may perpetuate conflict instead of cooperation. The situation is quite similar to that of spiral model of security dilemma in which parties are entrapped in an unending vicious circle of armament expansion. Following the strategy of Tit for Tat, one party retaliates against the other's defection by choosing defection. But if the other party retaliates against this defection by another defection, then it will result in an endless repetition of mutual defection. (Axelrod and Keohane 1985: 245). To remedy this, Axelrod proposes the concept of "forgiveness" in which, only after two consecutive defections of others, an actor retaliates against them by a single defection. He defines the concept as "propensity to cooperate in the moves after the other player has defected." Bigger gains can be made by more "forgiving" strategies than Tit for Tat (Axelrod 1984: 36, 39).

Despite these difficulties, neoliberalists argue that prisoner's dilemma is an effective model of mutual cooperation among states, and reciprocity strategies like Tit for Tat are effective strategies for cooperation under anarchy (Axelrod and Keohane 1985: 246).

The length of the shadow of the future is closely related to the issue of reciprocity. The repetition or iteration of game produces a possibility of punishing today's defective behavior with future sanctions. It opens the possibility of reciprocity. If the shadow of the future is long enough, future costs of the present defection will be greater than the benefit gained by it. Therefore, comparison of costs and benefits will induce rational states to cooperate with each other. Stable cooperation among states is formulated as equilibrium in infinitely repeated game of prisoner's dilemma. But the stability or equilibrium is maintained only as long as the punishment of defection is possible, or only if reciprocity is possible (Powell 1993: 213-214).

On these grounds, neoliberalists argue that cooperation among states is possible even under anarchy, if shadow of the future is long enough and reciprocation is possible.

In sum, neoliberalists see interstate relations as prisoner's dilemma, and argue that, even when each of the states behaves to maximize its profit, cooperation is possible in such a situation, as far as certain conditions are met. Two of them seem crucial; that is, shadow of the future and reciprocity.

We must point out a more basic premise for this argument of neoliberalists. As the solution of prisoner's dilemma assumes, a game should be repeated. Iteration is an essential prerequisite for reciprocity and shadow of the future. Only in such a game, a state is less motivated to defect because others retaliate by reciprocating defection (Axelrod and Keohane 1985: 232). In other words, the validity of neoliberal argument of cooperation depends upon the linkage of today's state behavior with future repetition of the game (Downs et al 1985: 128). Only when a game is repeated, one can adopt the reciprocity strategy in which one answer defection with defection or punishment, and answer cooperation with cooperation or reward. The more the game is repeated, the more reciprocity is guaranteed.

Neorealists are not convinced of these arguments of neoliberalists, and they have made serious criticisms. The criticisms by neorealists are based upon the (different interpretation of the) nature of anarchy. According to neorealists, states should give priority to their survival under anarchy, because anarchy means a possibility of attack from others. As neoliberalists misunderstand the nature of anarchy, they ignore the threat of war arising from it. This is why neoliberalists cannot recognize the importance of relative gains. Relative gains are major sources of obstacles to cooperation among states (Grieco 1988: 487、495). Why, then, are relative gains so important?

According to neorealists, the unequal relative gains of cooperation, whether in prisoner's dilemma or not, can be utilized to expand and strengthen military capabilities of a state or states. It is, therefore, natural that states fear that unequal gains of cooperation (relative gains) may be exploited overwhelmingly by their hypothetical enemy. When other states, especially the hypothetical enemy or enemies, benefit much more from cooperation, such fear prevents states from stable substantial cooperation. Thus, interest in relative gains prevents extensive cooperation among states (Martin and Simmons 1998: 738). Neorealists conclude that, when relative gains matter, cooperation under prisoner's dilemma is impossible.

Duncan Snidal makes a counter-argument. He demonstrates that, the greater the interest in relative gains is, the sooner the game changes into prisoner's dilemma (Snidal 1991: 710). According to him, when states pursue both absolute and relative gains, there is possibility of cooperation contrary to the argument of neorealists.

There is another type of criticism against the neoliberal thesis of cooperation. Powell argues that a model in international relations should not exclude the possibility of use of force. To include such possibility, two conditions should be satisfied. First, the model should explicitly include an option for the use of force. Secondly, the model should be able to deal with the possibility of the change of the system itself resulting from the use of force such as war (Powell 1993: 219).

Powell argues that the repeated game of prisoner's dilemma, or of any other type of game, does not satisfy the second condition. If the international system is viewed as a repeated game, the nature of the system (such as actors involved, their options and payoffs) is invariable. In short, under the assumption of repetition, the international system does not change at all. The assumption of repetition is tantamount to saying that the international system of 1939 is the same as that of 1945 or that after the end of the Cold War (Powell 1993: 219).

Powell concludes that, if (1) a state gets relative gains enough, (2) it has means to transform them to one's advantage and to other's disadvantage, especially in military terms, and (3) expected benefit of the use of force is greater than expected cost, then relative gains matter, and cooperation will be frustrated. If these conditions are not met, there arises a prospect of cooperation (Powell 1993: 226). If the utility of force is great enough, interest in the relative gains may prevent cooperation, but if it is not great enough, states are not much interested in relative gains and cooperation is more preferable (Baldwin 1993: 6).

Even if Powell's three conditions were satisfied, the existence of some central authority would be able to prevent war and rather force cooperation in a desirable future, though there is no such authority at present.

Perhaps Keohane's summary of gains debate is the best conclusion of our examination of the issue of conflict and cooperation in international relations.

> Relative gains are meaningful only in such rare situations where only two major actors are involved and one's relative gains decisively changes the power relationship of the two. The superpower arms race [...] may be rare example[s]. In these cases, relative gains are really important. [...] Though the concept of relative gains has only shown that cooperation is difficult when two actors are set in rivalry or in competition, it has never denied the general possibility of cooperation among states. (Keohane 1998: 88)

Even if cooperation does not always advance us toward the goal of peace, from the examinations above, we can hope for future cooperation among states, instead of war.

8. Theoretical Postscript: Whither Peace Studies?

8.1 Peace Studies and War

Several peace studies anthologies were published shortly after the end of the Cold War. They emphasized war, conflict and security issues (Balász 1993: 8, Boulding 1992: 1-2). Moreover, peace studies journals have recently tended to put a much greater emphasis upon the issue of war and conflict. For example, a cursory look at the recent issues of such journals as *Journal of Peace Research* will convince us that most of the articles and review essays address interstate and intrastate wars in some way or other, directly or indirectly. "Awakened" by the prevalence of local conflicts and the seriousness of their threat to peace, is peace studies now reverting to its earlier stage preoccupied with the issue of war? The answer is "yes" in a sense and "no" in another, as both Jeong (1999) and Alger (1999) suggest.

On the one hand, the answer is "no" because a simple return to the former stage is impossible especially once we know Galtung's theory of structural violence. It was, as it were, a river of no return, and we have already crossed it. The full realization of human potentials, or the realization of human rights in the deepest sense, will continue to be the common ultimate goal of peace studies. "Emancipatory knowledge interest," to borrow Heyward Alker's words (Alker 1988: 220), or the interest in the final emancipation of the human race from every thing which prevents the full realization of human potentials, will surely be shared by all peace researchers. It will constitute the common core of peace studies. And peace studies will be integrated by this common research orientation (Jeong 1999: 6).

In this sense, the point raised by the theory of structural violence will be inherited in its fundamental aspect. And peace studies will be interested in "transformative possibilities for the improvement of human well-being [such as economic development, environmental preservation, realization of social justice] as well as the prevention of [direct] violence" (Jeong 1999: 6). Peace studies can no longer revert to the stage before the theory of structural violence when one could speak of peace as the absence of war.

Probably it is upon this understanding of the goal of the discipline that many still advocate the broadening of the peace studies agenda. For example, many advocate the inclusion of environmental issues into the research agenda of peace studies, though their proposals are expressed by a variety of forms such as the "greening of peace research" (Pirages 1991), placing "ecopolitics in peace studies" (Kegley 1997) or the "notion of peace with nature or ecological justice" (Wenden 1995: 14) and so on.

On the other, as we saw above, leading peace studies journals are shifting their focus more and more toward the issues of war and conflict. Though Alger (1999) suggests the greater relevance of (shifting to) non-violent approaches in his evolutionary learning description, more than half of the 24 peace building tools which he enumerates directly deal with war and conflict. From these observations, it may be tentatively concluded that peace studies seems to be again moving its attention more and more to war and conflict. Though the scope may have shifted with the changes in the nature of conflict and insecurity, the purpose of peace studies has not changed. The main issue is to "prevent political violence" (Tromp 1992: 12). or "[the] goal [of peace studies] is now, as it was [at its birth], to render obsolete the field of security studies based on the military defense of nation-states" (Boulding 1992: 2)

Recent re-emphasis upon war and conflict reflects the judgment that war and conflict are the greatest obstacles to the ultimate goal of peace formulated above, and it also reflects the collective decision that peace studies should be devoted to the elimination of this obstacle, which has afflicted human beings from time immemorial. In an age when "democratic peace" and "the obsolescence of major wars" are asserted, wars and conflicts to be studied will not be limited to major wars in the advanced industrial world. But local wars and conflicts, and other forms of organized violence, especially their prevention and solution, should be given much more attention than before. In this sense, we can say that peace studies is now directing itself toward the elimination of the most serious hindrance, war, to its ultimate goal, peace.

8.2 Peace and Security

But the (re)orientation of peace studies faces a very difficult problem to solve, namely, the issue of security. The (re)orientation of peace studies should be considered in a broader context in its relation with security studies. And the concept of peace should be reexamined in its relation with the concept of security. It is because the concept of security has recently been expanded in the same way as the concept of peace was expanded a few decades ago (see 2.2.3 and 2.2.4 above). As a result, as some argue, peace and security studies are now converging (Kriesberg 2002: 587).

Security studies has been witnessing the same kind of dilemma, the "wide" versus "narrow" debate (Buzan et al 1998: 2, Shultz et al 1997: 1), as that between the broader and narrower agendas in peace studies which we sketched above (Wiberg 1992: 492, note 5). "Wideners" argued for expanding the scope of security agenda to include non-military sources of threat, while "traditionalists" argued for the established equation of security with military issues and the use of force (Buzan et al 1998: 1-2, Shultz et al 1997: 1-2). The broadened agenda usually includes environmental degradation (ozone depletion, global warming, scarcity of renewable and non-renewable resources), damages upon domestic economy caused by international capital, organized crimes like drug traffics, massive human rights violations, population explosions, refugees and uncontrolled population migration, infectious diseases (Patman 1999: 4, Roy 1997: 2, Shultz 1997: 43). And even those who are against the wider agenda admit that questions of civil liberties and economic welfare have always formed part of the broader security agenda. (Kennedy-Pipe 2000: 6).

The arguments of the proponents of the narrower traditional agenda are essentially the same as those raised against the broadening of peace studies, some of which were discussed above. In essence, they are against the excessive dilution and diversification of the discipline, though they don't deny the importance of the issues themselves such as environmental degradation and international economy. Even though he supports a wider agenda, Barry Buzan warns against the time when it becomes difficult to distinguish security studies from international relations studies (Buzan 1992:

483). Similarly, Richard Shultz Jr. and others argue that the expansion would risk "dilution and diversion [of the discipline] to such an extent that every critical national and international problem would be defined as a security issue," with the result that "security studies would subsume not only all of international relations, but much of domestic politics as well" (Shultz et al 1997: 3). Many agree that "if everything that causes a decline in human well-being is labeled security threat, the term loses any analytical usefulness" (Deudney 1991: 24).

Anyway, the concept of security has now been expanded to include many issues as is illustrated in Figure 25. As the figure shows, the concept of security has been expanded form the traditional national security of state both in "referents" and sources of threat (to security). Referents (those whose security should be guaranteed) now include not only states but also societies, internal groups and individuals. At the same time, sources of threat include nonmilitary threats like environment and economy. The expansion has now culminated in "human security."

Table 48 Security: Referents and Sources of Threat
source: based on Paris (2001), 98

		sources of threat	
		Military	military, nonmilitary or both
referents	states	**national security** conventional realist approach to security studies	**redefined security** e.g., environmental and economic security
	societies, groups and individuals	**intrastate security** e.g., civil war, ethnic conflict, and democide	**human security** e.g., environmental and economic threats to the survival of societies, groups and individuals

What is of relevance here, however, is not only the similarity of the debates in peace studies and security studies. But the broadening of the concept of security has also a direct consequence on peace studies. For example, recent peace studies anthologies increasingly emphasize the issue of security. They also point out the changes in nature and scope of security, or in sources of insecurity (Balász 1993: 8, Boulding 1992: 3-4), as is given in figure 25. Thus, the change or widening of the concept of security directly affects the peace studies agenda.

It is, therefore, appropriate to examine in some detail how the broadening of the concept of security affects peace studies. We will take up two issues: those of "environmental security" and "human security."

The broadening of peace studies agenda has recently been claimed on the ground that the issue in question, for example, environmental degradation, is a threat to human well-being, and hence a security issue in the broadened sense. Therefore, the issue should be included in the peace studies agenda.

To complicate the matter, however, there are actually two groups among the proponents of "environmental peace." One group emphasizes environmental degradation (including environmental scarcities or the resource depletion) as a cause of violent conflict (for example, Homer-Dixon 1994, Howard 1997: 64, Kegley 1997: 439). The other emphasizes it as a cause of the reduction in human well-being or as a kind of "structural violence." (For the criticism against the latter kind of argument, see Deudney 1991: 26-28). In this way, most of the argument emphasizes that environmental issues are security issues and hence peace studies issues.

On the one hand, the former fits rather well with the narrower definition of peace because the environmental issues such as resource depletion can be a serious cause of conflict. And, on the other, the latter argument can fit with the broader concept of peace proposed by Galtung. According to his definition, if environmental degradation causes a decline in human well-being, then it prevents the full realization of human potentials, and it should be regarded as a manifestation of violence, and should, therefore, be a legitimate research subject of peace studies.

In either case, the research object of security studies, environmental problems in this case, will be subsumed under peace studies as well.

The next issue is that of "human security." The concept of "human security" was first explicitly proposed in 1994 by the United Nations Development Programme (UNDP) in its annual report, *Human Development Report 1994: New dimensions of human security*. It emphasizes changes:

> from territorial [or state] security to people's security
>
> from security through armaments to security through sustainable human development (UNDP 1994: 24)

The first roughly corresponds to the expansion in referents from state to people (as a group or an individual) in Figure 25. The second corresponds to the expansion in the sources of threats. The listed threats to human security range from economic, food, health, environment, political to personal (bodily integrity) and community (survival of traditional cultures and ethnic groups) security (UNDP 1994: 24-25). It is "security in their daily lives." And it is a state in which "a more humane world is realized where people can live in security and dignity, free from want and fear, and with equal opportunities to *develop their human potential to the full*." (cited in Paris 2001: 91, emphasis mine).

There are many criticisms against the concept of human security. First, the concept is accused of lacking in a precise definition. The list given by UNDP is so broad that it is difficult to determine what, if anything, might be excluded from the definition of human security. Some protagonists argue that human security is "the totality of knowledge, technology, institutions and activities that protect, defend and preserve the biological existence of human life; and the processes which protect and perfect collective peace and prosperity to enhance human freedom." If human security is all these things, what it is *not*? (Paris 2001: 90-92)

From the above examination, the parallel between peace and security studies is clear. It can be illustrated schematically in Figure 26. And If we adopt broader perspectives on peace and security, it seems that there is a very great conversion between peace and security studies. In their broader perspectives, both these studies now address the issue of the full realization of physical and mental human potentials.

Perhaps, Ken Booth went the farthest in this respect. Instead of "freedom from threat" (Buzan 1992: 484) or "need for feelings of safety and survivability" (Kegley 1997: 439), he proposes "emancipation" as the key concept for the understanding of security. Emancipation means freeing people from such constraints as war, poverty, oppression, and poor education. Emancipation and security are two sides of the same coin. Emancipation leads to security (Booth 1991: 539). Though the concepts may have been reached through different routes, the similarity between "emancipation" and "positive peace" is obvious.

Figure 25 Peace and Security Studies

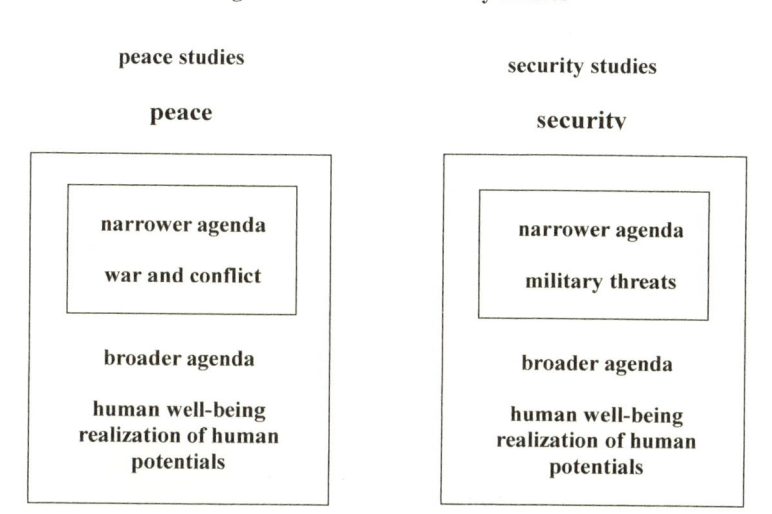

peace studies   **security studies**

peace   **security**

narrower agenda **war and conflict** broader agenda **human well-being** **realization of human potentials**	**narrower agenda** **military threats** broader agenda **human well-being** **realization of human potentials**

Peace studies now faces the questions whether peace is different from security in the broader perspective, and whether peace studies is different from security studies.

References

Albrecht, Ulrich, Dieter Ernst, Peter Lock and Herbert Wulf (1974), "Armaments and Underdevelopment," *Bulletin of Peace Proposals*, 5(2), 173-185

Alcock, N. Z. and Keith Lowe (1969), "The Vietnam War as a Richardson Process," *Journal of Peace Research*, 6(2), 105-112

Alger, Chadwick F. (1989), "Peace Studies at the Crossroads: Where Else?" *The Annals of American Academy of Political and Social Sciences*, vol. 504 (special issue on peace studies), 117-127

Alger, Chadwick F. (1999), "The Expanding Tool Chest for Peacebuilders," Jeong (ed.), 13-42

Alker, Hayward R. Jr. (1988), "Emancipatory Empiricism: Toward the Renewal of Empirical Peace Research," Wallensteen (ed.), 219-241

Aruga Tadashi et al (eds.) *Theories of International Politics (Kokusai Seiji no Riron)*, Tokyo: University of Tokyo Press (in Japanese)

Auvinen, Juha (1997), "Political Conflict in Less Developed Countries 1981-89," *Journal of Peace Research*, 34(2), 177-195

Axelrod, Robert (1984), *The Evolution of Cooperation*, New York: Basic Books

Axelrod, Robert and Robert O. Keohane (1985), "Achieving Cooperation under Anarchy: Strategies and Institutions," *World Politics*, 38(1), 226-254

Ayres, R. William (2000), "A World Flying Apart? Violent Nationalist Conflict and the End of the Cold War," *Journal of Peace Research*, 37(1), 105-117

Azar, Edward (1980), "The Conflict and Peace Data Bank (COPDAB) Project," *Journal of Conflict Resolution*, 24, 143-152

Balázs, Judit (1993), "Introduction," Balázs and Wiberg (eds.), 7-8

Balázs, Judit and Håkan Wiberg (eds.) (1993), *Peace Research for the 1990s*, Budapest, Akadémiai Kiadó

Baldwin, David A. (1993), "Neoliberalism, Neorealism, and World Politics," Baldwin (ed.), 3-25

Baldwin, David A. (ed.) (1993), *Neorealism and Neoliberalism: The Contemporary Debate*, New York: Columbia University Press

Ball, Nicole (1983), "Defence and Development: A Critique of the Benoit Study," Tuomi and Väyrynen (eds.), 39-56

Beaumont, Roger (1995), "Small Wars: Definitions and Dimensions," *Annals of the Academy of Political and Social Sciences*, 541, 20-35

Booth, Ken (1991), "Security in Anarchy: Utopian Realism in Theory and Practice," *International Affairs*, 63(3), 527-545

Boulding, Elise (1992), "Introduction: What Is Possible?" Boulding (ed.), 1-6

Boulding, Elise (ed.) (1992), *New Agendas for Peace Research: Conflict and Security Reexamined*, Boulder, Lynne Rienner

Boulding, Kenneth E. (1977), "Twelve Friendly Quarrels with Johan Galtung," *Journal of Peace Research*, 14(1), 75-86

Boulding, Kenneth E (1978), *Stable Peace*, Austin: University of Texas Press

Boutros-Ghali, Boutros (1992), *An Agenda for Peace: Preventive Diplomacy, Peacemaking and Peace-keeping*, New York: United Nations

Brecher, Michael and Frank P. Harvey (1998), "Conflict, Crisis and War: Cumulation, Criticism, Rejoinder," Frank P. Harvey and Ben D. Mor (eds.), *Conflict in World Politics: Advances in the Study of Crisis, War and Peace*, Houndmills and London: Macmillan, 3-29

Brecher, Michael and Frank Harvey (eds.) (2002), *Realism and Institutionalism in International Studies*, Ann Arbor: University of Michigan Press

Brown, Michael E. (1997), "The Causes of Internal Conflict," Michael E. Brown et al (eds.), *Nationalism and Ethnic Conflict*, Cambridge, MA: MIT Press, 3-25

Brush, Stephen G. (1996), "Dynamics of Theory Change in the Social Sciences: Relative Deprivation and Collective Violence," *Journal of Conflict Resolution*, 40(4), 523-545

Brzoska, Michael (1981), "The Reporting of Military Expenditures," *Journal of Peace Research*, 18(3), 261-275

Burns, Tom and Walter Buckley (1974), "The Prisoner's Dilemma Game as a System of Social Domination," *Journal of Peace Research*, 11(3), 221-228

Buzan, Barry (1992), "Response to Kolodzeij," *Arms Control*, 13 (3), 480-486

Buzan, Barry, Ole Waever and Jaap de Wilde (1998), *Security: A New Framework for Analysis*, Boulder: Lynne Rienner

Canberra Commission Home Page: http://www.dfat.gov.au/cc/cchome.html

Cashman, Greg (2000), *What Causes War? An Introduction to Theories of International Conflict*, Lanham: Lexington Books

Choucri, Nazli and Robert C. North (1975), *Nations in Conflict: National Growth and International Violence*, San Francisco: W. H. Freeman

Choucri, Nazli and Robert C. North (1987), "Roots of War: The Master Variables," Raimo Väyrynen (ed.), *The Quest for Peace: Transcending Collective Violence and War among Societies, Cultures and States*, London: Sage, 204-216

Cioffi-Revilla, Claudio (1990), *The Scientific Measurement of International Conflict: Handbook of Datasets on Crises and Wars, 1495-1988, A. D.*, Boulder: Lynne Rienner

Cliffe, Lionel and Robin Luckham (1999), "Complex Political Emergencies and the State: Failure and the Fate of the State," *Third World Quarterly*, 20(1), 27-50

Collier, Paul and Anke Hoeffler (2000), *Greed and Grievance in Civil War*, World Bank Policy Research Working Paper 2355, World Bank (http://www.worldbank.org/research/ PDF)

Collier, Paul et al (2003), *Breaking the Conflict Trap: Civil War and Development Policy*, Washington, DC: World Bank

Darnton, Geoffrey (1973), "The Concept <Peace>," *Proceedings of the International Peace Research Association Fourth General Conference*, 105-116

Dasgupta, Sugata (1968), "Peacelesness and Maldevelopment: A New Theme for Peace Research in Developing Nations," *Proceedings of the International Peace Research Association Second Conference*, Assen, The Netherlands: Koninklijke Van Gorcum & Comp, vol.2, 19-42

David, Steven R. (1998), "The Primacy of Internal War," Neuman (ed.), 77-101

Davies, John L. and Ted R. Gurr (eds.) (1998), *Preventive Measures: Building Risk Assessment and Crisis Early Warning Systems*, Lanham: Rowman and Littlefield

Davis, Byron L., Edward L. Kick and David Kiefer (1989), "World-System, Militarization, and National Development," Schaeffer (ed.), 27-45

Deudney, Daniel (1991), "Environment and Security: Muddled Thinking," *Bulletin of the Atomic Scientists*, 47(3), 22-28

Diehl, Paul F. (2002), "Chasing Headlines: Setting the Research Agenda on War," *Conflict Management and Peace Science*, 19(1), 5-26

Diehl, Paul F. and Jean Kingston (1987), "Messenger or Message? Military Buildups and the Initiation of Conflict," *Journal of Politics*, 49(3), 801-813

Doran, Charles F. (1983), "War and Power Dynamics: Economic Underpinnings," *International Studies Quarterly*, 27(4), 419-4411

Downs, George W., David M. Rocke and Randolph M. Siverson (1985), "Arms Race and Cooperation," *World Politics*, 38(1), 118-146

Dunne, J. Paul et al (2003), "Arms Race Models and Econometric Applications," Levine and Smith (eds.), 178-187

Eckhardt, William (1991), "War-related Deaths since 3000 BC," *Bulletin of Peace Proposals*, 22(4): 437-443

Eriksson, Mikael and Peter Wallensteen (2004), "Appendix 3A. Patterns of Major Armed Conflict, 1990-2003," Stockholm International Peace Research Institute, *SIPRI Yearbook 2004: Armaments, Disarmament and International Security*, Oxford: Oxford University Press, 132-143

Evans, Graham and Jeffrey Newnham (1992), *The Dictionary of World Politics: A Reference Guide to Concepts, Ideas and Institutions* (rev ed.), New York: Harvester Wheatsheaf

Fearon, James D. and David D. Laitin (1996), "Explaining Interethnic Cooperation," *American Political Science Review*, 90(4), 715-735

Fujiwara, Kiichi (2000), "Autocratic Peace: ASEAN in Comparative Perspective (Sensei no Heiwa Dango no Heiwa: Hikaku no nakano ASEAN), *International Relations (Kokusai Seiji)*, 125, 147-161 (in Japanese)

Galtung, Johan (1969), "Violence, Peace, and Peace Research," *Journal of Peace Research*, 6(3), 167-191

Galtung, Johan (1981), "Social Cosmology and the Concept of Peace," *Journal of Peace Research*, 18(2), 183-199

Geller, Daniel S. and J. David Singer (1998), *Nations at War: A Scientific Study of International Conflict*, Cambridge, Cambridge University Press

Gilpin, Robert (1981), *War and Change in World Politics*, New York: Cambridge University Press

Gleditsch, Nils Petter (1993), "The Most-cited Articles in *JPR*," *Journal of Peace Research*, 30(4), 445-449

Gleditsch, Nils Petter et al (2002), "Armed Conflict 1946-2001: A New Dataset," *Journal of Peace Research*, 39(5), 615-637

Goetze, David (1994), "Comparing Prisoner's Dilemma, Commons Dilemma, and Public Goods Provision Designs in Laboratory Experiments," *Journal of Conflict Resolution*, 38(1), 56-86

Goldblat, Jozef (2002), *Arms Control: The New Guide to Negotiations and Agreements*, London: Sage

Goldstein, Joshua S. (1985), "Kondratieff Waves as War Cycles," *International Studies Quarterly*, 29(4), 411-444

Goodhand, Jonathan and David Hulme (1999), "From Wars to Complex Political Emergencies: Understanding Conflict and Peace-Building in the New World Disorder," *Third World Quarterly*, 20(1), 13-26

Grieco, Joseph M. (1988), "Anarchy and the Limits of Cooperation: A Realist Critique of the Newest Liberal Institutionalism," *International Organization*, 42(3), 485-507

Grieco, Joseph M. (2002), "Modern Realist Theory and the Study of International Politics in the Twenty-First Century," Brecher and Harvey (eds.), 65-78

Gurr, Ted Robert (ed.) (1993), *Minorities at Risk: A Global View of Ethnopolitical Conflict*, Washington, DC: United States Institute of Peace

Gurr, Ted Robert and Barbara Harff (1994), *Ethnic Conflict in World Politics*, Boulder: Westview

Harff, Barbara (1992), "Recognizing Genocide and Politicide," Helen Fein (ed.), *Genocide Watch*, New Haven: Yale University Press, 27-41

Harff, Barbara and Ted Robert Gurr (1988), "Toward Empirical Theory of Genocides and Politicides: Identifications and Measurement of Cases since 1945," *International Studies Quarterly*, 32(3), 359-371

Henderson, Errol A. and John David Singer (2000), "Civil War in the Post-Colonial World, 1946-92," *Journal of Peace Research*, 38(3), 275-299

The Henry Stimson Center (1995), *An Evolving US Nuclear Posture*, http://www.stimson.org/zeronuke/evolve/summary.htm, pahse1.htm, etc

Herz, John H. (1950), "Idealist Internationalism and the Security Dilemma," *World Politics*, 2(2), 157-180

Hoivik, Tord (1977), "The Demography of Structural Violence," *Journal of Peace Research*, XIV(1), 59-73

Holsti, Kalevi J. (1991), *Peace and War: Armed Conflicts and International Order 1648-1989*, Cambridge: Cambridge University Press

Holsti, Kalevi J. (1998), "International Relations Theory and Domestic War in the Third World: The Limits of Relevance," Neuman (ed.) (1998), 103-132

Homer-Dixon, Thomas F. (1994), "Environmental Scarcity and Intergroup Conflict," Michael T. Klare and D. C. Thomas (eds.), *World Security: Trends and Challenges for a New Century*, 2nd ed, New York: St. Martin's, 290-313

Howard, Philip (1997), "Environmental Scarcities and Conflict: Assessing the Evidence in the Asia-Pacific Region," Roy (ed.) (1997), 64-75

Howell, Llewellyn D. (1983), "A Comparative Study of the WEIS and COPDAB Data Sets," *International Studies Quarterly*, 27(2), 149-159

Ishida, Takeshi (1969), "Beyond the Traditional Concepts of Peace in Different Cultures," *Journal of Peace Research*, 6(2), 133-145

Jeong, Ho-Won (1999), "Peace Research and International Relations," Jeong (ed.), 3-11

Jeong, Ho-Won (ed.) (1999), *The New Agenda for Peace Research*, Aldershot: Ashgate

Jervis, Robert (1978), "Cooperation under the Security Dilemma," *World Politics*, 30(2), 167-214

Kaldor, Mary (1986), "The Military in Third World Development," Mac Graham et al (eds.) (1986), *Disarmament and World Development*, 2nd ed. Oxford: Pergamon, 71-100

Kaldor, Mary (1999), *New and Old Wars: Organized Violence in a Global Era*, Cambridge: Polity

Kamo, Takehiko (1990), *Plan for International Security (Kokusai Anzen Hosho no Koso)*, Tokyo: Iwanami Shoten (in Japanese)

Kaufman, Stuart J. (1996), "An 'International Theory' of Inter-Ethnic War," *Review of International Studies*, 22(2), 149-171

Kegley, Charles Jr. (1997), "Placing Global Ecopolitics in Peace Studies," *Peace Review*, 9(3), 425-430

Kende, Istvan (1971), "Twenty-Five Years of Local Wars," *Journal of Peace Research*, 8 (1), 5-27

Kende, Istvan (1978), "Wars of Ten Years (1967-1976)," *Journal of Peace Research*, 15 (3), 227-241

Kende, Istvan (1989), "The History of Peace: Concept and Organizations from the Late Middle Ages to the 1870s," *Journal of Peace Research*, 26 (3), 233-247

Kennedy-Pipe, Caroline (2000), "Security beyond the Cold War: An Introduction," Clive Jones and Caroline Kennedy-Pipe (eds.), *International Security in a Global Age: Securing the Twenty-first Century*, London: Frank Cass, 1-8

Keohane, Robert O. and Elinor Ostrom (1995), "Introduction," Robert O. Keohane and Elinor Ostrom (eds.), *Local Commons and Global Interdependence: Heterogeneity and Cooperation in Two Domains*, London: Sage, 1-26

Klare, Michael T. (1989), "Low-Intensity Conflict: A Growing Threat to Peace," Linda R. Forcey (ed.), *Peace: Meanings, Politics, Strategies*. New York: Praeger, 113-120

Köhler, Gernot and Norman Alcock (1976), "An Empirical Table of Structural Violence," *Journal of Peace Research*, XIII(4), 343-356

Kozhemiakin, Alexander V. (1998), *Expanding the Zone of Peace? Democratization and International Security*, Houndmills and London: Macmillan

Krasner, Stephen D. (1996), "Compromising Westphalia," *International Security*, 20(3), 115-151

Krasner, Stephen D. (2001), "Problematic Sovereignty," Stephen D. Krasner (ed.), *Problematic Sovereignty: Contested Rules and Political Possibilities*, New York: Columbia University Press, 1-23

Kriesberg, Louis (2002), "Convergence between International Security Studies and Peace Studies," Brecher and Harvey (eds.), 584-597

Krippendorf, Ekkehart (1981), "Focus on: Peace, an Introduction," *Journal of Peace Research*, 18 (2), 109-110

Kuznets, Simon (1963), "Quantitative Aspects of the Economic Growth of Nations, VIII: The Distribution of Income by Size," *Economic Development and Cultural Change*, 11(2), Part II, 1-80

Lake, David A and Donald Rothschild (1998), "Spreading Fear: The Genesis of Transnational Ethnic Conflict," David A. Lake and Donald Rothschild (eds.), *The International Spread of Ethnic Conflict: Fear, Diffusion, and Escalation*, Princeton, NJ: Princeton University Press, 3-32

Larsen, Jeffrey A. (2002), "An Introduction to Arms Control," Larsen (ed.), 1-15

Larsen, Jeffrey A. (ed.) (2002), *Arms Control: Cooperative Security in a Changing Environment*, Boulder: Lynne Rienner

Lasswell, Harold D. (1941), "The Garrison State," *American Journal of Sociology*, XLVI(4), 455-468

Levine, Paul and Ron Smith (eds.) (2003), *Arms Trade, Security and Conflict*, London: Routledge,

Levy, Jack S. (1983), *War in the Modern Great Power System, 1495-1975*, Lexington, Kentucky: University Press of Kentucky

Levy, Jack S. (1985a), "Theories of General War," *World Politics*, 37(3), 344-374

Levy, Jack S. (1985b), "The Polarity of the System and International Stability: An Empirical Analysis," Sabrosky (ed.) (1985), 41-66

Lichbach, Mrak Irving (1989), "An Evaluation of 'Does Economic Inequality Breed Political Conflict?' Studies," *World Politics*, XLI (4), 431-470

Lichbach, Mark Irving (1995), *The Rebel's Dilemma*, Ann Arbor: University of Michigan Press

Lodgaard, Sverre (2000), "The Process of Nuclear Disarmament," Jozef Goldblat (ed.), *Nuclear Disarmament: Obstacles to Banning the Bomb*, London: I. B. Tauris, 17-28

Luard, Evan (1986), *War in International Society: A Study in International Sociology*, London: I. B. Tauris

Luckham, Robin (1984), "Armament Culture," *Alternatives*, x, 1-44

Mansfield, Edward D. and Jack Snyder (1995), "Democratization and the Danger of War," *International Security*, 20(1), 5-38

Martin, Lisa L. and Beth A. Simmons (1998), "Theories and Empirical Studies of International Institutions," *International Organization*, 52(4), 729-757

Matelly, Sylvie (2003), "The Determinants of US Military Expenditures in the Context of Arms Race," Levine and Smith (eds.), 158-177

Matsuo, Masatsugu (1983), *Analysis of the Meanings of "Heiwa" through an Association Experiment (Renso Chosa ni yoru "Heiwa" no Imi Bunseki)*, IPSHU Research Report (Institute for Peace Science, Hiroshima University) No. 8 (in Japanese)

Matsuo, Masatsugu (1985), "Japanese People's Image of Peace," *PSAJ (Peace Studies Association of Japan) Newsletter*, No.5, 8-10

Matsuo, Masatsugu (1995), "Peace Studies in Japan: The Current State," *Journal of International Development and Cooperation*, 1(1), 143-150

Matsuo, Masatsugu (2001), "Achilles and Turtle in Nuclear Disarmament or Pitfalls of Process Utopia (Kaku Gunshuku ni okeru Akiresu to Kame aruiwa Katei Utopia no Kansei), Instititte for Peace Science, Hiroshima University (ed.) *Japan and the Nuclear Issues in the Post-Cold War Era (Posuto-Reisen Jidai no Kaku Mondai to Nippon)*, 1-19 (in Japanese)

Matsuo, Masatsugu et al (1978), "Structural Characteristics of Information in Interdisciplinary Areas (with special reference to peace research), VI (Gakusai Ryoiki (Heiwa Kenkyu o Chushin to suru) ni okeru Joho no Kozo Tokusei VI),", *Information Management (Joho Kanri),* 21(7): 501-506 (in Japanese)

Midlarsky, Manus I. (ed.) (2000), *Handbook of War Studies II*, Ann Arbor: University of Michigan Press

Modelski, Geroge and William Thompson (1989), "Long Cycles and Global War," Manus I. Midlarsky (ed.), *Handbook of War Studies*, Boston: Unwin Hyman, 23-54

Møller, Bjorn (1999), "From Arms to Disarmament Races: Disarmament Dynamics after the Cold War," Ho-Won Jeong (ed.), *The New Agenda for Peace Research*, Aldershot: Ashgate, 83-104

Mousseau, Demet Yalcin (2001), "Democratizing with Ethnic Divisions: A Source of Conflict?" *Journal of Peace Research*, 38(5), 547-567

Mullins, A. F. Jr. (1987), *Born Arming: Development and Military Power in New States*, Palo Alto, CA: Stanford University Press

Mueller, John (1990), "The Obsolescence of Major War," *Bulletin of Peace Proposals*, 21(3), 321-328

Neuman, Stephanie G. (ed.) (1998), *International Relations Theory and the Third World*, Houndmills and London: Macmillan

New Agenda Coalition   http://www.clw.org/pub/clw/coalition/eigh0609.htm

Nicholson, Michael (1992), *Rationality and the Analysis of International Conflict*, Cambridge: Cambridge University Press

Nye, Joseph S. (1987), "The Long-term Future of Deterrence," Roman Kolkowicz (ed.), *The Logic of Nuclear Terror*, Boston: Allen and Unwin, 233-250

Nye, Joseph S. Jr. (2002), *Understanding International Conflicts: An Introduction to Theory and History*, 3rd ed., New York: Longman

Okamoto, Mitsuo (1982), "Possibilities of Peace Studies - With Special Reference to Its Institutional Aspects (Heiwagaku no Kanosei: - Tokuni sono Seidoteki Sokumen kara)," *Riso*, 1982, 8, 129-145 (in Japanese)

Okamoto, Mitsuo (1997),"Peace Studies in Colleges and Universities in Japan: A Second General Survey (Nippon no Daigaku ni okeru Heiwagaku Kanren Koza no Dainiji Jittai Chosa)," *Hiroshima Peace Science*, 20, 215-274 (in Japanese)

Olson, Mancur (1992), "Foreword," Sandler (1992), vii-xvi

Ordeshook, Peter C. (1986), *Game Theory and Political Theory: An Introduction*, Cambridge: Cambridge University Press

Ordeshook, Peter C. (1992), *A Political Theory Primer*, New York: Routledge

Quester, George H. (1989), "International-Security Criticisms of Peace Research," *The Annals of American Academy of Political and Social Sciences*, vol. 504 (special issue on peace studies), 98-105

Palmer, Glenn (1989), "Game Theory, Cooperation and Conflict," Linda R. Forcey (ed.) (1989), *Peace: Meanings, Politics, Strategies*, New York: Praeger, 177-188

Paris, Roland (2001), "Human Security: Paradigm Shift or Hot Air?" *International Security*, 26(2), 87-102

Patman, Robert G. (1999), "Security in a Post-Cold War Context," Robert G. Patman (ed.), *Security in a Post-Cold War World*, Houndmills and London: Macmillan, 1-12

Pearce, Jenny (1999), "Peace-Building in the Periphery: Lessons from Central America," *Third World Quarterly*, 20(1), 51-68

Pirages, Dennis Clark (1991), "The Greening of Peace Research," *Journal of Peace Research*, 28(2), 129-133

Posen, Barry R. (1993), "The Security Dilemma and Ethnic Conflict," *Survival*, 35 (1), 27-47

Powell, Robert (1993), "Absolute and Relative Gains in International Relations Theory," Baldwin (ed.), 209-233. Reprinted from *American Political Science Review* 85 (1991), 1303-1320

Rapoport, Anatol, (1969) *Theories of Modern War and Peace (Gendai no Senso to Heiwa no Rironn)*, Tokyo: Iwanani Shoten (in Japanese)

Rapoport, Anatol (1974), *Conflict in Man-made Environment*, Harmonsworth: Penguin

Rasler, Karen and William R. Thompson (2000), "Global War and the Political Economy of Structural Change," Midlarsky (ed.), 301-331

Regan, Patrick M. (1994), *Organizing Societies for War: The Process and Consequences of Societal Militarization*, Westport: Praeger

Richardson, Lewis F. (eds. by Quincy Wright and C. C. Lienau) (1960), *Statistics of Deadly Quarrels*, Pacific Grove, California: Boxwood Press

Roe, Paul (1999), "The Intrastate Security Dilemma: Ethnic Conflict as a 'Tragedy'?" *Journal of Peace Research*, 36(2), 183-202

Rosecrance, R.N. (1966), "Bipolarity, Multipolarity, and the Future," *Journal of Conflict Resolution*, 10(3), 314-327

Rosecrance, Richard (1986), *The Rise of the Trading State: Commerce and Conquest in the Modern World*, New York: Basic Books

Roy, Denny (1997), "Introduction: Old and New Agendas," Roy (ed.) (1997), 1-4

Roy, Denny (ed.) (1997), *The New Security Agenda in the Asia-Pacific Region*, Houndmills and London: Macmillan

Rummel, Rudolph J. (1994), *Death by Government*, New Brunswick, NJ: Transaction

Rummel, Rudoloh J. (1997), "Is Collective Violence Correlated with Social Pluralism?" *Journal of Peace Research*, 34(2), 163-175

Sabrosky, Alan Ned (ed.) (1985), *Polarity and War: the Changing Structure of International Conflict*, Boulder: Westview

Sagan, Scott D. and Kenneth N. Waltz (1995), *The Spread of Nuclear Weapons: A Debate*, New York: Norton

Sakamoto, Yoshikazu (1976), "Normative Approach: Approach to Peace Research 7 (Kihanteki Hoho Heiwa Kankyu no Hoho 7)," *Peace Studies (Heiwa Kenkyu)* (Peace Studies Association of Japan), 1, 46-51 (in Japanese)

Sakamoto, Yoshikazu (1990) *International Politics in a Global Age (Chikyu Jidai no Kokusai Seiji)*, Tokyo: Iwanami Shoten (in Japanese)

Sakamoto, Yoshikazu and Richard A. Falk (1980), "World Demilitarized: A Basic Human Need," *Alternatives*, VI (1), 1-61

Sample, Susan G. (2000), "Military Buildups: Arming and War," Vasquez (ed.), 165-195

Sandler, Todd (1992), *Collective Action: Theory and Application*, Ann Arbor: University of Michigan Press

Schaeffer, Robert K. (1989), "Introduction," Schaeffer (ed.), 1-8

Schaeffer, Robert K. (ed.) (1989), *War in the World-System*, Westport, CT: Greenwood

Schelling, Thomas C. (2002), "Foreword," Larsen (ed.), xi-xv

Seki, Hiroharu (1981), "Path to Peace Research and Its Prospect (Heiwa Kenkyu eno Michi to sono Tembo)," Hiroharu Seki (ed.) *Introduction to International Politics: Scenarios of Current Theory of International Politics for the Breakthrough of the Crises (Kokusaiseijigaku o Manabu: Kiki Jokyo Dakai no tameno Gendai Kokusai Seiji Riron no Shinario)*, Tokyo: Yuhikaku, 261-297 (in Japanese)

Shindo, Eiichi (1988), "Modern Wars – Theoretical Issues (Gendai no Senso – Riron jo no ShoMondai ni tsuite)," Hirofumi Uzawa et al (eds.), *Humanity in the Transition Period – What is State? (Tenkanki ni okeru Ningen – Kokka towa)*, Tokyo: Iwanami Shoten, 63-100 (in Japanese)

Shubik, Martin (1984), *Game Theory in the Social Sciences: Concepts and Solutions*, Cambridge, MA: MIT Press

Shultz, Richard H. Jr. et al (1997), "Introduction," Shultz et al (eds.), 1-12

Shultz, Richard H. Jr. (1997), "Introduction to International Security," Shultz et al,(eds.), 43-72

Shultz, Richard et al (eds.) (1997), *Security Studies in the 21st Century*, Washington: Brassey's

Singer, John David (1981), "Accounting for International War: The State of the Discipline," *Journal of Peace Research*, 18 (1), 1-18

Singer, John David (2000), "The Etiology of Interstate War: A Natural History Approach," John A. Vasquez (ed.), *What Do We Know about War?* Lanham: Rowman and Littlefield, 3-21

Singer, Max and Aaron Wildavsky (1996), *The Real World Order: Zones of Peace, Zones of Turmoil*, Revised ed., Chatham, NJ: Chatham House

Sivard, Ruth Leger (1987), *World Military and Social Expenditures 1987-88*, Washington, D.C.: World Priorities

Sivard, Ruth Leger (1989), *World Military and Social Expenditures 1989* (13th edition), Washington, D.C.: World Priorities

Sivard, Ruth Leger (1991), *World Military and Social Expenditures 1991* (14th edition), Washington, D.C.: World Priorities

Sivard, Ruth Leger (1993), *World Military and Social Expenditures 1993* (15th edition), Washington, D.C.: World Priorities

Small, Melvin and John David Singer (1982), *Resort to Arms: International and Civil Wars, 1816-1980* (2nd ed.), Beverly Hills: Sage

Small, Melvin and John David Singer (1985), "Patterns in International Warfare, 1816-1980," Small and Singer (eds.), 7-19

Small, Melvin and John David Singer (eds.) (1985), *International War: an Anthology and Study Guide*, Homewood, IL: Dorsey Press

Smith, Anthony (1986), *The Ethnic Origins of Nations*, Oxford: Basil Blackwell

Smith, Anthony (1991), *National Identity (Ethnonationalism in Comparative Perspective)*, London: Penguin

Smoker, Paul (1964), "Fear in the Arms Race: A Mathematical Study," *Journal of Peace Research*, 1 (1), 55-64

Snidal, Duncan (1991), "Relative Gains and the Pattern of International Cooperation," *American Political Science Review*, 85(3), 701-726

Snyder, Glenn S. (1971), "'Prisoner's Dilemma' and 'Chicken' Models in International Politics," *International Studies Quarterly*, 15(1), 66-103

Soroos, Marvin S. (1994), "Global Change, Environmental Security, and the Prisoner's Dilemma," *Journal of Peace Research*, 31(3), 317-332

Spear, Joanna (1997), "Arms and Arms Control," Brian White et al (eds.), *Issues in World Politics*, Houndmills and London: Macmillan, 111-133

Stein, Arthur A. (1990), *Why Nations Cooperate: Circumstances and Choice in International Relations*, Ithaca: Cornell University Press

Strange, Susan (1987), "The Persistent Myth of Lost Hegemony," *International Organization*, 41(4), 551-574

Strange, Susan (1994), "Wake Up, Krasner! The World Has Changed," *Review of International Political Economy*, 1(2), 209-219

Strange, Susan (1999), "The Westfailure System," *Review of International Studies*, 25(3), 345-354

Szentes, Tamas (1984), "The Economic Impact of Global Militarization," *Alternatives*, X(1), 45- 73

Takayabagi, Sakio (1983), "Heiwa Kenkyu (Peace Research)," Editorial Committee, Peace Studies Association of Japan (ed.) *Peace Studies - Theory and Challenges (Heiwagaku - Riron to Kadai)*, Tokyo: Waseda Univeristy Press, 3-13 (in Japanese)

Takayanagi, Sakio (1989). "Paradigm of Peace Research (Heiwa Kenkyu no Paradaimu)," Aruga et al (eds.), 299-330 (in Japanese)

Takayanagi, Sakio (1991), *Power Politics – Its Archetype and Transformation (Pawa Poritikusu – sono Genkei to Henyou)*, Tokyo: Yushin Do (in Japanese)

Tanaka, Akihiko (1989), "Theories of World System (Sekai Shisutemu Ron)," 237-265 (in Japanese)

Thakur, Ramesh (2000), "Envisioning Nuclear Future," *Security Dialogue*, 31(1), 25-40

Timberlake, Michael and Kirk R. Williams (1987), "Structural Position in the World-system, Inequality, and Political Violence," *Journal of Political and Military Sociology*, 15(1), 1-15

Tromp, Hylke (1992), "Peace Research at the End of the Cold War," Boulding (ed.), 9-12

Tuomi, Helena and Raimo Väyrynen (eds.) (1983), *Militarization and Arms Production*, New York: St. Martin's

United Nations Development Programme (UNDP) (2001), *Human Development* 2001, New York: Oxford University Press

United Nations High Commissioner for Refugees (UNHCR), (1997), *The State of World's Refugees, 1997-98: A Humanitarian Agenda*, Oxford: Oxford University Press

van den Dungen, Peter and Lawrence S. Wittner (2003), "Peace History: An Introduction," *Journal of Peace Research*, 40(4), 363-375

Vasquez, John A. (2000), "Introduction," Vasquez (ed.), xiii-xvii

Vasquez, John A. (ed.) (2000), *What Do We Know about War?* Lanham: Rowman and Littlefield

Väyrynen, Raimo (1983), "Semiperipheral Countries in the Global Economic and Military Order," Tuomi and Väyrynen (eds.), 163-192

von Neumann, John and Oskar Morgenstern (1944), *The Theory of Games and Economic Behavior*, Princeton: Princeton University Press

Wallace, Michael D. (1979), "Arms Race and Escalation," *Journal of Conflict Resolution*, .23(1),

Wallensteen, Peter (1985), "Incompatibilities, Militarization, and Conflict Resolution," Wallensteen et al (eds.), 219-234

Wallensteen, Peter (ed.) (1988), *Peace Research: Achievements and Challenges*, Boulder: Westview Press

Wallensteen, Peter, Johan Galtung and Carlos Portales (1985), "Preface," Wallensteen et al (eds.), xi-xiv

Wallensteen, Peter, Johan Galtung and Carlos Portales (eds.) (1985), *Global Militarization*, Boulder: Westview

Wallensteen, Peter and Margareta Sollenberg (1997), "Armed Conflicts, Conflict Termination and Peace Agreements, 1989-96," *Journal of Peace Research*, 34(3), 339-358

Wallensteen, Peter and Margareta Sollenberg (2001), "Armed Conflict, 1989-2000," *Journal of Peace Research*, 38(5), 629-644

Waltz, Kenneth N. (2001, 1959), *Man, the State and War: A Theoretical Analysis*, New York: Columbia University Press

Waltz, Kenneth N. (2000), "Structural Realism after the Cold War," *International Security*, 25(1), 5-41

Wayman, Frank (1985), "Bipolarity, Multipolarity, and the Threat of War," Sabrosky (ed.), 115-144

Weiss, Thomas G. (1995), "On the Brink of a New Era? Humanitarian Interventions, 1991-94," Donald C. F. Daniel and Bradd C. Hayes (eds), *Beyond Traditional Peacekeeping*, Houndmills and London: Macmillan, 3-19

Wenden, Anita L. (1995), "Defining Peace: Perspectives from Peace Research," Christina Schäffner and Anita L. Wenden (eds.), *Language and Peace*, Aldershot, Dartmouth, 3-15

Wiberg, Håkan (1981), "JPR 1964 - 1980 - What Have We Learnt about Peace?" *Journal of Peace Research*, XVIII(2), 111-148

Wiberg, Håkan (1988), "The Peace Research Movement," Wallensteen (ed.), 30-53

Wiberg, Håkan (1992), "(Re-)Conceptualizing Security," *Arms Control*, 13 (3), 487-492

Wiberg, Håkan (1993), "European Peace Research in the 1990s," Balázs and Wiberg (eds.), 9-25

Wien, Barbara J. (ed.) (n.d.), *Peace and World Order Studies: A Curriculum Guide*, 4th ed., New York: World Policy Institute

Wilkenfeld, Jonathan and Michael Brecher (2000), "Interstate Crises and Violence: Twentieth-Century Findings," Midlarsky (ed.), 271-300

Wright, Quincy (Abridged by Louise Leonard Wright) (1964), *A Study of War*, Second Edition, Chicago: University of Chicago Press

Yamakage, Susumu (1994), *A Theoretical Approach to International Relaions (Tairitu to Kyozon no Kokusai Riron)*, Tokyo: University of Tokyo Press

Yamamoto, Yoshinobu (1989), "Mathematical Models in International Politics (Kokusai Seiji ni okeru Suuritekina Moderu)," Aruga et al (eds.), 331-364

Zagare, Frank C. and D. Mark Kilgour (1998), "Deterrence Theory and the Spiral Model Revisited," *Journal of Theoretical Politics*, 10(1), 59-87

Zwicky, Heinrich (1989), "Income Inequality and Violent Conflicts in Developing Countries," Isidor Wallimann and Michael Dobkowski (eds), *Research In Inequality and Social Conflict*, Vol.1, Greenwich, Connecticut: JAI Press, 67-83